Providing
Safe Nursing Care
for
Ethnic People of Color

APPLETON-CENTURY-CROFTS/New York

Providing Safe Nursing Care for Ethnic People of Color

EDITORS:

Marie Foster Branch, R.N., B.S., M.A.
Program Director, Models for Introducing
Cultural Diversity in Nursing Curricula, Western
Interstate Commission for Higher Education,
Boulder, Colorado

Phyllis Perry Paxton, R.N., B.S., M.N.
Nursing Coordinator, Family Planning Nurse
Practitioner Program, UCLA Extension, Los
Angeles, California

FOREWORD BY

Barbara Rhodes, Ph.D.
Associate Professor, Pan African Studies, California State University, Northridge, California

Library of Congress Cataloging in Publication Data
Main entry under title:

Providing safe nursing care for ethnic people of color.

    1. Nursing. 2. Minorities--Medical care--United
States. 3. Nursing--Study and teaching. 4. Minorities
in nursing--United States. I. Branch, Marie Foster.
II. Paxton, Phyllis Perry. [DNLM: 1. Ethnic groups--
United States. 2. Nursing care. 3. Culture. WY100
P342p]
RT42.P78   610.73   76-6071
ISBN 0-8385-7943-4

Prentice-Hall International, Inc., London
Prentice-Hall of Australia, Pty. Ltd., Sydney
Prentice-Hall of India Private Limited, New Delhi
Prentice-Hall of Japan, Inc., Tokyo
Prentice-Hall of Southeast Asia (Pte.) Ltd., Singapore

Printed in the United States of America

Dedicated to
Rochelle
and
Terella

Contributors

Diane Adams, R.N., B.S., M.S.
*Assistant Clinical Professor, School of Nursing, University of California,
San Francisco, California*

Teresa Bello, R.N., B.S., M.S.
*Assistant Clinical Professor, School of Nursing, University of California,
San Francisco, California*

Marie Foster Branch, R.N., B.S., M.A.
*Program Director, Models for Introducing Cultural Diversity in Nursing
Curricula, Western Interstate Commission for Higher Education,
Boulder, Colorado*

Effie Poy Yew Chow, R.N., M.A., Ph.D.
*President, East West Academy of Healing Arts,
San Francisco, California*

Pauline Rodriguez Dorsey, R.N., B.S.
*Public Health Nursing Supervisor, Northeast Community Health Center,
Los Angeles, California; Past President of the Chicana Nurses' Organization*

Cecelia Gallerito, R.N., B.S., M.N.
*Lecturer, College of Nursing, University of New Mexico,
Albuquerque, New Mexico*

Barbara Lea Giles, R.N., B.S., M.N.
*Director of Field Services, City of Berkeley Health Department,
Berkeley, California*

Herlinda Quintero Jackson, R.N., B.S., M.P.H.
*Mental Health Counselor, East Los Angeles Mental Health Service,
Los Angeles, California; President of the Chicana Nurses' Organization*

Gladys Jacques, R.N., B.S., M.N.
Coordinator, Division of Nursing, UCLA Extension, Los Angeles, California

Jennie R. Joe, R.N., M.P.H.
*Doctoral Candidate in Medical Anthropology, University of California,
Berkeley, California; Member of Navajo Tribe*

Laura Martinez, R.N., B.S., M.A.
*Assistant Professor, College of Nursing, University of New Mexico,
Albuquerque, New Mexico*

Phyllis Perry Paxton, R.N., B.S., M.N.
Nursing Coordinator, Family Planning Nurse Practitioner Program,
UCLA Extension, Los Angeles, California

Josephine Pino, R.N., B.S.
Staff Nurse, Presbyterian Hospital, Albuquerque, New Mexico

Martina Carmen Ramirez, R.N., B.S., M.N.
District Director of Public Health Nursing, Northeast Health Center,
Los Angeles, California

Barbara Rhodes, Ph.D.
Associate Professor, Pan African Studies, California State University,
Northridge, California

Florence Martin Stroud, R.N., B.S., M.N., M.P.H.
Director of Public Health, City of Berkeley, California;
Doctoral Candidate, School of Public Health,
University of California, Berkeley

Ruth Ann Terry, R.N., B.S., M.P.H.
Assistant Clinical Professor, School of Nursing, University of California,
San Francisco, California

Esther Coto Walloch, R.N., B.S., M.N.
Assistant Clinical Professor, School of Nursing, University of California,
Los Angeles, California

Betty Smith Williams, R.N., B.S., M.N., M.S.
Assistant Dean, Academic Affairs, School of Nursing, University of California,
Los Angeles, California; Cofounder, Council of Black Nurses,
Los Angeles, California

Preface

The purpose of this book is threefold. Initially, the authors will describe how the deficit—deficient concept related to people of color has ignored the positive aspects of cultural health traditions and systems. Qualities, characteristics, and actions not held by Middle America are viewed as subordinate, insignificant, abnormal, and deficient. Cultural health practices are generally excluded from health care educational and delivery systems. The authors then will describe a set of new approaches to nursing care with outcomes redirected toward the enhancement of a state of wellness for people of color. Additionally, the authors will provide the reader with models for nursing education. The models are designed as supplements to existing curriculum models.

This book represents a collective effort and has been planned and developed by a group of ethnic nurses of color who are anchored in the perspectives of the constituent communities under discussion. These same individuals were instrumental in the historic development of the many action groups involved in identifying the need for cultural perspectives in nursing.

During the 1960s, various community action groups throughout the United States were instrumental in focusing on community needs as perceived by community residents. In the Southwest, nurses began to organize for action relevant to the expressed needs of residents of reservations, ghettos, and barrios. The primary concerns of the various nursing groups were the lack of accessible quality health services for ethnic people of color, the communication gaps between health professionals and consumers of health services, the lack of knowledge and interest demonstrated by health care professionals relative to the needs of community residents, the insensitivity of all segments of the health care delivery system to the plight of the oppressed, and the small number of ethnic people of color who were being educated in nursing schools for their R.N. licensure. The nurses realized that the focus on community needs, influenced by the activist movements of the 1960s, was losing momentum without implementation to improve the quality of life for poor people and ethnic people of color. The concerns of the nurses were validated by the Report of the United States Commission of Civil Rights.

In 1970, the Civil Rights Commission reported that overt racism had been a central part of American life for more than 300 years. Various racist laws, social institutions, living conditions, and distributions of political power had served to relegate subordinate positions to people of color. In spite of progress made in striking down legal support for overt racism during the 1950s and 1960s, the eradication of institutional racism has been distressingly insignificant. Health care still remains a commodity that is controlled by the power structure and is polluted with the contaminants of institutional racism. The authors and their associates were intent on developing strategies to minimize and eventually eradicate institutional racism from health care delivery systems.

"Dynamics of Prejudice: Implications for Nursing," a continuing education program, was developed to prevent a hiatus yielding eventual apathy. Funded by the National Institute of Mental Health and sponsored by UCLA Extension, the purpose of the program was to aid nurses in the identification and eradication of their own potentially racist attitudes. The project aimed to assist nurses in becoming agents of institutional change so that they would be more effective in working with student nurses, consumers of health services, and co-workers of various ethnic backgrounds. The program participants were asked to commit themselves to an action task on return to their agencies of employment. A group of nurses who participated in the first Dynamics of Prejudice Workshop in 1970 decided to form an organization entitled "Nurses for Action."

Nurses for Action was representative of various ethnic groups who felt the need to develop postworkshop activities geared toward improving the quality of life for ethnic people of color. These nurses realized that socioeconomic variables often affected the quality of life for a people. Further, there was the realization that relevant health care cannot be isolated from the life styles and patterns of the consumer. Members of Nurses for Action took their concerns to the California Nurses Association (CNA) in the form of a resolution. The resolution was introduced to and passed by the CNA House of Delegates in March 1971. The resolution mandated the establishment of a task force to study the status of minorities in nursing in the state of California and to make recommendations to the 1973 CNA House of Delegates for the eradication of racism from the nursing profession in California. The Minority Group Task Force was established, collected data on the status of ethnic people of color in the nursing profession, and submitted a number of recommendations to the House of Delegates in 1973. The recommendations were to be implemented through an Affirmative Action Program that was to be established within the structure of CNA. Although mandated by the 1973 House of Delegates, the recommendations made by the Task Force had not been implemented, nor had an Affirmative Action Program been established at the time of the 1975 convention.

Concurrent with the activities of Nurses for Action and the Dynamics of Prejudice Workshop, nursing educators began to voice a need for assistance in preparing students to meet the nursing needs of people of color. The educators were also aware of the gross underrepresentation of American Indians, Blacks, Chicanos, and other Spanish-speaking people in schools of nursing. It was with this awareness of the needs of nursing educators that the project "Faculty

Development to Meet Minority Group Needs" was developed. Funded by the W. K. Kellogg Foundation and sponsored by the Western Interstate Commission for Higher Education, project goals were to assist nursing educators in developing strategies to recruit and retain nursing students of color. In addition, faculty participants addressed curricular revisions necessary to meet the needs of ethnic communities. This led to the project "Models for Introducing Cultural Diversity into Nursing Curricula."

A network of resource persons emerged from participants of the Dynamics of Prejudice Workshop, Nurses for Action, the CNA Minority Group Task Force, and the Western Interstate Commission for Higher Education Faculty Development Project. Their activities were geared toward the eradication of racism from the health care delivery system.

It became increasingly apparent that, in the health care delivery and educational systems, increased emphasis was needed for the development of applicable knowledge and skills. Further, a search of the literature revealed a gross lack of information on physical assessment of people of color. Students were indeed being graduated and were not prepared to care for a significant portion of the population.

It was with this awareness of the gross gaps in health education and service that we endeavored to develop this text. Although a number of individuals contributed their ideas to the development of the text, a special thanks is extended to Ruth Gordon, Ph.D, and to Bill O'Banion whose ideas and philosophies are woven into the pages of the text. The final preparation of the manuscript was facilitated by Elsie Johnson, who patiently read the text for clarity and style. Acknowledgment is also made to K & S Graphics, illustrator.

Contents

Foreword

In this country we are becoming more and more aware of the debilitating effects of racism on all peoples — perpetrators and victims alike. We are also faced increasingly with conditions that confirm the reality that this mythology has seriously limited the development of whole races of people in the country. A cursory look at the conditions of people of color in the United States reveals that the wealth, technologic, and scientific development so proudly boasted of are not shared, indeed, by our people. Furthermore, such a look reveals that the contributions of people of color to this wealth and to the scientific and technologic fields are profoundly disproportionate to the returns they accrue in this society. And yet, despite these imposed limitations, this country's minorities have made significant contributions. Given this reality, it boggles the mind to contemplate the contribution of which this society has deprived itself because of the racism which has denied people of color the context in which to express our maximum potential.

The emergence of an aggressive front by peoples of color worldwide has had ramifications in this society, however, and is reversing this historic pattern. This is reflected in the determination of peoples of color not only to insist on their right to total development but their concomitant determination to explore carefully and to evaluate the experiences and knowledge resulting from our respective pasts and to reinforce the knowledge and insights so gained in their developmental process. Progress will not mean total embracing of models developed by the Western world, but development of new models which incorporate this significant input of both the past and present.

This new direction is one which is very much needed in the health field. The health of people of color in the United States reflects a peculiar irony. On the one hand, we are denied equal access to "modern medicine," while, on the other hand, we are conditioned to reject cultural health traditions as primitive and totally useless, a reflection on the ignorance of the user. Historically, when cultural health traditions and systems have been acknowledged, they have received a negative assessment and have been casually dismissed as nonscientific nonsense. No scientific method, except that articulated by the Western world, has been accepted as valid and, consequently, bodies of information have been ignored and relegated to eventual oblivion. Fortunately, the new direction emerging in the health field in which people of color demand consideration of our particular experiences will conserve some of this information. Additionally, it will correct those pages of history that denigrate the health practices of other cultures as being totally devoid of value.

xv

The reality is that, for millions of people over many, many years, cultural health traditions have functioned with varying degrees of effectiveness. A more than cursory review of these traditions and the systems developed for their delivery reveals their many positive aspects and discloses to many what might be an unsettling reality — that some of the most "modern" medicines and medical practices are incorporated in traditional systems that are centuries old. Further, such a review nurtures confidence in pursuing new models in health care systems and reinforces the awareness that, if health care systems are to effectively address the objective of achieving maximum wellness of recipients, they must be based on a sensitivity to and knowledge of the particular needs of the recipients and the characteristics of their environment — all of which affect the type and delivery of services.

It is overdue for racism to be rousted from its seat of power and that the medical field be about the business of pursuing the goal of better health for *all* people by *all* necessary means. Reevaluating the impact and import of traditional health practices and systems, developing new models for educating those in the medical field, and so forth, are necessary steps for the achievement of a health care system primarily concerned with the attainment of maximum wellness for *all* members of society.

For these reasons, a book which contains the collective insights of people of color from one area of the medical field is indeed a significant event. Hopefully, the interest in this particular aspect of the health field will be intensified and will give rise to more original and fruitful investigation, and this book will be the first of many to herald the dawn of an era where wellness will not be the exclusive domain of any one people.

Barbara Rhodes, Ph.D.
September 1975

PART I
Introduction

1

New Approaches in Nursing:
Ethnic Humanism Views

Marie Foster Branch

A prevailing opinion among ethnic nurses of color* is that the inclusion of ethnicity among the nursing ranks and in the curricula of schools of nursing will bring new life and fresh approaches to the profession. This opinion is a part of the "ethnic humanism view" which forms the basis for succeeding chapters.

The operationalization of the ethnic humanism view will require a reexamination of present methods employed in the teaching and practice of nursing. Also required is an extension of this view into the entire health field if nursing is to successfully implement new approaches for the specific improvement of services to ethnic people of color. It is expected that there will be continuing springboard benefits to clients from all racial backgrounds.

Nursing should take the lead for other health professionals in promoting humanism in the health fields and in reeducating its membership in the unique advantages of adopting ethnic views for health practice. After all, nursing generally is free to innovate and improve practice, having few change inhibitors common to other health professions, such as an elitist image, fees for service, and other fraternal and business ties that divert goals of service to goals of personal aggrandizement.

The challenge for nursing is to educate students and graduates in the ethnic humanism view. Reorientation is necessary for those who come from cross sections of a society that has programmed its members for stereotyped racial and class attitudes, for acceptance of oppression as a domestic and international necessity, and for comfortable levels as quiet participants in segmentalized health services that abuse the rights of some clients.

Preferred to the term "minority," which connotes inferiority.

3

Prerequisites for the reorientation process are not dictated by race, color, or cultural ties of the individual. Some ethnic people of color must adjust their ethnic view in order to practice humanistic nursing. On the other hand, some members of the white majority group have developed very effective ethnic views and are considered to be humanistic in their practice. For the most part, white majority persons and middle-class-oriented ethnic persons of color will have to supplement their life experiences in a purposeful way in order to become reeducated for ethnic practice. One might term this process "late life education" for practicing nurses. Hopefully, nursing students will receive education about ethnic and cultural diversity in the process of becoming nurses.

PERSONAL REEDUCATION

Personal reeducation involves participation in cultural awareness courses and experiences; examination of personal beliefs, attitudes, and behavior; and willingness to engage in continuous dialogue with ethnic people of color from different backgrounds. It is a process of developing a point of view and plan for practice which is flexible, changes with the times, and is in touch with community level movements among diverse groups.

REEDUCATION WITHIN THE NURSING CURRICULUM

A necessary first step for reeducation within schools of nursing should be to validate texts and other materials for accuracy of factual material, as well as for ethnic perspectives. Validation of material should be made by ethnic people of color belonging to the particular group under discussion at the time. Available resource persons are ethnic faculty from the school of nursing, faculty from ethnic studies departments on campus, and community persons who have first hand knowledge about the ways of the specific ethnic group. Next, faculty should make necessary revisions in the school's philosophy, learning objectives, theoretical framework, and teaching styles. The mission of the nursing program in philosophy, as well as fact, should reflect the needs of all students and all segments of the populations served by graduates of that program. This is not to say that every ethnic and cultural group should be included in the curriculum, but if students are given an opportunity to examine their feelings and behavior towards the major ethnic groups of color and are versed in the ways of adapting approach and practice for all groups, they will be able to make the necessary adjustments in another part of the nation or the world.

CONCEPTS FOR PRACTICE OF THE ETHNIC HUMANISM VIEW

Specific concepts form the ethnic humanism view and are necessary ingredients for the practice of safe, effective nursing care and for the provision of improved health services for ethnic people of color. The concepts incorporate a view for:

1. ethnic inclusion to provide skills for the practice of safe, effective nursing care
2. ethnic inclusion for purposes of enrichment
3. strengths and resources among ethnic people of color
4. holistic blends of traditional cultural and western healing practices
5. consumer participation in decisions which affect their welfare
6. accountability to ethnic communities of color

ETHNIC INCLUSION TO PROVIDE SKILLS FOR THE PRACTICE OF SAFE, EFFECTIVE NURSING CARE

The phrase "safe, effective nursing care" often is used to describe the type of care which nurses are expected to give in order to graduate from schools of nursing and to remain licensed.

Ethnic people of color are not receiving safe, effective nursing or medical care when considerations for cultural and ethnic differences are omitted from nursing care plans and the medical regimen.

On occasion, lifesaving measures are not taken because medical personnel lack basic knowledge necessary for the safety of the patient. An example of this is the ability to recognize respiratory distress in people with dark skin. The problem was brought into sharp focus through a recent incident in a midwestern hospital. A nurse was questioned about the seriously cyanotic condition of her patient who was a Black man. She replied, "I didn't know he needed oxygen; he was too dark." No doubt, variations of this problem will continue until all schools of nursing, medicine, and allied health fields are required to graduate practitioners who have proven proficiency in the recognition of skin tone variations which signal distress symptoms, such as cyanosis, jaundice, and skin rash in people of all hues from the lightest white to the darkest black.

There are other less dramatic but, nevertheless, important examples of the skills which should be required by schools of nursing and should be taught in in-service education classes before safe, effective nursing care can be provided for ethnic people of color. Hiring practice and performance ratings should include requirements for skills in communication, including fluency in languages of the community. In addition, job applicants and practicing nurses should demonstrate ability in the adaptation of special diets for cultural food patterns, and in the adaptation of nursing measures within the boundaries of cultural practices.

Communication Skills

Nurses and other key health workers should be fluent in the languages spoken by the predominant groups they serve. Otherwise, critical information cannot be shared for assessment and teaching purposes, and consumer participation in the planning and delivery of care is an impossibility. In the interim period, while language skills are being acquired by staff in hospitals and clinics with non-English-speaking patients, translators should be hired for all units. In addition, signs and paper forms should be translated. This example from a west coast medical center should never be duplicated. A Spanish-speaking teenage girl with terminal cancer did not understand why she was undergoing tests. She was labeled uncooperative by the nursing and medical staff and was sedated for routine x-rays because no Spanish speaking staff person was available to calm and reassure her. Her family was not able to cross the border to be with her. Eventually, a group of Spanish-speaking students from the nearby campus organized in shifts to visit the patient on a continuous basis until she died. Question the availability of safe, effective nursing care in this instance. Further, those who doubt the advisability of reinforcing language and traditions other than English should be reminded that the early European settlers in this country continued their language and cultural traditions from the old countries. They did not adopt the languages or cultural traditions of the groups which predominated in the country at that time, namely the American Indian tribes. Cultural identity is no less important to other ethnic groups.

Skills in the Adaptation of Special Diets for Cultural Food Patterns

A knowledge of cultural food patterns is essential for the nurse to be effective in adaptation of special diets for ethnic people of color. This is especially important for public health nurses, but nurses working in hospitals and clinics should also have this knowledge. An Asian man with hypertension said he would rather die than live without soy sauce and salty, pickled vegetables. With diet so important in the control of hypertension, creative approaches to his diet patterns were necessary before any progress could be made in treatment. The nurse worked with an Asian dietitian who devised a mixture of mustard and other seasonings, which was an acceptable substitute for soy sauce.

Food is important for health and healing. Special consideration should be given to the food preferences which, if not found on the hospital menu, could be brought in to the patients by their families.

Some cultural favorites, such as chilies, have nutritional value which is not ordinarily considered in the preparation of menus for regular and special diets. Until publications are available for this information, nurses and other health workers should collaborate with members of ethnic groups of color for a compilation of essential information.

Skills in the Adaptation of Nursing Measures within the Boundaries of Cultural Patterns

This principle incorporates a large number of skills which will be detailed in other chapters of the book. Suffice it to say that nurses who are not proficient in skills of making adaptations in their nursing practice for cultural patterns should seek educational opportunities which prepare them to do so. Opportunities are available through in-service seminars, professional institutes, and continuing education courses. It may be necessary to request that appropriate courses become a regular part of continuing education and in-service course schedules.

When plans for the care of ethnic people of color fail to meet objectives, close investigation often reveals omissions of protocols that include individual and family traditions. Often, these traditions are more pronounced among ethnic people of color. An example is the family tradition which is strong among many ethnic groups for the obtaining of group consent in many matters, including health. Members of the family would not act as individual agents and would obtain approval of other family members before appointments or having diagnostic tests. The individual family member might accept a clinic appointment just to be polite but might not appear for the session because the day and time was inappropriate for other family business. The creative nurse would explore this possibility with the patient and give instructions for selecting alternate dates and times in case a change in appointment is indicated after family council.

ETHNIC INCLUSION FOR PURPOSES OF ENRICHMENT

There are rich traditions among the diverse cultural groups in this country. Many of the ways of Asians, American Indians, Black Americans, and

Spanish-speaking Americans are unknown to white majority Americans, who are culturally deprived except through unreliable means. Examples are the mass media, textbooks, and informal information systems such as family and peer groups. The same deprivations exist interculturally so that few Black or Afro-Americans know about American Indians or Spanish-speaking Americans through first hand experience. Personal experiences with members of other groups can lead to personal and professional enrichment. Ethnic inclusion should be viewed as an opportunity for enrichment, rather than as a part of federally enforced regulations through the Civil Rights Act or as an appeasement of community pressure groups. Each individual can find fulfillment and can experience new dimensions of living by expanding beyond his or her boundaries and exploring the personal meaning of the experiences they have with people of different life styles and different world views.

STRENGTHS AND RESOURCES AMONG ETHNIC PEOPLE OF COLOR

Adoption of the strength and resource view requires the complete elimination of the deficit-deficiency view of ethnic people of color. That is, one must give up the notion that there are racial deficits which explain the differences in people. Instead, one searches for the strengths and resources among ethnic people of color and for explanations of style differences in attitude, behavior, and life style from the point of view of the ethnic group, rather than from the point of view of the majority society. The strength and resources concept has relevance for schools of nursing, as well as for health care facilities, and community-based agencies.

Examples of the strength and resources view are found among:

1. family ties among ethnic groups of color
2. ethnic organizations
3. life experiences in ethnic communities of color
4. inherited resistance to selected diseases

Family Ties

Strong family ties are common to most ethnic groups of color. The family is the source of strength, as well as of emotional and financial support during the many crises that ethnic people experience through poverty and other ills of oppression, such as unemployment or underemployment, poor housing, second class health care, inferior public services, etc.

Applicability to Schools of Nursing

The family can play a much more important role in the life of the ethnic student of color than is currently the practice. When close family ties require ethnic students to leave their course of study and return home for a family event, punitive measures are often taken by the instructors or administrators. This practice tends to discourage family participation in the education process and creates a conflict for the student, often resulting in academic failure. A creative approach would be to plan an ethnic inclusion program focus for ethnic students of color, including outreach for families of those students who have particularly traditional ties with family and community. The ethnic inclusion program should include a liaison person who is accepted by the families and communities in question and who can be invaluable in establishing long-lasting communication and understanding between the nursing faculty and the ethnic communities. Many schools of nursing are hiring ethnic student coordinators for this purpose. Such a program would include flexible curriculum modules and self-pacing courses that allow students with extended responsibilities to complete their studies without having to sacrifice their standing with family and community. Thus, upon graduation, the student is of value to the community which was the target for ethnic recruitment in the first place. Any faculty group not willing to make adjustments for the serious student with family and other cultural ties should reconsider its mission and include students who do not fit its regular requirements. The condition of many schools of nursing is such that ethnic students of color should be cautioned that they enter these schools at their own risk.

Applicability to Health Service Facilities

The family is also an important resource for ethnic patients of color. Creative approaches in health care facilities would include family members and peers as active participants in the care and cure processes. Families of ethnic patients of color often thrust their presence upon the hospital setting, much to the chagrin of the staff. How often have staff complained about the large numbers of family members present around the clock? Here is a clue for staff to include family in their plans for patient care, recovery, and the prevention of recurring illness.

Ethnic Organizations as Resources

Ethnic nurse organizations should be considered prime resources for the many ethnic inclusion activities discussed in this book, including recruitment and retention programs in schools of nursing, cultural awareness sessions in schools and in-service areas that plan for ethnic inclusion in the curriculum. Other ethnic organizations on campus and in the community are potential resources for nurses in all fields of practice.

Life Experiences for Strengths and Resources

Other strengths and resources among ethnic groups of color have been identified in recent literature, and many more can be identified by members of ethnic groups if they and those around them have a firm belief in their strengths. For instance, many persons from ethnic groups of color lead lives that are far from sheltered. They have experiences that have relevance for the demands of many life situations and that should be viewed for the advantage of strength rather than deficit. A nursing student who is a mother of five, head of the household, on welfare for years has much to teach other students and perhaps the instructor also. She is experienced in budget and family management. She is aware of innovative ways to apply principles of child psychology. She knows informal sources of information about community resources. She is skilled in nutrition management on a low-income budget, has used diversionary tactics for a host of political and social situations, can recognize childhood illness, and gives counseling and spiritual guidance in the face of overwhelming odds. This is part of an endless list of potential strengths, which will vary with the person and the circumstances. Creative instructors take advantage of such an opportunity to include in the curriculum a place for the student/mother to demonstrate her talents; thereby she is encouraged to recognize universal-experiences as strengths, and other students see her as a resource. The opportunity provides an enriched experience for all, including the faculty.

When a school of nursing declares an intention to prepare graduates for work with people of varying social classes and ethnic persuasions, it should not consider functioning without having, at all times, faculty and students who represent those social classes and ethnic groups.

Inherited Resistance to Selected Diseases

Although it is important to consider the negative effects of poverty and oppression on the health of ethnic people of color, too frequently these negative facts conceal the more positive facts about ethnicity and illness. There are inherited strengths among all ethnic groups just as there are inherited weaknesses. To name a few examples, Afro-Americans have low incidence rates of multiple sclerosis, gallstones, hip fractures, psoriasis, pyloric stenosis, and skin cancer. American Indians have a low incidence of duodenal ulcers, and Japanese have low frequency rates of acne vulgaris and congenital hip disease.* There are also other factors to be considered in this context. It is extremely important for nurses and other health workers to know the physiologic variations that are normal for particular ethnic groups of color. For instance, Black children reach developmental levels which are advanced for the norms based on white, middle-class children. Persons with dark skin normally have a purplish discoloration of the mucosa. Many Blacks have electrocardiogram patterns which differ from those of whites and which might be mistaken for pathology.†

It is important for nurses and other health workers to know the range of ethnic variations in natural resistance to illness and disease, as it is important to know the predispositions. Safe, effective care is possible only if this knowledge is put into practice on all levels of health education and service.

Style Differences from the Ethnic Point of View

In continuing the search for strengths and resources among ethnic persons of color, it is necessary to perceive differences in what might be termed a person's "style." This includes attitude, behavior, and life patterns. In order for effective intra- and intergroup relations to occur in health, nurses and others must examine their preconceived notions about why various groups act as they do (so-called stoic, passive, indifferent, hostile, etc.), and adopt an inquisitive search for valid reasons. The explanations must come from the persons involved and others among peer or other ethnic groups who understand them.

For more information, see Damon and Picazo et al in the bibliography at the end of the chapter.
†See Care of the Black Patient (paper) and Picazo et al in the bibliography.

Newly recruited ethnic students of color in schools of nursing provide examples of the way in which preconceived ideas about ethnic performance can interrupt their own learning and deprive majority students and faculty of positive experiences with persons who differ from them. The behavior profile in Table 1.1 is an illustration of common misunderstandings that frequently occur when groups of ethnic students of color are admitted to traditionally white schools of nursing.

The prevailing motive for interpreting behavior is related to preconceived ideas that the ethnic student is underprivileged and deprived, or in other words, has inferior status. The quiet student is viewed askance, as is the boisterous student. Most readily accepted is the ethnic student of color with features similar to those of whites; lacking this, next most acceptable are actions which identify the student as having white middle-class aspirations. This is a student profile which is not announced in school bulletins, but it is so operative that most readers will identify with it immediately, whether they are past recipients or perpetrators of such a profile.

HOLISTIC* BLENDS OF CULTURALLY TRADITIONAL AND WESTERN HEALING PRACTICES

The holism concept in health and the practice of nursing emphasizes balance states for the prevention of illness and restoration of health. The laying-on of hands is an important part of nursing as it is an important part of the healing traditions of many ethnic people of color. Consideration of the emotional state of ill persons, the relationship of the environment to illness and health, and the effect of nutrition on the body are areas of study which nursing has in common with cultural traditions for preventing or treating illness. The fact that these and other commonalities exist leads one to speculate about the ease with which the field of nursing will continue to integrate holistic principles of health into practice.

Nevertheless, changes are needed in order to formalize the incorporation of the traditional cultural methods and cultural appreciation into the teaching and practice of nursing. Drastic changes are called for in nursing curricula in order to have cultural perspectives understood, accepted, and acted upon in schools and in-service programs for practicing nurses. The goal is not to prepare culturally traditional healers — that is a function within each cultural group — rather, the goal is to introduce ethnic and cultural differences into the curriculum, to explore alternative healing

*Holism in health refers to the inclusion of the totality of those factors which affect the life of the individual for the prevention of illness, that is, holistic theory rejects the possibility of treating illness on the basis of germ theory alone, without including considerations of states of balance within the body and within the patient's environment.

Table 1.1
Behavior Profile for Nursing Students

	TRADITIONAL ETHNIC PERSON		
	Middle Class Aspirant	Low Ethnic Affiliation	High Ethnic Affiliation
1 Demeanor*	Responsive	Usually nonresponsive	Always nonresponsive
2 Social amenities†	Willing	Seldom willing	Never willing
3 Attitudes‡	Compliant	Resistive	Hostile
4 Dress§	Conventional	Semiconventional	Ethnic or other nonconventional
5 Communication‖	Straight, assumes understanding and fair play	Varies from straight to somewhat uncommunicative, assumes occasional understanding and occasional fair play	Uncommon, assumes rejection, dislike, and "rip-off"
6 Assertiveness#	Seeks assistance, assumes positive receptivity	Occasionally seeks assistance often after evidence of course trouble, assumes occasional receptivity	Seldom or never seeks assistance, assumes negativism
7 Group cohesiveness**	Incidental to the learning process	May or not be formed	Essential as emotional support group for learning

*Usual behavior for postsecondary students expected to succeed in professional programs. Conformist behavior expected although not included in writing in school bulletins. This type of behavior is rewarded in many of those situations in which the benefit of a doubt is operational.

†Manner of initiating greetings and small talk. The typical student is very verbal and has learned to please in order to succeed. He or she initiates conversation and greets faculty in the hallways and may even attend teas and receptions and enjoy being there.

‡Ethnic students of color are braced for institutional racism. Attitudes of resistance and hostility are often coping behaviors, interfering with the learning processes, especially if white faculty, inexperienced with mixed racial groups, respond to this type of coping behavior by becoming defensive and feeling rejected.

§Need for individual statements is frequently made through dress, hair style, and those few personal areas over which ethnic people have control. These styles are being adopted by the majority culture more and more as individuals seek expressions of individuality.

‖Compadre relationships exist among white students and their instructors (exceptions are white students considered to be deviant). This is seldom the case for ethnic students of color, especially those who are more traditional in life view and point of reference. Ethnic students of color in the high-profile group are most likely to be suspicious of whites and other ethnics in authority representing dominant groups with whom they, their families, and friends have had negative experiences.

#Frequently misunderstood posture. Values differ among groups. The less competitive and group-oriented students will not seek instructors for extra help with difficult class assignments. Often ethnic students are not accustomed to having informal discussions with instructor. The stigma attached to being an ethnic student in an all-white institution decreases chances of the student admitting problems since he or she is viewed as being the cause of the problem anyway.

**Ethnic students of color face what they perceive to be a hostile environment in the majority-populated school. Too frequently, this perception is validated during the initial phases of the first school term. A positive approach is taken by some schools which offer preentry programs and actually encourage group cohesiveness among ethnic students of color as a support group during at least the first year of the nursing program.

methods currently in practice in this country, and to bring knowledgeable persons into the classroom and in-service areas to explain the many ways in which nurses can incorporate into their practice a wide variety of alternative approaches to health including herbology, acumassage, relaxation, and exercises such as yoga and other exercise movements. A further challenge for nursing is the successful coordination of culturally traditional and western healing practices for clients who wish to use both.

CONSUMER PARTICIPATION

Nursing, of necessity, will become more responsive to the growing trends for consumers of services to have a part in making decisions which affect them. This concept can be applied to the student as a consumer, as well as to the patient as a consumer. Both may need preparation for this role.

The educational process will draw benefits from the participation of students and ethnic persons of color in forming curriculum theories and course outlines. The participation of ethnic persons from campus and from communities is essential for the validation of teaching materials with an ethnic focus.

In-service directors from clinics and hospitals can take clues from the examples of schools of nursing that have advisory committees for minority affairs. Such an advisory group is invaluable in providing ethnic input where it is not available from faculty and staff. It would be an innovation for hospitals and clinics, especially as holistic concepts are becoming incorporated into nursing practice.

One must caution against the use of students for ethnic input. They can be drawn from academic studies and must not be called upon for too many responsibilities. The same is true for ethnic faculty of color, who frequently are asked to teach ethnic content or oversee its preparation. This may become too burdensome for their schedules. If they are expected to take on responsibility for ethnic input in the curriculum, they should be given time free from other teaching responsibilities in order to do an adequate job and so as not to become "burned out." Resentment builds when fellow faculty have negative views on ethnic inclusion. Frequently, ethnic faculty are told: "If you want cultural content in the curriculum, you can teach it." Ethnic inclusion must be a shared effort among all faculty, as it is expected to be shared among staff in health service agencies. Hiring practices and performance evaluations in schools of nursing and health service agencies should reflect the commitment of schools and hospitals to include ethnic cultural content. All faculty and staff should be hired on the basis of their ability to teach and practice that content, and their evaluations should include assessment of their performance in this area, as well as in other areas in practice and teaching which are important to the safety and well-being of patients and their families.

ACCOUNTABILITY TO ETHNIC COMMUNITIES OF COLOR

Schools of nursing and health service agencies are accountable to the public, which includes ethnic communities of color. Accountability for ethnic inclusion is as vital as is accountability for fiscal and other responsibilities and should be in evidence in several ways including:

1. admission policies in schools of nursing
2. accreditation standards for schools of nursing
3. licensure examinations for registered nurses
4. employer requests
5. legislation for health services and professional education

Admission Policies

Nursing manpower shortages still exist among American Indians (including Alaskan natives), Black, and Spanish-speaking ethnic groups. Emphasis on recruitment and retention of ethnic students of color in schools of nursing is recent and needs to be emphasized as a priority for years to come. The emphasis will have to continue on a national, regional, and local level with participation from national, regional, and state nursing organizations, schools of nursing as well as from individuals.

Accreditation Standards

Currently, schools of nursing may become accredited without demonstrating intent to include ethnic groups of color among students, faculty, or staff, nor are they required to teach about ethnic and cultural differences. In the light of discussions in this and other chapters, the omission is a serious deterrent to the practice of safe nursing care for ethnic people of color.

Resolutions stating the need for ethnic inclusion as a part of accreditation standards were submitted to the National League for Nursing (NLN) Council of Baccalaureate and Higher Degree Programs by the University of California at the Los Angeles School of Nursing in March 1974 and to the League's Council on Associate Degree Programs by the San Jose City

College (California) Nursing Program in May 1975.* A support resolution was passed by the Western Council for Higher Education (WCHEN) and was submitted to the NLN in October 1974. Similar actions should be initiated now on the state level because many associate degree nursing programs are accredited only by state accrediting agencies. One cannot stress too much the importance of accreditation standards in providing assurance that all schools of nursing follow the lead of the many which have already initiated recruitment, retention, and curriculum change activities.

Employer Requests

There are constant searches conducted for ethnic persons of color who are prepared at all levels of nursing, including teaching. It is a responsibility of all employing institutions to make known their needs for prepared persons from ethnic groups of color. They should have serious communications with schools of nursing and leaders in continuing education programs. For example, if hospitals and clinics in a Spanish-speaking area cannot find enough nurses from the cultural and language groups in the community, their administrators should pressure local schools of nursing to meet their manpower needs. If there is a single graduate nursing program in a particular state, that school should receive regular requests for more nurses to become prepared at postbaccalaureate levels.

Health Legislation

If ethnic inclusion activities in nursing are to reach full circle, accountability at the legislative level must become a part of planning on national, regional, and local levels. In the spring of 1974, representatives of national nursing organizations rebuffed Senator Edward Kennedy's attempts to build accountability into legislation for nursing education. Testifying before a Senate committee in June 1975, representatives of the American Nurses' Association, the National League for Nursing, and the Student Nurses' Association spoke against a segment of a health bill which would have required schools of nursing receiving capitation monies (discretionary federal funds) to admit students who would consent to practice in underserved urban and rural communities for a designated period of time after graduation. This opposition was cited in *Capital Commentary* of June 1975 but received little national notice. It was inappropriate for organized nursing to reject legislation aimed at meeting critical health manpower needs. It would have been appropriate for organized nursing to initiate

Resolutions available from the Western Council of Higher Education for Nursing, P. O. Drawer P, Boulder, Colorado 80302.

self-directed plans for insuring accountability within nursing education. These initiatives will come from sources other than organized nursing, and they will be perceived as pressure tactics unless the profession's spokespersons begin to take leadership for insuring accountability on a consistent, nationwide basis.

SUMMARY

Nursing education and service has before it today every opportunity to create change in teaching and practice. If the initiatives for ethnic inclusion are joint ventures between institutions and communities, the result will be that safe, effective nursing care will become a reality for all people. The concepts which are prerequisites for these changes have been included in this preliminary discussion, and details are included in subsequent chapters.

Bibliography*

Archer S, Fleshman R: Community Health Nursing Patterns and Practice. North Scituate, Mass. 1975
Arehart-Treichel J: What we can learn from Chinese medicine. Science News 107, 1975
Baca JE: Some health beliefs of the Spanish-speaking. Am J Nurs 1852–1854, October 1972
Bilagody H: An American Indian Looks at Health Care. Delivered at the Ninth Training Institute for Psychiatrist-Teachers of practicing Physicians. Western Interstate Commission of Higher Education, June 1969
Beergest DR: Racism in everyday speech and social work jargon. Social Work 18:4, 1973
Blue Spruce G: Needed: Indian health professionals. Health Serv Rep 88:8, 1973
Branch M: Nursing Faculty Development to Meet Minority Group Needs (Final Report). Western Interstate Commission for Higher Education, August 1975
Care of the Black Patient. Papers from conference in May 1974 on Continuing Education in Nursing at University of California, San Francisco
Damon A: Race, Ethnic Group and Disease. Soc Biol (formerly Eugenics Quarterly) 16:69–80, 1969
Davis LG: The Black Family in Urban Areas in the United States, 2nd ed. Illinois, Council of Planning Librarians, 1975
Development of Projections of the Number of Minority Persons, Women, and Minority Women Who Will Be Active in the Health Occupations. Contract 231–75–0014 (Pursuant to section 8(a) of the Small Business Act as amended), Washington, D.C.
EPIE Career Education Set: How to Detect Racism and Sexism in Classroom Materials. New York, EPIE Institute

Most are general references, except those specifically cited in text.

Fersh S: Learning About Peoples and Cultures. Evanston, Ill., McDougal, Littel

Gaitz CM, Scott J: Mental health of Mexican-Americans: Do ethnic factors make a difference? Geriatrics, November 1974

Goldsmith WC: The ghetto as a resource for Black Americans. J Am Inst Planners 40:1, 1974

Griggs A: Alaskan natives face urbanization. Race Relations Reporter 4:16, 1973

Hess G, Stroud F: Racial tensions: Barriers in delivery of nursing care. J Nurs Admin, May-June 1972

Hill RB: The Strength of Black Families. New York, National Urban League, 1961—1971

Hilliard AG III: The intellectual strengths of black children and adolescents: A challenge to pseudoscience. J Non-White Concerns, July 1974

Humphrey P: Learning about poverty and health. Nurs Outlook 22:7, July 1974

Jablonsky A: Curriculum and instruction for minority groups: An annotated bibliography of doctoral dissertations. Doctoral Research Series 4, October 1973

Jones RL (ed): Black Psychology. New York, Harper, 1972

Karno, MD, Edgerton R: Perception of mental illness in a Mexican American Community. Arch Gen Psychiatry 20, February 1969

Longres JF: Racism and its effects on Puerto-Rican continentals. Soc Casework, February 1974

Morales A: The Mexican Community Looks at the Physician. Delivered at the Ninth Annual Training Institute for Psychiatrist-Teachers of practicing Physicians. Western Interstate Commission for Higher Education, June 1969

Murray TR: A pattern for teaching indigenous culture. Comp Ed 10:49—55, 1974

Picazo ME, et al: Integration of Community/Academic Education to Meet Future Health Manpower Needs of Minorities Now. Bay Area Raza, Coalition for Health, 1974

Raya AE: Imaginative Approaches to Health Problems in the Southwest States. Office of Secretary for Health and Scientific Affairs, DHEW

Samuda RJ: From ethnocentrism to a multicultural perspective in educational testing. J Afro-Am Issues 3:1, 1975

Sinnette CH: Genocide and black ecology. Freedomways, First Quarter, 1972

Smith EM: Chicana/Chicano Bibliography. California, Center of Mexican-American Affairs, Whittier College

Suzuki PT: Minority Group Aged in America. Illinois, Council of Planning Librarians, 1975

Textbook Bias Toward Alaskan Natives: Document. Interpreted Education 9:2, 1971. Report by Department of Education, University of Alaska 1969, part 2. Leary's subcommittee on Indian Education of Senate Commission on Labor and Public Welfare, 1969

The Rights of Hospital Patients. New York, Avon, Paperback No. 380—22459—150.

Thomas A, Sillen S: Racism and Psychiatry. New York, Brunner/Mazel, 1972

Torrey EF: The Irrelevancy of Traditional Mental Health Services for Urban Mexican-Americans. Department of Psychiatry, Stanford Medical Center, 1969

Vasquez HI: Puerto Rican Americans Nat Elem Princ L:2, 1970

Wang LC: The Chinese community in San Francisco. Integr Ed, March/April 1971

Willie C, Kramer BM, Brown BS: Racism and Mental Health. Pittsburgh, University of Pittsburgh Press, 1974

White WW: Sex and White Racism. Development of Anti-Racism Training. Indiana Interreligious Commission on Human Equality

2

Historical Review of Ethnic Nurse Associations

Betty Smith Williams

INTRODUCTION

Professions and their professional associations fulfill a distinct function in the social structure of our society. The professional association has become the mechanism for protecting and developing power, status, and prestige, as well as setting norms and values for its practitioners and clientele.

Nursing, although viewed as a subprofession by some, has acquired the trappings of an autonomous profession. It has highly organized systems for the promotion of nursing education and practice, ranging from local clubs to national and international associations and federations. In the United States, the American Nurses' Association has become the dominant instrument for shaping the nursing profession.

In recent years, there has been an emergence of nursing associations based upon ethnic groupings. This trend can be viewed as consistent with the activist movements of ethnic people of color during the 1960s and 1970s. This development has created a new voice for the nursing professionals who lay claim to the right to define the nursing care practice and education for safe, effective service to their respective ethnic groups.

This chapter will focus on the ethnic nursing associations, their relationship to the traditional control associations, and their impact and potential. Whether the associations are and will be regarded as deviant or will rise to be determinants for the profession of nursing, is in question. Sociologic theory of professional associations as social institutions of control will be used to establish a framework for this analysis.

An historical perspective of such professional associations will be presented as background for understanding the problems that precipitated this revolution in the organization of professional nurses associations. The National Black Nurses' Association will be described in greater detail because of this author's direct knowledge and involvement in its development and because the history of the group is well documented in its integration efforts with the American Nurses' Association.

This author hypothesizes that ethnic nurses of color will set new norms and values and will strengthen professional nursing associations. Thus, they will no longer be defined as deviants, but, instead, as determinants or pacesetters.

HISTORICAL PERSPECTIVES: BLACK NURSES AND THE AMERICAN NURSES' ASSOCIATION

Rigid patterns of segregation and discrimination existed in 1876, when the American Nurses' Association was founded. The ANA was typical of other professional organizations, including medicine and law, in that members of the national associations were first accepted for membership by the local units. If racial discrimination was practiced on the local level, ethnic people of color in those locals were not eligible for membership in the ANA. This was a time of "Black Codes," frequent lynchings, and the rights of Negroes as freedmen were in great jeopardy. Negroes* were not admitted to the schools that had alumni entry into the ANA. Mabel Staupers recounts that, other than a few Negro nurses, mostly graduates of the New England Hospital, no Negro nurses were eligible for ANA membership in 1908.[1] It was against this background that several Negro organizations came into existence; the National Association for the Advancement of Colored People (NAACP) is the most prominent example.[2] The National Association of Colored Graduate Nurses (NACGN) was created as a mechanism for Negro nurses to pursue their defined mission. They sought equal access and equity in the profession.

The NACGN adopted the following goals:

1. To advance the standards and best interests of trained nurses.
2. To break down discrimination in the nursing profession.
3. To develop leadership within the ranks of Negro nurses.[3]

The Association organized, with officers and a Board of Directors, held national conventions, and developed local chapters to promote the cause.

The term Negro is used in its historical context to indicate terminology in popular use at the time.

The members cooperated with the National Medical Association, the Negro physicians' professional organization.

The struggle for survival and growth was marked with strife to develop schools of nursing for Negroes; to obtain licensure (take state board examinations) in the various states; to be allowed to join the ANA; and to gain admission of Negroes to "white" schools. The NACGN had heavy financial needs, as do many associations. At times, they found support for this separate effort from a few white philanthropists.

The first official attention given by the ANA to the NACGN is recorded as a 1926 meeting of committees representing both organizations to discuss ways in which NACGN members who were excluded from state ANA units because of their race could join ANA as direct members. Unfortunately, very little progress was made during this session.[4] The Depression and war years passed before the ANA launched a campaign in 1946 to encourage all state and local associations to drop racial barriers to membership.[5]

During the period from 1946 to 1951, negotiations between the ANA and NACGN were intensified. In 1948, a special class of direct membership was created by the ANA to allow Negro nurses to join in states where membership was withheld because of race. Leaders of both associations moved to formalize relationships with a momentum which culminated in the vote for dissolution of the NACGN on January 26, 1950 and its formal merger into the ANA in 1951.[6]

A careful review of the historical account of this merger as chronicled by Mabel Staupers, the last president of the NACGN, reveals that Negro nurses negotiated a series of agreements with the ANA. In 1950, a Committee on Intergroup Relations was formed as a major vehicle of the ANA for full integration of Negro nurses into its membership. The stated program was as follows:

1. Clarification in the minds of nurses about the nature and implications of racial and cultural discrimination in nursing, and about the profession's responsibility for the quality of racial and cultural relations existing among and between nurses, their patients, and their colleagues.
2. Establishment of long-term and current goals in intergroup relations by the American Nurses' Association, and adoption by it of policies to guide and support nurses in their actions on racial and cultural issues.
3. Inspiration and psychological support given by the ANA along with technical guidance and assistance to nurses, as they have sought to understand and act in accord with the human relations philosophy of their profession.

4. Development of a climate throughout nursing which encourages nurses to discuss racial and cultural relations, and to seek the assistance they need to improve intergroup relations.
5. Adoption by governmental, religious, and other civic bodies of unequivocal policies in support of "liberty and justice for all" in America.[7]

The merger represented ANA's commitment to enable Negro nurse members to participate in the total program and to insure that the program would contribute to the welfare of all Negro nurses. It was not until 1964, 13 years after the merger, that all state and district associations had removed all racial barriers to membership.

Black nurses moved into a new era without an association, but with hope of integration. With the formal network of the national association dismantled, the control and influence of these nurses became dependent upon faith in the ANA for carrying out its commitment. Local clubs of Black nurses persisted in a few cities, functioning largely as social organizations which contributed scholarships to students attending nursing schools. For example, the Mary Mahoney Club of Seattle, Washington, named after the first Negro nurse, was formed in the late 1940s. Its continued existence was testimony to the felt need for Black nurses to relate to one another, and their distinct cultural orientation.

Chi Eta Phi, founded in 1932, is a national sorority of registered nurses. It became the only such group nationally organized with a largely Negro membership. Its motto, "Service for Humanity," has been carried forward by its chapters. The members are encouraged to participate actively in the ANA.[8]

Other ethnic nurses of color, the American Indians, Asians, Chicanos, and other Spanish-speaking nurses, were not organized into associations during these years, but in subsequent years have formed local and/or national groups.

SOCIOLOGIC THEORY AS APPLIED TO PROFESSIONAL NURSING ASSOCIATIONS

Some sociologists view professional associations as having roles and functions which are part of the fabric of the total social system. Each part operates to control the problems faced within its domain. The dominant professional associations gain support by official and quasiofficial means; thus, they exercise great influence in all matters of that profession. If such an association has rising dissident factions, its power structure may act to contain them by devaluing them, discrediting their behavior, and by labeling them as deviants. The deviant faction may be viewed as trying to redefine the values and norms of that professional association. The competing deviant, if successful, can produce the new dominant ethic of that professional association, and thus become the determiner, the pacesetter for the new values of the profession.

Eliot Friedson contends that a profession is distinguished from an occupation because a profession possesses autonomy and the right to control its own functions. Nursing, by its dependence on medicine for certain authority, is viewed as paramedical; however, he notes that nursing seeks professional status. Those seeking professional status usually attempt to create many of the same institutions as those possessing that status.[9] The professional nurses' associations exemplify such institutions.

Professional associations, historically, have worked to achieve control over their own work. They have claimed a core body of knowledge which they seek to be legitimatized as exclusive to their practitioners. Codes of ethics are developed which enumerate the humanitarian purpose of the profession and set highest values on such characteristics as honesty, equality, excellence, fair play, and charity. Responsibility as a basic trait is emphasized, and the claim that professionals may work conscientiously without supervision is made. Control of entrance into the profession and attention to education or adequate training are prominent aspects of the programs of these associations.[10]

"The Inner Fraternity" control group is described by Oswald Hall[11] as typical of professional occupations. His studies reveal that in the medical profession, ethnicity and religion were the most significant variables in the recruitment process. This inner fraternity operates largely through the control of professional associations in a sponsorship process. This relatively small group of insiders shapes both informally and formally the development of the profession. The established members will, in the course of time, develop a subgroup which functions to provide order, to ascribe and maintain status, to control the conduct of members, and to minimize competition and conflict. This sponsoring subgroup develops an orderly manner of incorporating new members into their community and of repelling unwanted candidates and intruders by allocating rights and privileges. The protegé who is selected thus attains smooth entrance and obtains appointments to positions of power as he becomes a colleague. The process goes full circle, thus maintaining control by the dominant power group.

Any deviance from the orderly process, including efforts to acquire entrance to the inner fraternity, is dealt with from within by negative sanctions and penalties. Assuming that these fraternities, circles, or networks are created on the basis of common standards with permissive limits, deviants may be excluded from one circle but may find another that may accept them. Friedson identifies the boycott as a major sanction.[12]

Deviance from a set of norms developed by professional associations creates a social problem for those who view this as a threat to maintenance of their control. No longer are those things which the dominant group has identified as normal and proper for the profession the only options. As indicated earlier, certain limits of differing values are planned for and tolerated. What then are the breaking points? When does social deviance threaten the power structure of an organization? Deviance is a label or concern of the definer who imputes certain behaviors as threats to the norm. This belief occurs as an evaluation of a state or situation.[13]

The previously mentioned social analysis applies to the ANA. It is similar to other professional associations in that it develops power and acts to retain control. One would conclude that the sharing of the power and status of the organization was at stake, based on the accounts of the exclusion and later reluctant inclusion of "intruders," Black nurses, into the ANA. The ANA managed to position itself as the dominant force and literally engulfed the intruders during times of great social pressure for integration ie, the armed forces and public schools. ANA dominant groups were left in control to reward on a token basis the entry of certain Black nurses. This created the illusion of integration. A group of Black nurse protegés was selected. They brought prestige to the organization, creating the impression of a progressive professional group who truly sought to give service to all people in equity. The reward to the "new" members was the promise of intergroup relations programs and the continuance of the Mary Mahoney Award for the nurse who made a significant contribution toward integration. Black nurses were allowed considerable control in the selection of the recipient; thus, the illusion of their power was maintained.

The emergence of new ethnic nurse associations, on the other hand, was due to the fact that the ANA did not keep pace with the core needs of ethnic nurses of color in a time when more participation and power were needed. The current generation of nurses, many highly prepared educationally and aware of themselves as competent people, are in tune with the times, ready to be the definers of their destiny, and ready to strike out on their own for institutional change.

CURRENT ETHNIC NURSE ASSOCIATIONS

The desire for social intercourse with those doing the same work and facing the same problems is cited by Saunders and Wilson[14] as the immediate motive for professionals seeking one another.* Ethnic nurses of color had

*From *Carr Saunders and Wilson: The Professions: 1933. Courtesy of the Oxford University Press, Oxford.*

this need to know one another and to identify and gain strength in unity toward facing the challenges presented in the late 1960s and early 1970s. A decade of activism had swept the United States. Revolutionary momentum had inspired new hope in deprived and oppressed people.

Two patterns appear to have set the course of various professional ethnic people of color during those times. In certain communities, these professionals began to form groups which established, from a grass roots base, organizations to articulate their causes. The other approach was through the formation of caucus groups at various national professional association meetings. Both of these approaches led to the creation of new networks for discourse between ethnic professionals. Ethnic nurses of color pursued both courses, with resultant emergence of new groupings of ethnic nurses.

LOCAL ASSOCIATIONS EMERGE

In Los Angeles, The Council of Black Nurses was formed in 1967. By 1970, the Los Angeles and San Francisco Bay area Black Nurses' Associations had met and planned the first statewide conference of Black nurses. This conference attracted Black nurses from places as far away as Miami and New York City. Within a year, these cities and others reported formation of Black nurses' associations. The major purposes of these organizations were to improve the health care of Black people, and to safeguard the professional status of the Black nurse.

The Chicana Nurses' Organization was established in Los Angeles in 1969. In a joint meeting with the Los Angeles Council of Black Nurses, the two groups shared experiences and planned organizational strategies. Unity of purpose was clear in this meeting. The desire to mobilize to improve nursing care to persons of the respective communities was the overriding theme. The need for increased numbers of Chicano nurses was recognized as crucial to creation of the improvement needed in the health care of Chicano people. Focal issues included recruitment, admission, and retention of Chicanos in schools of nursing. Further, obtaining positions on policy-making levels was identified as a means for Chicano nurses to exert influence on their destiny. The Latin American Nurses' Association emerged in northern California in 1972. Subsequently, other local units have organized in Colorado and other states and a national Latino nurses' association has been formed.

The Korean Nurses' Association of Southern California was founded in 1970. There is also a Northern California Korean Nurses' Association and several other local associations throughout the United States. The goals of these associations include increasing the effectiveness of the Korean nurses in order that they, in turn, can deliver the highest quality nursing care to Korean-Americans. Korean nurses who are new to the United States must obtain licensure and learn the American health delivery methods. Philosophical differences in Korean nursing and Western nursing, as well as language barriers, are identified problems. The Korean Nurses' Association in southern California conducts continuing education programs monthly to assist in the acculturation process.

The Philippine Nurses' Associations are located in southern California, San Francisco, Seattle, and other major population centers of the United States and Canada. They are chapters of the International Philippine Nurses' Association, incorporated on May 9, 1948. The southern California chapter was established in October 1960. Among their broad goals is that of assisting nurses coming into this country from the Republic of the Philippines to become licensed. These associations also address the problems of acculturation and adjustment to life in the United States. They conduct activities to improve the health of the Filipino people in particular, and of society in general. These include sponsorship of clinical and scientific workshops and seminars. The question of starting a separate American Filipino Nurse Association is being considered by some members of that nursing community.

NATIONAL ASSOCIATIONS EMERGE

National Black Nurses' Association, Inc.

A caucus session was held during the national meeting of the American Nurses' Association in Miami in 1970 by Black nurses. The session resulted in the establishment of a steering committee. The committee members, who were from most geographic areas of the country, were to continue the communication and dialogue which emerged from the caucus. On December 22, 1971, a group of Black nurses called by the steering committee chairman, Dr. Lauranne Sams, met in Cleveland, Ohio, to examine the status of the Black nurses' movement. It was at this weekend retreat in the home of Dr. Mary Harper than the motion to form the National Black Nurses' Association was unanimously passed. Interim officers and committee chairmen were selected from those present, and the tasks basic to formal organization were identified and assigned.

The impetus for the decision to organize a special association for Black nurses came from a recognition that the ANA lacked focus for Black and other ethnic concerns. The need for a Black Nurses' Association was emphasized at the 1971 National Conference on the Status of Health called by the Congressional Black Caucus at Meharry Medical College, Nashville, Tennessee. Leaders of Black health and welfare professional associations throughout the nation were gathered to assess and strategize to improve health care for Black people. Black nurses lacking an association were not formally included. A congressman, when approached regarding this, stated, "You (Black nurses) have no organization, no agreed upon leaders for us to include." Although other Black health professionals, physicians, dentists, pharmacists, have gained entrance to the dominant organizations, they still maintained their national associations through the years.

Clearly, the decision to establish the National Black Nurses' Association, Inc., was the means for Black nurses to get back their voices, to send forth messages that "Black nurses have the understanding, knowledge, interest, concern and experience to make a significant difference in the health care status of the Black Community."[15] Through subsequent meetings, the National Black Nurses' Association, Inc. (NBNA) objectives were agreed upon as follows:

1. Define and determine nursing care for Black consumers for optimum quality of care by acting as their advocates.
2. Act as change agents in restructuring existing institutions and/or helping to establish institutions to suit our needs.
3. Serve as the national nursing body to influence legislation and policies that affect Black people, and work cooperatively and collaboratively with other health workers to this end.
4. Conduct, analyze, and publish research to increase the body of knowledge about health care and health needs of Blacks.
5. Compile and maintain a National Directory of Black Nurses to assist with the dissemination of information regarding Black nurses and nursing on national and local levels by the use of all media.
6. Set standards and guidelines for quality education of Black nurses on all levels by providing consultation to nursing faculties, and by monitoring for proper utilization and placement of Black nurses.
7. Recruit, counsel, and assist Black persons interested in nursing to insure a constant progression of Blacks into the field.
8. Act as the vehicle for unification of Black nurses of varied age groups, educational levels, and geographic location to insure continuity and flow of our common heritage.
9. Collaborate with other Black groups to compile archives relevant to the historic, current, and future activities of Black nurses.
10. Provide the impetus and means for Black nurses to write and publish on an individual or collaborative basis.[16]

These objectives were utilized in the NBNA's incorporation in the State of Ohio in 1972.

One of the first programmatic efforts to increase the focus and visibility of the NBNA was its participation in the symposia of the 1972 ANA Convention. These sessions stirred a great response in the ANA, which will be described later in an analysis of the dominant organization's response to "deviants."

It became clear to the NBNA interim steering group that if a separate organization was to be a fact, they would have to change the nature of participation in the ANA national meetings. Plans emerged for a separate national Institute and Conference under the direction and control of the NBNA. The first Conference was planned for the fall of 1973, months away from the spring meeting of ANA. The purpose was to draw out Black nurses who would have a more singular purpose for attendance: the content of the NBNA program.

The theme for the first NBNA Institute, held in Cleveland, Ohio, was "Emerging Roles for Black Nurses: Responsibility, Accountability, and Militancy." Unable to secure an outside grant, members of the steering committee advanced their personal funds to provide the necessary seed money to finance this Conference. As Gloria Smith poignantly describes, "the spirit of that meeting was a fusion of great joy and immense pain — the joy arising out of the relief of no longer having to be isolated, and the pain from the disappointment in the old system."[17]

The 1974 Institute was held in Miami, Florida. The focus was "Institutional Racism: Impact on Health Care Delivery." An election of officers was held, which changed some members of the now official Board of Directors; notably, a student nurse assumed the office of National Second Vice President. This was the beginning of a formalized means of training for the future leadership of Black nursing.

The next milestone of national conference programming will be the Third Institute, planned for October 1975, in St. Louis, Missouri. By mandate of the prior Institute, the theme is "The Black Family — The Black Experience: Implications for Nursing Intervention." The innovations of having clinical papers and family studies, along with panels, speeches, and symposia, suggest a movement in the professional association's traditional format.

American Indian Nurses' Association, Inc.

The American Indian Nurses' Association (AINA) began viable organizational efforts in 1971.[18] The Association's goals are

1. To promote optimum health among the American Indian people
2. To promote a more equitable number of American Indians within the nursing profession through recruitment and through development in nursing education
3. To educate the Indian and non-Indian population about the specific health needs of Indian people
4. To recommend proper solutions to the health problems of Indian people[19]

The AINA credits the Association of American Indian Affairs for both moral and monetary assistance in the development of its organization, which was formally founded in 1972.

The AINA, as expressed by its goals, moved to attain visibility and focus upon the plight of Indian nurses and the Indian people. It has become an incorporated organization with headquarters in Norman, Oklahoma. The association also has been able to employ an executive director and staff. AINA activities are influenced by the treaty status of American Indian nations. They are in a unique position. Treaties with the United States government promised a variety of services in exchange for land. AINA is requesting that the Indian Health Service fulfill its commitment.

Among efforts to fulfill its goal of dealing with inequities in health care to Indian people, the AINA has three major projects. These are (1) the identification and recruitment of American Indian nurses into the labor force; (2) the recruitment of American Indian women into nursing education programs; and (3) the obtaining of Allstate Scholarships for American Indian nursing students.

AINA has surveyed schools of nursing in the western United States to determine the number of Indian students and faculty and the extent to which curriculum content emphasizes health and nursing needs of Indian people. This content is believed to be an integral part of nursing science. They have established the Ethel Wortis Fund as a revolving emergency fund for American Indian nursing students.

"Perspectives in Nursing in the American Indian Community" was the theme of the first national conference sponsored by AINA in April 1975, at Haskell Indian Junior College, Kansas. The purpose of the conference was to provide a means for American Indian nurses to collaborate with nursing colleagues, members of other health disciplines, and various agencies for the advancement of health care in the Indian community. At the same time, the membership saw an opportunity to provide the students and faculty of Haskell with exposure to professional Indian nurse leaders. They had hopes of influencing recruitment to the profession.[20]

CAUCUS WITHIN ANA EMERGES

In June 1974, the Spanish Speaking-Spanish Surnamed Nurses' Caucus of the American Nurses' Association was established. Its purpose is to integrate Spanish-speaking nurses into the structural and decision-making level of ANA, and to have a voice in the planning of health service delivery to Spanish-speaking citizens and residents of the United States. The present project is the compilation of a "talent bank" of Spanish-speaking nurses, with their areas of specialization and expertise. The future program plan is to survey health services rendered to residents of Spanish-speaking communities, as well as the services needed. In addition, research to identify the contributions of Spanish-speaking nurses to nursing practice and nursing education is envisioned.

This subgroup within ANA may be an example of ethnic nurses of color working within the dominant professional nursing association to influence responsiveness to their groups' concerns. Is it possible to attain ethnic goals by internal organizational strategies? The caucus clearly seeks access to power from within. Implicit in this ethnic caucus formation must be the conviction that the ANA priorities, resources, and skills can be reordered to effectively meet their needs. The impact of this approach should be carefully examined to enhance the knowledge base regarding institutional change.

ETHNIC ASSOCIATIONS' THEMES

There are several themes pervading the reasons for development of the new ethnic nurse associations: (1) the concept of ethnic nurses as best able to identify the nursing needs of their unique ethnicity; (2) the recognition of the desirability and need for increasing their numbers on all levels and positions in the nursing profession; (3) the desire for equity; and, (4) the conviction that there is strength through group action. Further, there was the common thread identifying the American Nurses' Association as having one set of functions separate from those of the ethnic nurses' associations. The associations feel the need to influence ANA's decisions and to become strengthened in order to create better nursing care for all.

ANA RESPONSE

The American Nurses' Association's response to the ethnic group activities has varied. There were those within the organization who were acutely in tune with the need for change. The ANA president, having learned of the National Black Nurses' Association's activities, invited Dr. Lauranne Sams and two other nurses of her choice to lunch in Detroit in 1972 with the ANA executives. As a participant in that luncheon, this author assesses that the real question, separatism, was never asked. There was a discussion in which ANA's good intentions were expressed. Although the leadership was unable to influence ANA membership to focus upon a commitment to Black nurses, hope was expressed for the improvement of the situation with the passage of the pending Affirmative Action Resolution (see Appendix). Notably, the ANA President-elect recognized the potential that an ANA spokesman could have had for moral guidance in promoting equity for all nurses.

For the first time in ANA history, a Black nurse, Ethelrine Shaw, Columbus, Ohio, was elected third vice-president at the 1972 meeting. In addition, the Affirmative Action Resolution was approved that ANA should meet its old commitment to the National Association of Colored Graduate Nurses. Shortly thereafter, an Affirmative Action Task Force was formed. Its membership was Black, Chicano, and American Indian, along with a nonethnic nurse of color.

The task force has published a plan for action which was passed by the 1974 house of delegates of the ANA.[21] The plan defined the Ombudsman role and recommended the establishment of an independent Ombudsman Committee. Both had been instituted by Board approval and appropriation. A unique meeting was held by the task force, with all minorities holding positions on ANA structural units having the responsibility of promoting unity and of developing concerted program thrusts. The group determined that the ANA should develop a major national project which would both improve the health situation of minority people, and, at the same time, demonstrate the power of professional nurses to positively change a health state. The recommended focus was the problem of maternal and infant morbidity and mortality. This problem area was identified as being particularly responsive to nursing intervention modalities. The task force has sought a permanent place for its work through a commission on nursing and through guidelines for affirmative action among state and local units of the ANA.[22]

The ANA is collecting ethnic membership data and has learned in 1975 that ethnic nurses are joining at a rate higher than other nurses. This phenomena may well be the result of increased activity of ethnic nurses of color in their own professional nursing organizations throughout the United States. The ANA was given federal funds to increase the number of minority nurses with Ph.D. degrees. The first doctoral fellowships were awarded during the summer of 1975.

During the early meetings of the task force, it was immediately obvious that this enormous job would require basic institutional change. The task force was limited by its formation as a committee, rather than as a commission within ANA. Such a commission has been proposed by the task force. The ANA provision for institutionalization of these actions by creation of a commission on multiracial concerns will be the strongest expression yet of its commitment to ethnic concerns.

IMPACT UPON NURSING

Social theory explains professional associations as a means for the attainment of control of the content, goals, standards, education, and practice of a given occupation. The development of multiple ethnic associations in the nursing profession has been described. One could expect the occurrence of conflict of such a nature as to weaken the central purposes of nursing associations. The conflict would most likely occur in areas where more than one group claims domain. The very fact that ethnic nurse organizations are becoming a reality indicates that there are some areas of conflict. From an analysis of their respective goals, the conflict appears centered upon priorities of the traditional professional nursing association, specifically the ANA priority, action toward the inclusion of ethnic nurses in substantial roles, and the attention to the health care needs of ethnic people of color.

A comparison of ethnic nurse associations reveals similarities between the groups, such as nationally incorporated groups with local chapters, units, or affiliates. The ANA By-Laws state its purposes as follows:

The purposes of the American Nurses' Association shall be to foster high standards of nursing practice, promote the professional and educational advancement of nurses, and promote the welfare of nurses to the end that all people may have better nursing care. These purposes shall be unrestricted by considerations of nationality, race, creed, color, or sex. [23]

The ethnic nurse associations' purposes are focused upon consideration of ethnicity, declaring urgent special needs and specialized expertise. The attainment of equity in health status for ethnic people is argued to need positive, aggressive action. This is quite different from the more palliative term, "unrestricted."

The search for autonomy, the key concept of professionalization advanced by Eliot Friedson,[24] was earlier expressed as a problem for nursing which keeps it on a pararelationship with medicine, which controls many of nursing's actions. Health professionals have not designed a successful way of meeting the health needs of ethnic people of color. It is believed that if organized nursing is going to reorder its priorities, it may be possible to create a nursing domain in which autonomy would be a reality. It has been proposed that ethnic nurse organizations will be key factors in this role for professional nursing. This belief is not advanced in naiveté, for experience has shown that what is painful and outmoded in our system is being strongly expressed by desperate ethnic groups, and also supported by many enlightened members of the dominant group.

The pain of being dehumanized, treated as an object, will no longer be tolerated. Ethnic nurse groups call for humanism, which is lacking in medicine and which has been diminishing in nursing. Personalization, reflected by concern for the whole being, his/her dignity and worth, must become a primary and integral part of all nursing care. The centralization of power and control in the hands of the power elite is destined for a very slow demise. The sponsorship and inner fraternity systems are being exposed as patronage. Certainly, the nursing professional associations are not exceptional. New systems will emerge, and their definition can be influenced by unification of nurses who have goals of equity and humanistic health care for all people.

The power of the American Nurses' Association has both grown and diminished. Increased numbers of ethnic members bring a creative potential heretofore not available or explored. The sharing in decisions, including priority setting among a broader base of professional nurses, will diminish older elite group control. The outcome may depend upon the development of new systematic means for input of all members, for all nonprotegé nurses feel alienated and powerless. This discussion has focused on ethnic nurses of color; however, there is also a story to be added about other "deviant" nurse groups. Increasingly, white "deviants" are vocalizing their dissatisfaction with the system. This evidence of discontent should be examined. The challenge is there; will the ANA take the venture?

Will ethnic nurse associations survive and grow as determiners of the practice of nursing? Only some future social observer will be able to document and thus answer this rhetorical question. Ethnic associations will need to produce quickly — to obtain visibility and credibility. Utilization of their expertise to accomplish short-range value goals should increase their support base. They should benefit by avoidance of interethnic competition which can absorb needed energy and thereby dilute and weaken the movement. Where mutual goals can be served, affiliation with like-minded colleagues, regardless of ethnicity, should be encouraged for strength in working toward their goals. The unique knowledge that the given ethnic group brings to nursing must be nourished by systematic maintenance of a "reality base" grounded in the roots of their community.

Reality orientation to the respective communities can be continued by planned input and feedback through regular contact with the people and priority issues. Direct professional nursing care within one's own ethnic community will give the individual nurse the opportunity to provide and influence others toward the provision of the highest quality humanistic health care.

The multiracial society we have is not likely to decrease in the United States, considering the fact that most of the peoples of the world are of color. The reason for ethnic nurse associations to promulgate and plan should increase by demand. This will occur, not because of the present dominant nursing associations' desire to give away their control, but because of the recognition that guidance, determination, and pacesetting from the ethnic groups is necessary for nursing's very survival as an independent profession. The movement of ethnic nurses to this position of leadership can be theirs to choose.

CONCLUSIONS

The emergence of ethnic nurses of color in formal nursing associations in the late 1960s and early 1970s has been described and discussed as a challenge to the American Nurses' Association for self-determination. Professional associations as institutions for control and definers of an occupation are firmly based in societies. Nursing seeks full professional status and autonomy and possesses the same types of systems for selection of the power elite. Ethnic nurses, after years of exclusion, are defining their own domain. With this emergent trend, it has been shown that ignoring them or treating them as deviants has been unsuccessful. Since the ANA can obtain new strength from accepting and utilizing "new" resources, the changes are inevitable and can be incorporated to produce higher status and prestige for the whole nursing profession.

Some changes as a result of the impact of ethnic nurses' associations are identifiable. There is determination for pacesetting. Resistance is also evident, so ethnic nurses' associations will need to maintain momentum and resist coercion to secure new ground.

The concept of caring is often cited as the unique capability of a nurse — caring for the total person's mental and physical well-being. Capitalization upon this by truly operationalizing this skill, with resultant increased value to *all* members of this multiethnic society, could propel nursing into true autonomy and professionalization. Nursing would then, in fact, be able to establish domain in which no other professional/occupational group has demonstrated the capability.

APPENDIX

RESOLUTION ON AFFIRMATIVE ACTION PROGRAM*

WHEREAS, in 1951 a merger of the National Association of Colored Graduate Nurses and the American Nurses' Association was effected which resulted in the dissolution of the National Association of Colored Graduate Nurses with a subsequent commitment by the American Nurses' Association that the participation of black nurses in the American Nurses' Association would receive major promotional efforts, and

WHEREAS, "It was recognized that if Negro nurses were to receive complete and adequate services within the American Nurses' Association, provision must be made by the ANA for staff and facilities which would enable Negro nurse members to participate effectively in the total program of the organization and ensure that the program would contribute to the welfare of all Negro nurses,"† and

WHEREAS, the Committee on Intergroup Relations, which was established as the vehicle to implement the Intergroup Relations Program, was dissolved by the ANA in 1962 before the objectives of the program were achieved, and

WHEREAS, In the 21 years since the merger of the National Association of Colored Graduate Nurses and the American Nurses' Association, black nurses have noticeably been excluded from elected office and appointed positions on committees, commissions and boards within the organization and the inclusion of black nurses on policy and decision-making bodies in nursing and related health care groups has remained limited, and

WHEREAS, Increasing numbers of black nurses are finding it necessary to organize in caucus groups and associations to meet the needs created by the failure of the American Nurses' Association to discharge its obligation; therefore be it

RESOLVED, That the American Nurses' Association honor its commitment by taking immediate steps to establish an Affirmative Action Program at the National level which will rectify this failure; and be it further

RESOLVED, That such steps shall include:

Submitted by ANA Commission on Nursing Research.
†*Staupers, Mabel K., No Time for Prejudice, New York: The Macmillan Co., 1961, p. 138.*

1. *Appointment of a Task Force composed of nurses representative of minority groups (which shall also include white nurses) to develop and implement such a program, and*
2. *Appointment of a black nurse to the ANA staff to work with the Task Force developing and implementing the program, and*
3. *ANA shall actively seek greater numbers of minority group members in elected, appointed and staff positions within ANA and urge states and districts to do likewise; and be it further*

RESOLVED, That the ANA encourage and promote Affirmative Action Programs on the state and local levels; and be it further

RESOLVED, That an ombudsman be appointed to the ANA staff.

References

1. Staupers MK: No Time for Prejudice. New York, Macmillan, 1961, p 15
2. Hughes L: Fight for Freedom. New York, Berkeley, 1962, p 22
3. Staupers, op cit, p 17
4. Idem, p 24
5. Steiber J: Public Employee Unionism. Brookings Institute, 1973, p 78
6. Staupers, op cit, p 143
7. Idem, pp 146—47
8. Idem, pp 193—94
9. Friedson E: Profession of Medicine. New York, Dodd, Mead, 1973, p 76
10. Idem, p 76
11. Vollmer H, Mills D (eds): Professionalization. Englewood Cliffs, N.J., Prentice-Hall, 1966, pp 329—30
12. Friedson, op cit, p 194
13. Idem, p 215
14. Carr Saunders AM, Wilson PA: The Professions. Courtesy Oxford University Press, Oxford, 1933
15. National Black Nurses' Association, Inc.: Constitution and By-Laws. 1973
16. Idem.
17. Smith GR: From invisibility to blackness: The story of the National Black Nurses' Association. Nurs Outlook 23:228 April, 1975
18. Newsletter of the American Indian Nurses' Association: Vol. 2, No. 2, 1975
19. American Indian Nurses' Association: Perspectives in Nursing for the American Indian Community. A Nursing Conference Brochure, 1975
20. Newsletter of the American Indian Nurses' Association: Vol. 1, No. 2, 1974
21. Bello T, Mathwig G, Ruffin J, et al: Affirmative Action in Action. A report. Kansas City, Mo., American Nurses' Association, 1974

22. Ruffin, J. Affirmative Action Programming for the Nursing Profession Through the American Nurse's Association, Kansas City, Mo. The American Nurses Assn, 1975 M-23 5M 11/75
23. American Nurses' Association: By-Laws. As amended June 1974
24. Friedson E: Professional Dominance: The Social Structure of Medical Care. New York, Atherton, 1970

Bibliography

Alexander RP: The black lawyer and his responsibility in the urban crisis. Negro Digest, June 1969

Bigham G: To communicate with Negro patients. Am J Nursing 64 (9), 1964

Harvey L: Educational problems of minority group nurses. Nurses Outlook 18(9): 1970

Hess G, Stroud F: Racial tensions: barriers in delivery of nursing care. J Nursing Assoc, May/June 1972

Mosley D: The nursing profession and the urban poor. NCRIEEO Tip Sheet No. 11, April 1973

Parsons T: Definitions of health and illness in the light of American values and social structure. In Jaco EG (ed): Patients, Physicians, and Illness. New York, The Free Press, 1955

Parsons T: Essays in Sociological Theory. New York, The Free Press, 1954, p 34

Resolution on Affirmative Action Program, Adopted by the American Nurses' Association, 1972 (Appendix)

Robinson A: Why so few blacks in nursing? RN, July 1972

Staupers M: Story of the National Association of Colored Graduate Nurses. Am J Nursing, 1951

PART II

Cultural Health Traditions: Implications for Nursing Care

CULTURAL HEALTH TRADITIONS: AN OVERVIEW

Cultural health encompasses large categories of preventive and healing arts practiced by people who live close to their cultural traditions throughout the world. Many of these practices for the maintenance and restoration of health have been described from observations of nonwestern cultures. For the purposes of this book, the discussions of cultural health traditions will center on four major ethnic groups of color in the United States. The authors hope that readers will be encouraged to search for information on other ethnic groups in this country with health traditions similar to those described in Chapters 3 through 6.

Throughout history, people have searched for the causes of the imbalance which is termed "dis-ease." That search continues today. We do not have satisfactory explanations for the many variables of illness. Why does one group of people contract communicable disease while another does not? Why do other major illnesses affect some and not others? Can we identify the proportion of factors necessary for illness to occur? If such were the case, we would be predicting lifelong patterns of illness from conception to death. Conceivably, one's chart for wellness and illness would follow a formula based on knowledge of one's heredity, immunity, susceptibility, exposure to germs and toxins, environment, behavior, predisposition, life style, diet, thought patterns, life stresses, etc.

Cultural health and healing follow traditions based on knowledge which, in the cases of many groups, has evolved over centuries. The information that forms the body of knowledge for the cultural traditions is the result of explorations into the physical and spiritual relationships between people, nature, and the universe. Belief systems for the practice of this knowledge have been developed by each cultural group. Basic to most of these belief systems is the holistic view that there is harmony among the triad: the person, the earth, and the universe. A disruption of this harmony creates an imbalance which may result in illness of mind, body, or spirit, or which may cause other disasters which affect the person. It follows then that healing or the reestablishment of harmony dictates an approach which is inclusive of the triad: the person, the earth, and the universe.

Practitioners of western technologic medicine are beginning to "discover" the holistic view to healing. Although the discovery process is incomplete and the practices are still used separately, for the most part, some proponents of the usual treatment modalities are adding to their practice modalities such as biofeedback, biorhythms, relaxation exercises, hypnosis, and other approaches which assist individuals to restore innate balancing mechanisms. An ideal practice of the healing arts in the United States would combine knowledge and practice from a variety of belief systems for the creation of a holistic approach to the maintenance and restoration of health with heavy emphasis on the prevention of illness.

The chapters in this section are intended to impart to the reader new knowledge of and appreciation for health practices which have been labeled as superstitious nonsense by the unknowing and the insensitive. This section should be used as the basis for the creation of one's personal view of health. We are wise to adopt the notion that a personal view of health evolves continually as does one's personal view of life. Such a view is influenced by new knowledge and experience, is never static or stale, but hopefully, moves towards the ultimate truth.

3

Cultural Health Traditions:
The Latino/Chicano Perspective

Pauline Rodriguez Dorsey
and Herlinda Quintero Jackson

What you want to know makes no sense. . . .The trouble with you is
that you understand things in only one way. You don't think a man
flies; and yet a brujo can move a thousand miles in one second to see
what is going on. He can deliver a blow to his enemies long distances
away. So, does he or doesn't he fly?

Admonition by Don Juan[1]

Differences in perceptions and orientations among people are culturally defined. The mode of expression of emotions, as well as the way in which daily activities of living are performed, are determined by the input from the environment. The learning process begins from the beginning of life, and reinforcement or molding of behavior takes place constantly. Consequently, behavior deemed as "unacceptable" by one group of people may be an accepted practice to another group.

This chapter will explore perceptions of illness among Latino/Chicano people and will present some of the reasons for the survival and flourishment of folk health practices. The emphasis of the chapter will be on achieving some degree of coherence among the health ideologies and practices coming from a group of people known nationally as Latinos. This group of people is often referred to as Hispanos, Spanish-Americans, Latin-Americans, Mexican Americans, Chicanos, or Boriqua. Many writers agree on generalizations about the Spanish-speaking of America. However, accurate and relevant descriptions must be made for the many ethnic groups that make up the Latino population of the United States. Cultural similarities or variants occurring within Latino groups must be recognized. Although there exists a diversity of values, beliefs, and morals among the groups referred to as Latinos; we will make an effort to bring together the most common of these. It will become clear that all Latinos, their health beliefs and values, do not come from one mold. Many of the examples given in this chapter will refer to Chicano folk health practices, as they represent the largest group of Spanish-speaking people in the United States, and because of the Chicano culture's predominant influence throughout the Southwest. The conceptual framework for the understanding of Latino folk health practices will be that of the Chicano culture because the authors' familiarity and basis for folk beliefs and practices are strongest in the Chicano experience.

A review of the literature reveals little documentation regarding the prevalence and incidence of patronage of folk healers by Latino/Chicano people. Much exploration has been done in terms of examination of folk medicine as an institution within Latino/Chicano culture.*[2,3] Observations have been made also of Chicanos seeking "modern" medical assistance while still continuing to use folk remedies prescribed by folk healers.[4]

Cabrera points out that available information on folk health tends to portray Mexican Americans in a negative stereotypic manner, often excluding or slighting their contributions, the result being exclusion from historical or literary roles.[5] Typically the Latino/Chicano has been portrayed as being strongly influenced by mystical, sacred, and ritualistic practices. Little investigation is made into the cause-effect aspect of the curative healers. Consequently, a void is left in terms of the implications and positive contributions made by Latino/Chicano folk practitioners.

There has been a recent trend within the dominant society to use herbs, certain foods, special diets, and natural curative measures. Recent movements in ecology, naturalism, and self-preservation have added impetus to this rush "back to nature." Although a few conscientious persons have utilized these practices throughout the centuries, naturalism is enjoying a glorification and a rebirth among members of the dominant society. Information and statistics regarding the deleterious effects of additives and caustic preservatives have produced an increased concern for using natural foods and nonharmful substances. With the help of consumer advocates, there has been an acknowledgment by the general public that modern medicine does not have all the answers. Certain diseases — acute, chronic, or incurable — have no remedy today, despite modern technology. In the race away from the shackles of industrialization, the public is searching to regain a sense of well-being outside of the boundaries of modern medicine. These attempts at self-cure often step beyond the limitations of Western thought.

The authors suggest that the reader recognize the limitations of these studies. Their presentation here does not imply acceptance of their premises or conclusions regarding folk practices. We cite these authors only in reference to the findings of their investigations and not as to their conclusions.

Traditionally, the dominant society views the disease process as a result of germs, microorganisms, or a myriad of symptoms which can be diagnosed and treated. The Latino/Chicano views disease as having spiritual, social, and consequential ramifications far beyond the biologic context of a microorganism.[6]

Kiev indicates that culture influences the form that illness takes and, consequently, the type of treatment developed to deal with the illness. He speaks of "culture specific" methods of treatment for disorders and/or conditions that are culturally determined.[7] Therefore, illness is viewed within a social context by the Latino/Chicano and is approached with a sociocultural perspective. The Latino/Chicano utilizes people, artifacts, and materials that are familiar and within his experience. Octavio Romano describes the concept of "charismatic medicine" in the role of the delivery of health care:

> *The concept of charismatic medicine postulates that a complementary and charismatic component simultaneously exists in (a) the healer role as such, and in (b) the healer as an individual occupies that role, he may bring to it personal qualities which sustain without significant alteration the preexistent forms, or, he may enhance the charismatic attributes of the healer role through his own qualities as a distinct personality. The interplay of these two factors, as they "successfully" affect the clientele, is here called charismatic medicine.*[8]

The importance of charisma and the prestige and respect attributed to the healer are important components of the folk health system. This concept of charismatic medicine will be discussed further in the chapter.

HISTORICAL BACKGROUND

The roots of Latino/Chicano folk health knowledge derive from the diverse Indian civilizations of Latin America. Another contributing influence is traditional fifteenth- and sixteenth-century European medicine and practices.[9] The use of medicinal herbs and plants as cathartics, diuretics, emetics, etc. has been documented in early Egyptian and Greek writings and later influenced Spanish medicine. In terms of North American civilization, there exists clear evidence of the use of folk medicine and practices throughout the transitional periods of the Mayan and Aztec civilizations to those of the American Indians of the Southwest and extending through the era of the Spanish conquistadores.

Further, folk healing can be traced through the middle cultures of Mexico and the Southwest which are forerunners of twentieth century lifestyles.

Determinant Characteristics in the Utilization of Folk Health Practices

The following represent the five factors which determine the use or adherence to folk health practices among Latino/Chicano people:

1. Accessibility
2. Degree of acculturation and language
3. Family generation and familial practices
4. Religion
5. Age

ACCESSIBILITY. The East Los Angeles Health Report of 1970 documents the shortage of bilingual medical personnel and services in one of the nation's largest barrios. Compounding this shortage is the lack of bilingual health providers within the institutions and agencies that service the predominantly Spanish-speaking area.[10]

The same report documents the poverty level of the Mexican American community as being $3500 annual income.[11] At present, the income of Spanish-speaking, Spanish-surnamed persons living in rural and inner city areas is at or well below poverty level. Money is spent on food, housing, and other day-to-day survival needs. Illness and diseases, which are manifestations of poverty, often run their course without the benefit of medical attention. As Cabrera points out, "people suffer, not because they are fatalistic, but rather because they are powerless to alter the course of events".[12] Health maintenance, although a priority, is often a luxury due to social circumstances.

The plight of the rural Chicano can be typified by citing the conditions of the *bracero* or farmworker. Galarza, MacWilliams, and Chandler describe the adverse working conditions of the migrant farmworker.[13-15] No research exists about the type of health services offered to this group of workers. However, the speeches and endeavors of Cesar Chavez, leader and spokesman for the United Farm Workers, have exposed the inadequacy or lack of health care facilities for farmworkers throughout the nation.

Faced with the lack of health services, an individual must seek out and utilize those resources most appropriate, accessible, and functionally relevant. An example of the utilization of familiar and relevant resources is the patronage of neighborhood Latino stores, which carry staples, common herbs, and spices familiar to the culture. These stores, found in all Latino/Chicano communities, carry remedies for home treatment, as well as herbs, religious artifacts, and oils from Mexico or the mother country (Fig. 3.1).

Cabrera supports the thought that where geographic or social isolation is a fact, old-country cultural ways may be more commonly observed. He further points out that this may be true of all poverty or low-income groups in the United States.[16]

DEGREE OF ACCULTURATION. Whether Chicanos accept or reject folk medical beliefs and practices indigenous to their culture is related to the theoretical argument that a person's perceptions of illness and its treatment are basically culturally and socially determined.[17] Saunders in studying cultural differences in medical care stated:

Illness and disease, it must be remembered, are social as well as biological phenomena . . . on the social level they include the meanings, roles, relationships, attitudes, and techniques that enable members of a cultural group to identify various types of illness and disease, to behave appropriately, and to call upon a body of knowledge for coping with the condition defined as an illness. What is recognized as disease or illness is a matter of cultural prescription, and a given biological condition may or may not be considered an illness, depending on the particular cultural group in which it occurs. . . . What should be done about a given condition defined culturally as "illness" and the proper relationships of a sick person to other people are also culturally prescribed.[18]

Clark and Saunders, in their respective studies, argue that the use of folk medicine depends significantly on the commitment by Chicanos to their culture.[19,20] Madsen has studied the significance of folk illnesses among acculturating Chicanos.* He notes that one of the functions of folk illnesses was to provide a mechanism to avoid situations involving a conflict between Mexican and American values. Thus, according to Madsen, folk disease represents a means of retreat to the conservative role of Latino society.[21] He believes that class differences have some relationship to the use of folk practices. He observes lower class people as depending more heavily on the services of *curanderos*† rather than on modern medicine, the lower middle class as manifesting more skepticism regarding folk cures but using folk medicine in addition to modern medicine, and the upper middle class as regarding going to a physician as a prestige act but also relying upon prayers as essential to cure. The latter class is more apt to consider medical explanations of illness first and resort to folk healers only as a last

This posture does not represent the authors' viewpoint. It is only because few authorities have attempted to study folk health that we are prompted to investigate and cite his findings. Octavio Romano has contested Madsen's interpretations, and the reader is referred to his work for in-depth detail.

†Note: The suffix "os" in the Spanish language denotes both sexes and should not be interpreted in a sexist manner.

FIG. 3.1. Pharmacy advertisement listing of herbs and home remedies (Courtesy of Luis Duarte, Farmacia Villa-Real, Los Angeles, California)

Extenso y Variado Surtido de
YERBAS DE MEXICO

A
Alfalfa Semilla
Alucema
Amole
Anacahuita (ramas)
Anacahuita (Flor)
Azafran
Azhar de Naranjo
Ajenjible
Artemisa
Aniz Estrella
Aniz Semilla
Aniz Yerba
Alamo-Cascara
Azhar de Boldo
Agria-Cana
Albacar
Abrojo Rojo
Angelica
Aholva
Ajenjo
Azucaran
Ahuehuete
Aceitilla
Amargon
Abeduol
Aguacate (hojas)
Alfilerillo
Ajonjoli

B
Borraja
Barba de Elote
Boldo
Buchu
Brazile - Palo
Black - Walnut
Betonica
Bardana

C
Cadillo
Cascalote
Cascara de Alamo

Cascara de Encino
Castilla Rosa de
Cola de Caballo
Chia
Can-Yerba
Cocolmeca
Copalquin
Chuchupaste
Cramaria
Cuachalada
Cuassia
Canutillo
Colorada-Raiz
Canaguala
Cana-Fistula
Cana-Agria
Chucata
Culantrillo
Cascara de Granada
Cachanes
Cedron
Colorines
Contra-Yerba
Cardo Bendito
Cascara de mezquite
Chicoria
Cenizo
Coyote Yerba
Consuelda Mayor
Carrizillo
Cominos
Copal Goma
Cilantro
Costomate
Cascara Sagrada
Chaparro-Amargo
Chaparral Yerba

D
Damiana
Danielon Root
Diente de Leon

Dill Seed
Desierto-Te-Del
Doradilla
Duerme de Noche
Drosera

E
Elote Macho
Elote, Barba de
Encino
Estafiate
Eucaliptos
Enebro
Espinozilla
Epazote de Zorrillo
Epazote de Comer
Escobilla
Escorcionera
Espliego
Estopa de Coco

F
Fencucreco
Fistula Cana
Flor de Pena
Flor de Tila
Flor de Sauco
Fistula
Flor de Jamaica
Flor de Violeta
Flor de Manita
Fumaria
Fuminaria
Flor de Sempual
Flor de Navidad
Flor de Noche Buena
Frangula
Flor de Guaiacan
Flor de Trompillo
Flor de Malva
Flor de Granada
Flor de Tabachin
Flor de Rosa de Castilla

Flor de Mimbre
Flor de Anacahuita
Flor de Piedra
Flor de Magnolia

G
Genciana
Gobernadora
Golondrina
Gordolobo
Guaco Palo
Guachichile
Goma Mesquite
Goma (Insienso)
Granada Cascara
Guacima
Guata
Guacan
Guayacan
Guayabo
Guayabo Hojas
Golpe Yerba
Gato Yerba
Goma Copal
Gediondia
Genjibre
Grama
Guamis
Guajes Ciriales
Guajes Cirianes
Gualtecomate
Guisaso de Caballo

H
Hinojo
Hamula
Hipazote de Zorrillo
Hipazote de Comer
Hojas Zapote
Hoja - Sen
Hojas de Nogal
Hojas de Fresno
Hojas de Guayabo

FIG. 3.1 (cont.)

Hojas de Aguacate
Hojas de Naranjo Agrio
Hoja Santa
Huachichile

I

Ipazote de Zorrillo
Ipazote de Comer
Incienso
Istafiate
Itamo Real
Inmortal
Indio-Yerba

J

Juniper
Jericol
Jamaica Flor
Junipero
Jojobas

L

Laurel
Lampaso
Lanten
Lupulo
Lemon Balm
Limon Te
Linden Flowers
Lavandula

M

Malabar
Malba
Manrubio
Manzanilla
Manzo
Masto
Matarique
Mora
Mezquite Goma
Mezquite Cascara
Menta
Magnolia-Flor
Manita Flor
Matico
Molonge
Moztaza Negra
Moztaza Amarilla
Mirra en Grano
Mejorana
Miona
Mirto
Melisa
Malvavisco
Mala Mujer
Mastranzo

Muicle
Micle

N

Nogal Negro
Nuez Moscada
Neldo
Negrita
Naranja Agria (hojas)
Negro Yerba
Navidad Flor
Noche Buena Flor

O

Orchata
Oregano
Orguela de Raton
Oruzus Orozas
Ortiga
Otate
Ocote
Ocotillo
Ortiga Muerta
Oxoco Pague

P

Palo Guaco
Popotillo
Palo Dulce
Prodigiosa
Pena Flor de
Pasmo
Pamita
Peppermint
Pionia
Pirule
Palo Mulato
Palo de Brazil
Paviflora
Pinguica
Pinguica Hojas
Palo Aliso
Pollo Yerba
Pinguica Fruta
Peonia
Perro Yerba

Q

Quassia

R

Rosa de Castilla
Raiz de Valeriana
Romero
Raiz del Manzo
Raiz Colorada
Rhatania
Retama

Ruda
Raiz de Zarsaparrilla
Raiz Angelica
Raiz Pionias
Raiz del Cocolmeca
Raiz del Indio
Raiz Inmortal
Raiz Tumba Vaquero
Raiz Escorcionera
Raiz de Abrojo
Raiz de Mala Mujer
Raiz de Rubarbo
Raiz de Valerina
Raiz de Genciana
Raiz de Gato
Raiz de Oso
Regaliz

S

Sanguinaria
Sanguinaria Raiz
Sanguinaria Flor
Senna Leaves
Sarsaparrilla
Sangreado
Sauco
Sassafras
San Nicolas
Santa Yerba
Spearmint
Salvia Real
Simonillo
San Juan
Santa Maria
Semilla de Alfalfa
Senizo
Sapo Yerba
Sempual Flor
San Pedro
Sangre del dragon

T

Tabachin
Tumba Vaquero
Tlachichinole
Torojil Morado
Tila
Tatalencho
Te de Senna
Trompeta
Tronadora
Tripas de Judas
Tomillo
Tesota
Tejocote
Tejocote raiz
Te de Limon

Tesquequite
Tepeguaje
Tamarino Fresco
Tamarindo
Teposan
Tibinagua
Trevol de agua
Trompetilla
Trompillo

U

Una de Caballo
Uva Ursi

V

Verbena
Vivora
Valeriana
Ventocidad
Violeta
Venado Yerba
Violeta Flor

Y

Yerba del Perro
Yerba de Can
Yerba del Manzo
Yerba de Vivora
Yerba de Mora
Yerba Aniz
Yerba del Pasmo
Yerba Santa
Yerba del Aire
Yerba del Indio
Yerba del Golpe
Yerba del Perro
Yerba del Pollo
Yerba del Venado
Yerba Luisa
Yerba del Zapo
Yezgo
Yerba del Negro
Yerba del Coyote
Yerba de la Pastora
Yerba de La Virgen
Yerba del Pantano
Yerba Buena
Yerba del Christo
Yerba del Sol

Z

Zorrillo Ipazote
Zapote Blanco
Zarsaparrilla
Zassafras
Zemual Flor
Zorrillo Ipazote
Zapo Yerba
Zapote Blanco hojas

FIG. 3.1 (cont.)

PROTEJA SU SALUD CON

CAPSULAS DESENFRION, su Resfrio
Alergias, Sinusitis y demas sintomas de resfrio.
16 Capsulas por $1.50

COMBATA

Su Tos con **"KONTRATOS" MAYORES,** es un Jarabe
aprobado y perfeccionado para la tos de los adultós.
Frasco de 4 oz. $1.50

COMBATA LA TOS

DE LOS NIÑOS
Con **KONTRATOS–NIÑOS**
Delicioso y agradable al paladar con sabor a naranja.
Preparado especialmente para niños de todas las edades.
Frasco de 4 oz. $1.50

PROTEJA SU ATRACTIVO PERSONAL CON LA

SOLUCION "ACNE–SEPTICA"
Especial para granos, espinillas, barros y erupciones de la piel.
4 oz. $2.00

NO SE RESIGNE A SU DEBILIDAD, TOME EL

ACEITE PURO DE CAHUAMA
Marca Baja, Calif.

Es un Aceite sin alteraciones, extraido cuidadosamente
de las Cahuamas que se producen en el Golfo de Baja California.
Cuando usted lo necesite, pidalo directamenta a sus distribuidores.
FARMACIA VILLA–REAL
12 oz. $2.00

PARA LA DEBILIDAD EN GENERAL, TOME LAS

FAMOSAS CAPSULAS DE CAHUAMA

Dan fuerza, vigor y actividad en su vida
100 capsulas $2.00
Pidalas directamente a la FARMACIA VILLA–REAL
2331 Brooklyn Ave. – Tel. 261-0348
Los Angeles, Calif. 90033

Mandenos el importe de su pedido y lo recibira a vuelta de correo PORTE PAGADO por nuestra cuenta. Ordenelo C.O.D. y pague al Cartero al recibirlo.

FIG. 3.1 (*cont.*)

resort, he says. The elite rely entirely upon physicians and prayer. Only in extreme situations (ie, terminal illness, chronic disorders) would a folk cure be sought.[22]

Due to the influence of the dominant society's orientation toward the "germ theory," many acculturated Latino/Chicano people will ridicule folk medicine and even deny its existence. The individual oriented toward dominant culture values will tend to devalue folk health beliefs and regard them as naive. Condescension is a familiar posture of the dominant community towards Latino/Chicano folk culture and folk medicine practices. The theoretical basis for this attitude can be seen in the discussion of nativism or "fear of the foreign" by Krofcheck and Jackson. They concluded that the dominant culture will reject or ostracize things not familiar to that culture.[23] Therefore, although Latino/Chicano folk practices are not new but deeply rooted and indigenous to America, they are perceived by the dominant culture as "foreign" or "different" and, therefore, are feared.

Because of the before mentioned influence of the dominant culture, many Anglicized Latinos look down on the use of folk practices. However, their own relationship to extended family group members, who believe in folk medicine, may link them to the beliefs and practices. In reference to the Chicano population of the Southwest, Cabrera reminds us that, while some patients seek out "modern" medical treatment, they, at the same time, solicit the services of *curanderos* and use their folk remedies.[24]

Language also plays a role in acculturation. People who are less acculturated or assimilated into the dominant society will most likely be Spanish-speaking. Communication, which is an important factor in the diagnosis and treatment of an ailment prompts these individuals to seek out Spanish-speaking, traditional or nontraditional health providers.

Facility with English cannot be closely associated with a decreased use of *curanderos* or folk healers, as personal interviews with *curanderos* and *espiritualistas* demonstrate a high incidence of English-speaking consumers.

The degree of acculturation can therefore, be affected by the following factors: (1) Influence of the dominant culture on the individual; (2) Degree of kinship ties and traditions; (3) Social class differences; (4) Influence of the language.

FAMILY GENERATION AND FAMILIAL PRACTICES. The Latino/Chicano family structure can be characterized as a strong social unit. Murillo points out that among the Latino/Mexican American society, the family is the main focus of social identification.[25] The family structure of the dominant society includes the parents and their offspring. The aforementioned nuclear family is also present in the Latino/Chicano culture but is not limited to those components. The range of kinship is extended to relatives (grandparents, aunts, in-laws, etc.) and also encompasses the Latino "compadre system." Literally, the *compadre* is a "coparent" or one who will assume the parenting role should anything happen to the natural parents. This *compadre* system can be either a formally defined role, having religious connotations (baptism, confirmation, etc.), or it can be an informal endearment, having implications of mutual aid and respect. The *compadre*, consequently, is included within the extended family, although frequently no actual blood relationship exists.

The roles of the family members are clearly defined, with the male typically being the head of the household. Anthropologic studies conducted by Rubel establish two components of interaction within the family structure of the Chicano: first, respect and obedience to elders; second, male dominance.[26] Children are taught to share, cooperate, and work harmoniously for the good of the family members. A strong sense of obligation exists within the family unit. One must keep in mind the constant dynamics of change which affect the culture and, consequently, family structure. It is the authors' viewpoint that the Latino/Chicano family structure is a system that is not a static unit. Contemporary Chicano families and their life-styles must be viewed "in the spirit of the times" (eg, *movemiento feminil*). Definitely, the increased participation of Latina/Chicana women in the feminist movement will have implications for the future family structure. For our purpose, it will suffice to point out the existing relationships between familial attitudes and structure, and the usage of folk health practices. Typically, in the event of milk sickness, the mother or grandmother will treat the illness at home; if they are unsuccessful, another key family member, elderly female relative or *comadre* with special knowledge of folk medicine will be consulted. Severe illnesses (*mal ojo, susto*, etc.) are referred to *curanderos*. If the individual is born far from his family's country of origin he often becomes less familiar with its traditions, beliefs, and customs. However, if the family and significant others still adhere to certain folk practices, the individual is more likely to also utilize those practices.

Cabrera's study indicates that some families who have lived for several generations within the United States, report that they adhere to some health beliefs which can be categorized as folk practices.[27] Case studies collected by the authors further document the extent to which folk health practices are relied upon today within the Chicano community. Consequently, it can be observed that folk health practices and modern medical treatment can and do in fact coexist within the Latino/Chicano experience.

RELIGION. The influence of the Church on people of Latin America and Mexico has received much attention and documentation. The Church places emphasis on Divine Will. Happiness and peace are associated with keeping God's commandments and leading a good life. The concept of God-given health greatly affects the Chicano's perception of illness/wellness. Illness may be viewed as a *castigo de Dios* (a punishment from God). Priests are often summoned for special blessing and special patron saints will be called upon to intercede on behalf of the sick person. Many homes in the barrios have shrines to the Virgen de Guadalupe or a family altar laden with holy images, flowers, candles, and sometimes pictures of deceased relatives. During an illness, family members will gather and pray for the recovery of the afflicted person.[28]

Closely associated with religious beliefs is the use of religious artifacts, special rituals, and a respect, albeit fear, of the supernatural. Since health is viewed as God-given, many religious rituals are utilized in the healing process. The combination of religious and mystical beliefs actively demonstrate that folk health and religion are not in conflict.

According to several authors, disease among Mexican Americans is perceived in two major categories: (1) "good" or "natural" illnesses, which come from violating the balance of the natural world controlled by God; and (2) "supernatural" illnesses or bewitchments sent by human adversaries utilizing evil satanic forces.

A natural illness is corrected by restoring the particular balance that was disrupted. Bewitchment is cured by countermagic or by removing the immediate source of harm. In both cases, specified rituals are utilized to combat the illness or condition and to restore equilibrium. All techniques of folk curing are accompanied by prayers and petitions to God and to saints.

AGE. Prior to the late 1960s it was postulated that older Chicanos would be more likely to retain traditions of their homeland by clinging to folk traditions and being deeply involved in folkways and customs. In a study by Nall and Speilberg,[29] the assumption was made that older adults were more likely to be integrated into the ethnic subculture than younger persons. It was found that age was clearly related to the acceptance of the treatment of tuberculosis among the Chicanos sampled. Presumably, an adult has more interaction with the dominant culture than a child and, consequently, may be more influenced to assume the customs of the dominant culture. It follows that a young child will be influenced by the practices of the family unit. One might speculate that older Chicanos might cling to folkways, younger Chicanos might be influenced by the dominant culture, and the youth might be influenced by the home practices. The reader is cautioned against prematurely arriving at these conclusions.

Currently, we are experiencing a rise in political consciousness resulting from the Chicano movement of the late 1960s. Nationalism has become a strong unifying feature within the Chicano movement. A deliberate rediscovery of ethnicity and determination to revitalize the past has resulted in increased self-awareness. People of *La Raza* are attempting to perpetuate cultural and ethnic identity and to improve social, economic, and political conditions for Mexican people in the United States.

The Chicano movement or *La Causa* has increased awareness of existing racism and oppression. It has had its impact upon politics and subsequently upon education, employment practices, and housing. As a direct result of this increased awareness of self, many Latino/Chicano people are openly admitting to the practice of folk health. No longer feeling the pressure of guilt or shame, we are freed to recognize the contributions made by folk healers to the delivery of health care.

The authors believe that health providers will see an increase in the numbers of Latino people of all ages utilizing both traditional and modern folk practices in the maintenance of health.

Historical Perspective of Folk Health Practices

The Latino/Chicano culture is rich in both Indian and Spanish influence. The Inca, Maya, Toltec, Zapotec, Mixtec, Tarascan, Aztec, and many other Indian civilizations all predate the culture of white middle America. Dr. Ignacio Gonzales Guzman, in his chapter entitled "Biologia Medica," points out that the civilization of the Indians was, in many ways, superior to that of the white men landing on its shores. The Aztec and Mayans were familiar with medicinal plants, terrestrial or aquatic, that had curative properties. Records of these plants and their indications were kept in texts which document the early practice of pharmacology among the Indians.[30] These writings were handed down from generation to generation, constantly being augmented by new findings.

With the arrival of the Spanish came the influence of European medicine and practices, as well as the moralistic influence of the Church. Attitudes of "right" and "wrong," fear and punishment, still influence Latino thought today.

Folk healers, medical beliefs, and practices, have roots in both Indian and Spanish custom. Belief in supernatural powers, reliance upon ritual, and knowledge regarding medicinal use of plants, can be directly traced to the Mestizo Indian. Fear of punishment and the wrath of God, devotion to religious rites, and the introduction of European medicine, can be attributed to the Spanish.

Perpetuation of folk health knowledge can be partially attributed to early writings of the Indians and the Spanish friars. Books such as *El Libro de Fray Anselmo,* and *Medicamentos Indigenas,** among others, document

*Rusca, A: *El Libro Fray Anselmo.* Mexico City, Hermanos Brothers; Pompa, G: Medicamentos Indigenas. Miami, Florida, Editorial America S. A., 1972.*

early treatments used to cure certain conditions. Although some books illustrate the early use of indigenous medicine, the most common method of transmission of folk health practices is from generation to generation by word of mouth.

Of course special powers possessed by certain folk healers cannot be "passed on" in this manner; one must be born with the power or with the attribute. Interviews with *curanderos* document a popular belief that, if a child cries while still in his mother's womb, this child will possess certain mystical powers.

The legacy of the Chicano/Latino, then, is a rich composite of Spanish and Indian cultures. It is a legacy abundant in folkways and customs and one which has many implications for modern medicine.

DEVELOPMENT OF A CONCEPT OF WELLNESS

In order to understand the folk health beliefs and practices of the Latino/ Chicano family, it is essential to explore the health philosophies and ideologies of the culture that dictates these practices.

The basis for many of the beliefs is the concept of equilibrium, a balance between man and nature. The natural and supernatural are not taken as separate entities as in the dominant culture and Western thought. Rather, a person is seen in a global way, as a being whose health and welfare are guided by the maintenance of a balance between the natural and supernatural world. A loss of this equilibrium is considered to be the basis for illness, emotional, physical, or mental.

In striving to maintain a balance between the environment and the individual, most Latinos take on preventive-oriented behavior. Prayers, relics, and good faith are used to ward off maladies; herbs and spices are commonly used to decrease susceptibility to disease or to prevent complications of chronic illness. A discussion of the actions and indications of these herbs will follow later in this section.

The prevention of bodily imbalance prevails among Latinos. Latinos are known to use commercial products of modern medicine, along with their folk medicinal herbs to attempt to maintain good health.

The theory of "balance" extends to several beliefs in Latino/Chicano folk health practices. In maintaining good health, the *curandero* encourages the consumption of foods that are compatible and which maintain balance in the body. Foods are so classified according to their effect, ie, chili and meat are hot foods, because chili burns the mouth, and a heavy meat or pork dinner late at night may cause indigestion; ice cream and cucumbers are cold foods, soothing and fresh to the body. In terms of illness, these hot and cold foods are consumed with regard to the appropriateness to the conditions of the patient, ie, cool liquids and fruit to combat fever.

Pregnancy is considered to be a delicate and perilous time for the fetus. Latinos maintain the belief that any emotional, physical, or spiritual trauma may cause an imbalance in the body of the mother and therefore be harmful to the child. If trauma occurs, it will have bad effects on the health and development of the fetus.

Once more, the evidence of the powerful and supernatural forces accompany the natural phenomena that can deform the infant. For example, throughout the United States, the practice of wearing keys on the night of a lunar eclipse is prevalent. This practice is to protect the fetus from effects that may cause deformities and is viewed as a preventive measure. Although childbirth is seen as a natural process in life and as harmonious with nature, a commonly used expression for the announcement of the birth is ¡Ya se alevio! (She is well!).

In order to maintain harmony with the universe an expectant mother is encouraged to maintain her diet, to exercise, and to take the herbs and teas recommended by the local yerbero or key family member. The practice of this activity reinforces the concept of harmony between the natural and supernatural forces of the world.

The Latino/Chicano family is usually somewhat familiar with the illnesses that are more commonly cured by the curandero in the home setting. These illnesses are treated through prayers, diet, rituals, and herbs. Among the most familiar of these illnesses are the following.

Mal Ojo

This illness results from the influence of someone outside the family, or extended family, on a person. This influence is seen in terms of a desire, or envy of the victim, or another similar imbalance of the relationship between the victim and the intruder. Most often, as a consequence of unspoken emotions, there exists a mystical or psychological interplay in this condition. Children are most frequently affected.

CASE STUDY

It was a cool summer evening when baby Adrian suddenly became restless, feverish, and refused to eat at all. Similar symptoms were present the following day, and his parents began to trace their activities of the week.

One incident that stuck out in their minds was a situation that occurred while purchasing their new car. Adrian's parents noticed that an older Anglo couple had been admiring the child. They further recalled that although the couple talked about him and smiled at him, they never touched him. With the fear that he might have been given ojo, *the family took Adrian to his grandmother; she would know,* era la que sabe *(key family member).* Sra. H. *visited her grandchild, and the diagnosis was confirmed.*

That evening family members were called together as she prayed over Adrian. They were involved in the healing by their prayers and their presence. She then took an egg, and, as she prayed, she passed it over his body three times, stopping at his forehead and lips to make the sign of the cross. More prayers were recited and responses given. Sra. H. *then lifted her grandson and passed him over a candle that lay on the floor, three times in circular motions. At the same time she prayed in inaudible words.*

One hour later, the egg was cracked into a bowl of water, and the bowl was placed under a crib. The child was massaged and laid in the crib to sleep.

In the morning, his mother went to the crib and checked her child. Though he was restless and weak, his fever had broken. Beneath the crib, in the bowl, was a semi-poached egg that had taken the form of an eye. Sra. H. *was called back to remove the egg and the diagnosis was confirmed. Her explanation to the authors was that, by some process, the fever was drawn into the water and cooked the egg.*

Caida de la mollera

A common ailment of infancy, this illness is one most often treated by the key family member mentioned earlier. This syndrome resembles dehydration and may be caused by a fall or the child having been dropped. This carries the implication of neglect or poor care of the child and therefore carries an emotional or psychological implication. Guilt by the parent or person in charge of the child when the accident occurred is common and is difficult to deal with. Kiev attributes this phenomena to the importance that is placed on adequate parenting in this culture.[31] He discusses a cycle by which parents, especially the mother, are locked into a pattern of dependency on their children for emotional security and respect, and thus they constantly strive to conform to the model of the devoted parent. This opinion has not been found by other researchers of this illness, and, therefore, is taken only as an opinion.

Susto

Susto or fright is associated with a traumatic situation experienced by the patient at some time prior to onset of symptoms. The individual is said to have been frightened at some point in early childhood or adulthood. Symptoms include anxiety, insomnia, indigestion, palpitations, and anorexia. Often this illness may be precipitated by the loss of a loved one through death.

The *espiritualista* who is called upon to perform the healing exercises may use herbs, rituals, and prayers to cleanse and heal the victim. It is thought that the frightening experience makes the soul or spirit leave the body. It becomes necessary to restore the balance that was left with this separation of soul and body.

CASE STUDY

> *Sra. J. lived in a small town. Following the unexpected death of her daughter, she became suddenly ill, started to lose weight, was unable to eat, experienced weakness, and epigastric pain. She had all the symptoms of* susto. *After several visits to a physician without symptomatic relief she contacted a* curandera. *She was given a concoction of an herb mixture and was instructed to take the mixture for nine days. She was instructed not to drink any tea or coffee, but only to take chicken broth. After a month, she began to gain weight, and she followed the bland diet the* curandera *had advised.*

Empacho

Empacho is another childhood illness, which is said to be caused by the ingestion of bad foods by the child. Once more, guilt may be a presenting factor, as the infant or child is said to have been neglected while he consumed whatever it was that made him ill. Also, this may be caused by an emotional experience during meal time, or by eating heavy foods such as bananas, beans, potatoes, or pork, in the evening. The latter indicates a lack of supervision of the child's eating habits and therefore may be a source of accusations towards the parents. Interviews with *curanderos* and *yerberos* indicate that this is a common illness, however, and does not necessarily occur because of poor parenting. In *empacho*, undigested food is said to form a sticky ball (bolus) on the wall of the stomach or upper intestine and is cured by massage and herbs. Manipulations of the stomach and back with sacred oils, by a *sobador*, aid the bolus in moving down the intestinal tract and out of the body.

Mal Puesto

A disease or illness brought on by a *brujo(a)* at the request of another person. This may occur through the use of magical devices and rituals in order to manipulate or cause a *mal* (bad deed) on the victim. Symptoms associated with the illness are paranoia, restlessness, and anorexia.

A man who suddenly may become dependent and passive is not easily tolerated in the Latino culture. Therefore, it is often said that such behavior results from a *Mal Puesto* caused by a witch who has attempted to dominate his soul and mind.

CASE STUDY

Sra. R.'s daughter informed the nurse that her mother had been experiencing mood swings in which she became angry, cried frequently, or behaved "different" than usual. Upon exploring the situation the daughter revealed that her mother had confided in her that she was having heavy and prolonged menstrual bleeding. The mother believed a Mal Puesto *(hex) had been placed upon her by an adversary. This* Mal Puesto *resulted in the heavy bleeding and the accompanying behavior.*

Comparative Identification of Folk Healers

Folk healers are not professionals in the sense that they have formal training in the act of medicine or earn their living by their practice; they are members of the community who are regarded as specialists because they have learned more of the popular medical lore of culture than have other barrio people; use language which the patients understand and vocabulary familiar to patients; never dictate what must be done, advise the patient what she or he considers appropriate. [32]

The above quote is thorough in its description of folk healers in general. A more specific account will provide an awareness of the difference in functions and status of various folk healers. The following are main practitioners of Latino folk medicine.

Key Family Member: *El/la que sabe*. In Latino families, a mother, grandmother, grandfather, or another elderly relative who has special knowledge of folk medicine. Mild illness, ie, *caida de la mollera*, is treated in the home by this person, as folk diseases unrecognized by modern medicine are not referred to physicians unless there is doubt about diagnosis or suspicion of complications amenable to supplementary scientific treatment. This person is so designated and is given the reverence and honor due him by all family members.

Yerbero: (also known as *yerbista* and *yerberito*): This person is an expert in the origin, functions, and derivatives of herbs and spices for curative and preventive reasons. His role in the practice of folk medicine has been one of growing, sorting, and distributing herbs and spices, and of sharing his knowledge of them. Expertise is gained from ancestors and their teachings and by exploring the use of these herbs and through experimenting with them. His position in his community is one of respect and esteem.[33]

Curanderos: "The *curandero* is a full or part-time specialist who heals by virtue of a 'Gift from God,' typically revealed and confirmed in dreams . . . may be male or female (*curandera*), often see themselves, and are seen by others as having unusual qualities . . . *curanderos* cure by means of elaborate rituals, as well as herbal decoctions, massage, and ventriloquism. The performance of a healing ceremony by a *curandero* is typically complex, impressive, protracted, sometimes involving weeks of prayer and treatment."[34]

Some *curanderos* may cure bewitchments with cleansings but will not perform counter-magic against the witch who has performed a *Mal Puesto*. Yet Madsen reminds us that the dominant culture and some anglicized Latinos may, in reference to witchcraft, speak of curers and witches as being the same. He further says that *curanderos* have expressed fear of this label and often refuse to treat bewitchment cases, lest they be suspected of possessing evil powers.[35]

Sobadores: Specialists in massage treatment and muscle and bone manipulations. He (she) is well trained in the bony structure of the body, as well as the muscular system. This training may be from another *sobador* or knowledgeable family member. A specialty under this field is the *huesero*, a bone specialist or chiropractor.[36]

Espiritualista (also known as *Espiritismo*): Male or female having the ability to analyze dreams, premonitions, cards, etc. More akin to the *brujo* than to the *curandero*, because of this power, he (she) is a person who has been sought for comfort, advice, and purifications or cleansings. He (she) has the power to *adevinar* or see the future and can warn his clients of oncoming danger or wrath, thereby averting tragedy, as they modify perilous or careless behavior. In Latino/Chicano folklore, he (she) is usually a person who was heard to cry while still in his mother's womb, and therefore is revered as gifted since birth.

The *espiritualista* maintains a position of respect and esteem in his barrio. He is sought after not only for curing or cleansing oneself, but also for prevention, usually in the form of magical protection, ie, medals, prayers, rituals. Through the use of amulets and prayers, the *espiritualista* can protect the individual from further bewitchments.

Brujo(a): Male or female having extensive command of the malevolent and benevolent techniques of witchcraft and is therefore sought after or feared. *Brujas* bewitch their victims by placing hexes upon them or other magical means. His (her) status in the community is one of power and prestige, and he is often honored, out of fear rather than respect. Counter-magic by a witch is supposedly performed by specialists only, ie, *espiritualistas* or other witches.

FOLK MEDICINE AS A SCIENCE

Concept of Wellness

The authors have established that Latino/Chicano health is viewed holistically as a state of equilibrium between the physical and social environment and the individual. Unlike Western medicine, folk medicine does not treat symptoms alone or disease conditions. The focus of Western medicine has been upon epidemiology and pathophysiology. The ritual of healing in Western medicine involves attaching a biomedical category to a group of presenting symptoms, thus arriving at a diagnosis. Once labeled, this entity is then examined, tested, and probed, using elaborate tools and devices. Treatment might often include massive doses of synthetic drugs, removal of body parts, or referral to a psychiatrist if none of the former work.

Within Western medicine, the patient thus has the choice of dying from the caustic effect of drugs or from the disease. The human body is divided and subdivided according to the speciality of the practitioner — not particularly according to the needs of the patient. The dichotomy of mind and body lends itself to the belief that, if an illness does not respond to traditional therapy, it is "all in the patient's head," and, consequently, in the realm of the psychotherapist. Folk medicine, in contrast, approaches the sick individual as a whole psycho-physio-cultural-spiritual being in relationship with his environment. This approach presents a totally different dimension to well-being and the maintenance of health.

Fabrega has done research into what he terms "ethno medicine" among the Mayan Indians (Zinacantecans) of Mexico. He points out that within this branch of medicine, illness can be analyzed in three ways: (1) as indicating a stress and dysfunction in the sociocultural unit;[37] (2) in terms of how religious and other supernatural ideas are expressed in ritual and practice; (3) as an example of the way sociocultural patterns shape the expression, the dynamics and the treatment of the illness.

Mal ojo and *susto* defy treatment utilizing the Western approach, yet the illness states are quite real. The rituals and rites involved in treatment include participation by key family members, investigation into social and environmental causative factors, and enlistment of the individual's own inner healing energies. This use of one's own inner energies as a source of healing is a concept of great importance to the *curandero(a)*. It is used in the laying on of hands, in many curative rituals, cleansing, and treatments. The spirit of the individual is summoned to look favorably upon the afflicted person. States of warmth, coolness, and tranquility are generated without outside assistance. Also associated with this concept is the transfer of energy from the healer to the afflicted. Many *curanderos(as)* and other folk healers utilize this transfer of energy in healing to the extent that they feel physical exhaustion (*siento debil* — feeling drained) following the healing session.

Conversely, the sick person will experience improved health and ease. One might relate this feeling to the religious experience of being absolved from one's sins by a priest and the accompanying feeling of being at ease.

Currently, meditation and biofeedback practices look to the utilization of inner energies as a means toward relaxation, distraction, suggestion, and sense of control. Esoteric exercises which are centered within the body also call upon the inner strength and potential of the person. Clearly, the roots of these "modern" trends within Western thought have their roots of origin in folk healing practices.

This meeting of ritual and rites with technology and treatment emphasizes man's uniqueness as a whole, rather than a separate mind—body—soul entity. This being the focus of folk medicine, it can be seen that illness, disease, and death are inseparable from personal, interpersonal, spiritual, and social matters.

The folk medicine practitioner utilizes his skill (or clinical judgment) along with his charismatic attributes to heal the whole person. The practitioner is knowledgeable in physiology of body systems, has an understanding of the illness process, and is sensitive to the manifestation of illness among his (her) people. Consequently, the folk practitioner validates the disease experience of the individual.[38] This was diagramatically illustrated by Dr. Dominquez Ybarra (Fig. 3.2).[39]

In modern medicine, the patient lists symptoms to a physician, who then prescribes and treats the condition or symptom. The *curandero* validates the disease experience with the individual, interacting in such a way as to help him reach a state of equilibrium with his environment. The specific treatment depends on the social, physical, and emotional spiritual components of the disorder (ie, holistic approach).

Scientific Method

Scientific investigation involves the process of observation, interpretation, prediction, experimentation, and validation. Costly equipment and elabo-

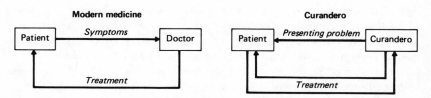

FIG. 3.2. Traditional Mexican process of diagnosis/academic process of diagnosis

rate data collection systems are not prerequisite for accurate conclusions. Unquestionably, many important discoveries have occurred through simple trial and error, as well as through inductive and deductive thinking. Persons who have little knowledge regarding folk health may view this discipline as being "primitive," "exotic," and completely "unscientific." One need only review the scientific method of inquiry to see that the *curandero(a)* utilizes this process in healing. The *curandero(a)* has a similar role to the Western physician and similarly relies upon a body of knowledge, as well as experience and tradition, in arriving at methods of treatment. As mentioned before, treatment for the known folk practices embodies a holistic approach.

When ill with recognizable symptoms, the Latino/Chicano will first utilize self-contained measures such as prayers, dietary restriction, and household remedies. The individual might consult a *yerbero* or *yerbista* and then a *curandero*.

Initially, a friend or relative will consult the *curandero* and request a visit. The visit for work-up may take place in the home of the *curandero(a)* or in that of the patient. A diagnostic evaluation of the patient's situation is then performed (ie, history and physical examination). The *curandero(a)* validates the illness process and will give suggestions and advice regarding treatment; thus confirming the illness by diagnosing it.

The *curandero* may look at the presenting symptoms and explore the situation further in the following manner.

In order to investigate the cause and environment of the condition, he may establish a process of inquiry as: Was there a person who was in disagreement with the patient? Was there a person who favored the child but did not have physical contact or touch him? (as in *mal ojo*). This establishes the quality of the disequilibrium initiated by the power or energy of another person.

In arriving at a diagnosis, the *curandero* works at involving key people and family members from the start. He questions them: When did they first note any changes? When did any symptoms start? What are their impressions of the condition? How do they feel about the implications of what they see as the condition? In doing this, he brings together the emotional, social, and physical phenomena that may affect the patient's recovery. He also acknowledges the family members as significant and recruits them as assistants in the healing process.

Further inquiry involves questions to the family such as: To whom did you go before coming here? Did you try to treat this on your own? Have you seen a *yerbero* for consultation? What has he advised? What herbs, spices, or ointments are now being utilized?

The patient is now observed physically for other symptoms, and the *curandero* then may offer an individualized type of care by touching, talking, and providing feedback to the patient, thereby identifying symptoms the patient may have, although he has not yet verbalized them.

As is evidenced by the previous information, the method of observation of the *curandero* will involve more active participation in the diagnostic process than is used in Western medicine. Based on his past experiences, his clinical knowledge and training, he is more apt to take positive steps towards inquiry. He will interpret these symptoms in terms of psycho-social-spiritual aspects of the individual at this time. Based on the information collected, he will predict or hypothesize an outcome and prognosis and set the tone for a positive action towards restoration of equilibrium. He then initiates the treatment, once more involving the patient and his family members and other key witnesses (to the illness) in the use of treatment measures that may include use of herbs, spices, rituals, or rites. These measures are then validated to determine the effectiveness of the treatment.

The effects of certain environmental phenomena on the body that are categorized as "hot" and "cold" are also dealt with in those terms. Having an awareness of the physiologic implications of hot and cold and their effects on the body function provides the nurse with an operational basis for this discussion.

Western medicine provides a basic knowledge and understanding of the implications of hot and cold on the human body systems, ie, circulation, respiration, etc. In folk medicine there also exist categories of illness which are considered hot or cold conditions. These conditions are treated by the application or removal of hot or cold foods, ointments, devices, or conditions. One such example, which is indicated for *resfrios* (chills caused by fever) and *phegma* (bronchial congestion), is the application of *plantas de tomates*, a treatment that employs the same principle as a mustard plaster or facial. The action of the treatment increases circulation and draws out the impurities of the body.

This treatment illustrates the use of heat in dealing with an illness that is hot, ie, fever. The *curandero* or key family member will apply hot compresses of whole stewed tomatoes to the plantar regions of both feet, the palms of both hands, and to the chest. Clean cloths are placed over these areas tied to secure the compresses. Several hours later, when cooled, the compresses are removed and if necessary the procedure is repeated the following day. Scientifically, one might justify this treatment by considering the following facts: (1) Tomatoes have a significantly high content of vitamin C that can be absorbed through the skin. (2) The hot compresses cause peripheral blood vessels to dilate, an action which promotes healing by increasing the blood supply to the area. (3) An increase in blood supply will decrease congestion by carrying away infected and accumulated fluid.

Also indicated in the treatment of *resfrio* and *phegma* are teas made from some broad spectrum herbs and plants. They contain the same substances found in several drugs prescribed by modern medicine.

It has been documented that South American Indians used the drug quinine from the bark of the cinchona tree for the treatment of malaria. There is also documentation of the early use of curare for killing animals or humans by immobilization. This drug depresses respiration function and may lead to asphyxiation. Today both of these drugs are used in Western medicine; the former for its antipyretic effect and the latter as a muscle relaxant during surgery requiring general anesthesia. As previously described, Mayans, Incas, and Aztecs had very sophisticated medical and surgical skills. They knew how to set bones in casts, suture wounds, give injections, and use irrigations. The use of herbs and potions as stimulants, depressants, and hypnotics was common among Mexican and South American Indians.

Today the use of such drugs has been considerably reduced due to laws governing their use. The *curandero* will utilize herbs that possess similar properties in the treatment of such conditions (Table 3.1).

TYPES OF HEALING

The previous section dealt with medicinal measures and illnesses in terms of the physiology and scientific justification. This section will focus on the types of *remedios* (remedies) employed and the different approaches which lead to healing and the restoration of equilibrium, or the prevention of disequilibrium.

Table 3.1
Categories of Medicinal Herbs

HERB OR PLANT	INDICATION	ACTION	ADMINISTRATION
Curative			
Ajo (garlic)	Anorexia Stomach distress Snake bites High blood pressure Toothache pain Bowel discomfort Chronic bronchitis Skin callus Fever	Stimulates appetite and digestive process; antiseptic effect on digestive system; hypotension; analgesic antiseptic; stimulates peristalsis; expectorant action in liver and kidney; softens skin for easy removal of callus	Used in small amounts; used in cooking; mashed juice of *ajo* in combination with another liquid; *not cooked,* distilled in water, eaten with a meal to prevent irritation of stomach mucosa
Oregano (plant herb)	Fever Dry cough Asthma Nervous tension Anxiety Intestinal colic Amenorrhea	Expectorant; sedative effect; antiseptic action; antispasmodic; stimulates circulation and flow of blood	Taken in hot teas, (*infusiones al vapor*) leaves soaked in water
Rosa de Castillo (rosewater)	a) Fever Cold sweats Gastroenteritis b) Infant diarrhea Colic c) Tonsillitis	Astringent quality; purgative (heavy dosage); stimulates peristalsis; diminishes inflammation	a) Cool teas are taken orally b) Taken on a fasting stomach c) Gargle with water
Romero (contains camphor)	Indigestion Gastritis Rheumatism Arthritis Venuralgia Contusions Menstrual distress of a "cold" origin	Acts on mucosa; balsamic effect; antispasmodic effect; relaxes the muscles; decreases pain	Drink teas Apply *romero* soaked in alcohol Vaginal douches "Warm" *romero*
Zapote (found in semitropical regions; seeds are used for teas)	Arterial hypertension Insomnia Headaches	Sedative qualities; anticonvulsive properties; hypnotic analgesia; heart depressant; cerebral relaxant	Teas taken warm or cold

Table 3.1 (cont.)

Categories of Medicinal Herbs

HERB OR PLANT	INDICATION	ACTION	ADMINISTRATION
Broad spectrum *Yerbabuena* *(Yerba buena;* mint)	Indigestion Stomach pains Anorexia, nausea (caused by ingestion of "cold" foods) Earaches, ringing in ears Fever	Analgesic; antiemetic; antipyretic	Teas taken orally Teas taken with honey Apply lotion directly to ear; place leaf over ear
Manzanilla (chamomile flowers)	Stomach and intestinal pain Uterine pains and cramping Menstrual cramps Anxiety, insomnia	Antispasmodic; muscle relaxant specific to uterine action; hypnotic effect	Taken in teas with honey or sugar
Linaza (linseed)	Constipation Ulcers Respiratory congestion, dry cough Inflammation of mucus membrane, bladder, rectal, vaginal mucosa Scalp dryness and itching, dermatitis, skin burns	Balsamic effect; coats the stomach; decongestive action; expectorant effect; soothing and healing; analgesic; calms itching and burning; coats and soothes irritation	Teas are taken daily until change in condition Mixed with oregano and lemon to make a syrup Washings Laxative Use gummy substance as a liniment (combined with *aqua de cal* [lye])
Corazoncillo	Heartburn Intestinal gases Diarrhea Hemorrhoids Scanty and painful menstruation Headaches and fever Joint pains, arthritis, cuts, bruises Ulcers	Antispasmodic; increases flow of blood; antipyretic effect; antiinflammatory; soothes irritation; balsamic effect	Taken orally in teas Teas and cool baths Lotions applied topically

Table 3.1 (cont.)
Categories of Medicinal Herbs

HERB OR PLANT	INDICATION	ACTION	ADMINISTRATION
Preventive Gordolobo	At onset of colds to prevent bronchitis, hemorrhoids, and varicose veins	Balsamic effect; reduces inflammation; expectorant; works on the venous system to diminish congestion; constricting effect; stimulates pulmonary circulation	Stems and leaves used for teas
Oregano	Prevents menstrual cramps Prevents infection Prevents liver disorders	Relaxes uterine muscles; stimulates and regulates menstrual flow (contraindicated during pregnancy); antiseptic effect; stimulates flow of gastric juices; analgesic; antiseptic	Taken orally in teas *al vapor* Placed topically Taken in small amounts with meals Cotton placed on tooth
Alde verde *(aloe verde)*	Burns Sunburn	Juice at bottom is an analgesic; antiseptic effect; prevents blisters	Placed directly on mild burns and scalds to stop blistering and peeling
Sacramental *Ajo* (garlic)	Prevents harm from befalling the patient		Put into small sacks and carried on the person
Osha	Good luck, keeps away evil spirits		Used during spiritualism: on the patient or in concoctions
Altamisa	Brings good luck *Dolor de espalda* (pain in shoulder caused by the stress of a *mal puesto*)		Leaves of this flower are heated on a hot plate and then soaked in alcohol

Remedios (remedies)

The Latino/Chicano culture is rich in *dichos* and *consejos* (sayings and advice) which caution the individual regarding certain behavior. One must keep in mind the importance of the concept of balance between hot and cold in order to comprehend the implications of these *consejos*.

Mojando la cabeza: A warning to wet the top of the head (*la mollera*) whenever the lower torso or the body is in water. This promotes the state of equilibrium to the entire body.

Consejos sobre la regla: While menstruating, the woman is cautioned against eating acidic foods or spicy foods (mustard) due to the increased likelihood of cramps. Acidic foods and pepper of heavily seasoned foods are classified as hot. The menstrual period is also considered to be a hot condition. Therefore, these two hot factions would result in an imbalance in equilibrium and would have the consequence of increased menstrual flow or cramping.

Escalofrios (chills): The warm person is cautioned to keep away from draughts (*corrientes de aire*) or from breathing cold air, or from eating or drinking cold foods. The obvious effect would be a shock to the body due to the disequilibrium generated.

Spiritualism

Spiritualism is a type of healing which is employed predominantly in conditions that are considered of supernatural origin. Within the Latino/ Chicano culture, healing can also take the form of a spiritual activity, and mysticism is also utilized to some extent in the performance of exorcism and "calling on the spirits." This is influenced by religious beliefs; however, it is distinct in terms of its elements and consequences. Medicinal measures and treatments involving heat and cold have already been discussed.

While some somatic illness may be simultaneously treated by prayers and rituals as well as physical activities, these supernatural conditions, *mal ojo, susto,* and *brujeria* are the primary foci of spiritualistic acts.

Spiritualism relies on the phenomena of faith; the rites or rituals are permeated by prayers and chants to God and the spirits for restoration of health. Often, the spiritualist or *espiritualista* will involve the patient in the process and, thereby, distract his attention from his problems. In assigning the patient a significant role in the ritual, he provides activities that are meaningful to the patient. This also serves as an anxiety-diminishing action, as it is comforting to the patient to implore and expect results from a just and loving God. The family or significant others are also involved in litanies or chants by means of a rite and response process.

Any instruments, medals, holy water, etc., used during this healing process are blessed and prayed over before they are used on the patient. This prevents any harm that could further befall the patient. Prayers or speech requests may be written on paper or on tree bark, folded and placed in sacramental urns in front of candles. Rituals may include the placing of protective devices such as amulets, holy water, and blessed herbs on the patient's person. This serves to prevent further harm to the patient.

In order to understand some of these health needs and practices of the Latino/Chicano family, it is essential to explore the values and the culture that dictate these beliefs and actions. The basis for the integration of physical and metaphysical acts of healing is presented here. The natural and supernatural are not taken as separate entities as it is in the dominant culture and Western God thought. Rather a person is seen as a being one whose health and welfare are guided by the maintenance of a balance between the natural and the supernatural, and a loss of this equilibrium is considered a basis for illness — emotional, physical, or mental.

There are several perspectives as to why people seek out the services of folk health healers. Some of these perspectives reflect narrow attitudes and little knowledge of the history and tradition of the Latino/Chicano cultures. Some of the factors that affect the use of *curanderos* have already been discussed, and therefore, we will focus on what motivates the Latino/Chicano to use the *curanderos* rather than the factors that prevent use.

Some of the prevailing perspectives of sociologists and anthropologists reflect stereotypic thinking. As an example, one author states in his discussion of this subject that "folk healers are better than no health care at all."[40] This derogatory tone shows little sensitivity to and understanding of the significance of folk health in the history of culture. This view minimizes the effectiveness of folk healing practices. As a statement, it implies that Latinos/Chicanos go to *curanderos* because they are forced to economically, and, as a last resort, rather than by choice.

There is no documentation found to support this attitude. Also, there is no documentation that the poor utilize the services of folk healers exclusively or more so than does the middle-class Latino/Chicano. Based on the research of the literature and interviews conducted, the authors take an opposite posture. It is our feeling that the Latino/Chicano will seek the services of the folk healer of his ethnic group by choice. No matter how articulate or *inglesado* (Anglicized) the Latino/Chicano is, he still maintains some credence in the *dichos* and *consejos* passed to him by his culture. Also, social class has not been demonstrated to be a barrier to use of the *curandero*.

A more positive and functional attitude taken by some Latinos/ Chicanos is that people will use both systems of health care simultaneously, along with the *curandero* and the *yerbero*: that Latinos will also utilize modern medicines from local drug stores and the local public health clinics.

In further response to the question of why people go to *curanderos*, we must acknowledge a realistic factor, that the present health care delivery system has not offered a means through which the poor can receive care that is comprehensive, relative to their needs, or sensitive to their culture or economic situation. Accessibility to health care, especially in rural areas has been documented repeatedly as poor and inadequate.

Often most of the staff is monolingual, and there is little doubt as to how this handicap limits the effectiveness of the care provided. Therefore, it is inevitable that the poor, or anyone for that matter, will seek a health care provider who is accessible, both financially and logistically speaking.

The importance of receiving individualized care cannot be emphasized enough. This value, no doubt limited to the middle and upper classes, is universal. Often, the patient will visit the *curandero* in his own home, or if too ill, will be visited by the healer. In visiting the home of the *curandero* he (she) finds an atmosphere that is very similar to that in his (her) own home. The warmth and serenity of the environment allows and encourages the patient to feel relaxed and comfortable before seeing his (her) mentor. This facilitates openness and freedom in the interaction between patient and healer.

The *curandero*, as stated before, usually lives in the community he serves, knows the community he serves, and is aware of the dynamics and can be seen as an established pillar of the *barrio*. Therefore, his constant presence there makes him a more accessible provider of health care than is the district health office or the private group practice.

The key motivator, however, of the Latino/Chicano folk healer is the practitioner himself. *Curanderos* usually become known in their communities as they become successful in treating family and intimate friends. As a key family member he becomes known in his field of healing, his neighbors and their family seek their aid for their own personal ailments. Thus begins an informal referral system that is guarded, as well as expanded. This is understandable in view of governmental restrictions and codes on who will practice healing measures. The *curandero* will thus attract clients, and his clearness of expression and forceful manner in which he approaches the patient will serve to instill confidence and hope in the person. The patient will return and probably refer a *compadre* (*comadre*) or *amigo* (*amiga*) when appropriate.

Another dynamic in discussing the question of what motivates people to seek out *curanderos* is faith. Though it is difficult for one to have faith during illness as stated before, the *curandero* encourages prayers and faith and discourages self-pity. He will recruit the patient's own energies, and he constantly reminds the patient that, as it is natural to want to be healthy, it is unnatural to wallow in sorrow and against nature to fear and doubt and thus perpetuate the illness. As this provides the patient with emotional support, reassurance and confidence, it is inevitable that he (she) will return to the health care provider.

Health maintenance also motivates a person to seek out the *curandero* or *yerbero* for optimum health and a long life, free of disease.

It is a generally held health belief among folk healers that nature alone is the primary healer, and therefore treatments, medicinal measures, and activities must be in congruence with nature. Unnatural agents and synthetic drugs produced by pharmaceutical companies are frowned upon. The mind and mental condition is thought to influence the body and vice versa, and therefore a clean, pure blood stream is absolutely essential for clean, pure thoughts. Therefore, foods ingested must be natural and pure. The body will react when acts against nature occur, and the inevitable law of compensation will be met by the indulger, ie, *"empacho."*

Herbs

The very first and only true medicines ever used by man and animals alike were those derived from the plant kingdom. Herbs act as astringents, alkalinizers, acidifiers, tonics, laxatives, euphorics, etc. Plants and their derivatives have effect upon circulation, respiration, muscle responses and irritability, and the intellectual psyche. Clearly, Latinos/Chicanos through the ages have recognized the medicinal properties of plants and have utilized them as part and parcel of their health maintenance.

The following list constitutes only a small number of curative herbs used within the Chicano community.

It is hoped that the readers will gain some understanding of their use and indications. Admittedly, this is a fundamental approach. However, for the sake of explanation, we have chosen to present a few of the more common types of herbs and have categorized them as follows: preventive, curative, sacramental, broad spectrum, etc. It should be pointed out that many herbs can, and are, used in combination with other herbs. Also, certain herbs can function in more than one category. It should also be noted that the authors intentionally omitted precise dosage and preparation so as to discourage experimentation.

The use of fresh herbs and plants, without chemically induced changes, have been found by Mexican physicians and pharmacologists to be quite productive to the restoration and maintenance of health. It is understandable that they may contain electrolytes (salts) and minerals that are more pure in their natural form and therefore more potent than the same drug derivatives that modern medicine produces in pharmaceutical laboratories.

In his manual, *Plantas Curativas de Mexico,* Dr. Luis Cabrera describes the action of pure herbs and plants as potent because ions and other substances have not changed their properties through chemical alterations. He refers to *moleculas vivas* in their pure form as unaltered and, therefore, of full potency. The action of these plants and herbs are seen as biologic rather than chemical. Medicinal herbs that are widely used by Latinos/ Chicanos, both north and south of the border, are recorded in Cabreras' manual. The uses of these have also been validated by the author's interviews, and knowledge of use by *curanderos, espiritualistas,* and Latino/ Chicano families.

The utility of these plants far extends the boundaries of the more specific-acting drugs of modern medicine. They may be employed for their preventive, as well as curative effects. Simply by modifying the dosage or the combination with other herbs or plants, the potency and functioning changes. As these plants are considered broad spectrum, their actions are more general than specific. Medicinal herbs that are commonly used and merit mention are listed below.

Anise for painful gases, stomach upsets, and colic. Anorexia and bronchitis are also treated by this herb. Breast-feeding mothers whose milk is diminishing are encouraged to take teas of anise.

Cedron en ayunas (fasting before breakfast) is taken as a tea and is indicated for a nervous stomach. It has an antispasmotic effect.

Cola de caballo (shave grass) is utilized for treatment of kidney disease (for its diuretic property), to reduce hemorrhage, and for tuberculosis.

Eucalipto (eucalyptus) has been demonstrated to contain in its leaves an odoriferous substance that has an antiseptic and disinfectant effect. This is said to be produced by the combination of *canforico* (camphor) and *aceite volatil* (oil) contained in the leaves. For *aire* (earache, stiff neck, colds or headaches), a condition which results from a cold draft or chill, the *curandero* will use a warm treatment — inhalation and sweating therapy. Stones may be heated in boiling water with eucalyptus and juniper oil and the patient will sit bent over, and inhale the vapors. (This illness reflects the hot and cold effects on the body; upsetting the equilibrium is avoided as it produces *aire.*)

Yerba glondrina makes a sweet-tasting tea and is used to treat rheumatism, toothaches caused by the "cold," and urine problems. The daily application of the liquid will also assist in removal of calluses and corns.

Lemon juice and glycerine oil in combination is used to soften dry hands. Glycerine may also be combined with rosewater (*rosa de Castillo*) and honey or olive oil to make ointments and salves for treatment of dermatitis, dry scaly skin, and blisters.

Camphor is a substance found in several herbs and plants and is sought for its relief of pain and rheumatism.

Romero, an herb that contains camphor, may be cut from the home garden and soaked in alcohol for several hours. This provides a good rubbing lotion for painful muscles and arthritis.

Liniments are prepared from herbs and oils by crushing an herb or plant into a powder and mixing it with oil.

A massage given with mixtures of camphor, *alcoholato de romero*, and *corazoncillo* are often used to warm and relax the nerves and decrease pain, arthritis, and muscle tightness that form as a result of tension and over-work.

Mexican physicians and pharmacologists have written books devoted solely to *ajo* (garlic) and its function. Garlic has long been used for diphtheria prevention and treatment, and also for its sacramental qualities. Herbs and plants that contain *"aceites esenciales"* (essential oils) work as balms on the mucous membranes to increase movement and slough off infected tissue, thereby stimulating the functions of these organs.

Cool rice water is universally employed for the treatment of diarrhea. With a tablespoon of vinegar it is used for gargling in cases of tonsilitis. Table 3.1 describes in more detail a few of the classified herbs and plants.

IMPLICATIONS FOR MODERN MEDICINE

Throughout this chapter, the authors have established the importance of maintaining an open and accepting attitude in the assessment of patient needs. As indicated by Haley, there are three major ways of viewing one's role relationship; (1) a within-self view, ie, seeing one's world as comprised of a collection of individuals; (2) as an interpersonal view, in which the world is seen in terms of dyadic relationships; (3) a systems view, in which interpersonal fields are the focus.[41] Each view has implications for the perceptions and behavior of the nurse and the patient. The authors would add a fourth category, that being a holistic view, in which the individual is seen as a whole psycho-social-physical-spiritual being within the dynamics of the environment. This view necessitates a willingness on the part of the nurse to suspend judgment, develop an open attitude, and develop aware-ness of the factors which have effects on the individual.

In contrast, persons not familiar with the Latino/Chicano culture may experience cultural dissonance or incongruence, brought about by the maintenance of a middle-class perspective or posture. Terms such as "culturally deprived" or "disadvantaged," are examples of labels attached to groups of people by persons who view their environment in terms of their own values. Implicit in the professionalization process is adherence to the middle-class values and norms of the dominant society. Schools which prepare health professionals traditionally offer only one frame of reference, that of the dominant culture. This perspective is used as a yardstick against which other cultures are measured.

As mentioned previously, the health professional can approach someone from outside of his (her) culture by retreating to nativism or fear of the unknown, with the viewpoint that the other culture is strange, exotic, primitive, different, and consequently less acceptable. This approach can lead to ridicule of family practices and traditions, stereotyping, and racist attitudes. These behaviors all reinforce cultural incongruence and create cultural dissonance, the end result being inadequate health care delivery. Maladaptive coping mechanisms which result from cultural incongruence include: tunnel vision — narrow perspective, judging all cultures from one frame of reference; blocking — refusal to see or consider culture as a variable; denial — rejection or refusal to admit the importance of a culture.

The opposite, more positive reactions to cultural incongruence are characterized by an open-minded approach, acknowledgment of differences among groups, and nonjudgmental acceptance of the whole person. All of these lend to a development of insight into the culture and its unique features. With this frame of reference, the health practitioner is more likely to assist the patient to reach an optimum of health maintenance.

The various responses to cultural incongruence as discussed, can be more clearly understood by the development of a paradigm illustrating the continuum of responses to the incident of cultural incongruence (Fig. 3.3).

A second area which has implications for health personnel is scientific incongruence, best defined as the use of scientific practices which are divergent or which have different frames of reference from those of the health practitioner.

It has been established that folk health is both an art and a science. Although the two schools of thought can coexist, it is essential to have an understanding of the different viewpoints regarding the illness process. As discussed earlier, the approach of pathophysiology is important, yet limited, in assessing the patient's interaction with his sociocultural background.

The third factor of folk health which has implications for the role of the health provider is the fact that the role of the nurse is one which is culture-bound. There is no equivalent role ascription in folk health for the nurse. As previously discussed, the folk health practioner will utilize the key family members and/or other significant individuals in the healing process.

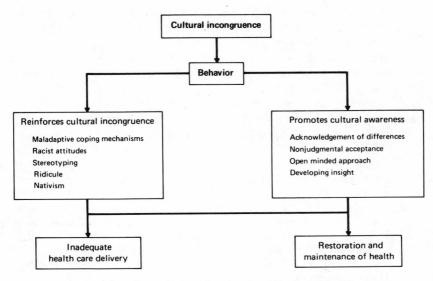

FIG. 3.3. Outcomes of culturally relevant and irrelevant health care

The nurse then, must define her role within that individual's family structure. Utilizing nursing skill and knowledge, the health professional should assess the patient's needs from a holistic standpoint and provide for patient care which is comprehensive and congruent with his way of life and his space orientation.

Role of the Nurse

The authors encourage the health professional to strive toward behavior which will lead to cultural awareness. The health professional must constantly reassess his/her own attitudes and judgments in terms of the continuum previously provided.

Nursing must institute a viable and socially relevant approach to the delivery of health care. This approach must respect the Latino/Chicano beliefs in the existence of real though intangible nonobservable entities of living that are deeply rooted in hundreds of years of folk history.

To achieve this level of awareness, the nurse must develop insight into her (his) own attitudes and beliefs. In order to do this she (he) must explore and reexamine the foundation for those attitudes and beliefs. The foundation selectively forms one's value system. Having reached this level of consciousness, the nurse can move from the role of an observer to one of a participant.

This awareness of self will allow the nurse to have a nonjudgmental approach because she (he) will be aware of the biases and prejudices that would otherwise perpetuate cultural incongruence.

Having attained a level of awareness, the nurse can proceed to relate to the health needs of the Latino/Chicano person. Any reversal of this process will result in inferior health care delivery and erroneous assessment of needs. Ignorance and imposition of Western thought and concepts will only serve to alienate the person and impede the process of nursing.

Some behavioral objectives for nursing include:

1. Delivery of holistic patient care which emphasizes the integral relationship between the psycho-social-spiritual-environmental aspects of the person
2. Facilitation of the nurse-patient relationship through the development of special skills (ie, Spanish proficiency, and the inclusion of bilingual—bicultural nursing personnel)
3. Establishment of family involvement in the healing process
4. Obtainment of knowledge of nontraditional community resources (Latino stores, etc.)
5. Assessment of signs of illness and referral to appropriate folk health practitioners
6. Enlistment of the help of folk health practitioners for culture specific conditions
7. Establishment of in-service programs in places of employment which will further explain folk health practices specific to that locale
8. Promotion of the concept of cultural pluralism in the education of nurses. This type of nursing education will prepare practitioners to assist persons with different cultural backgrounds, values, beliefs, and practices regarding health care maintenance.

SUMMARY

The Latino/Chicano culture is not a static entity which can be examined and conceptualized. Many destructive stereotypes have resulted from this type of examination. Rather, the Latino/Chicano culture must be viewed as the interaction of a diverse people (*La Raza*) within the constantly changing conditions, places, and circumstances of the times.

Folk health practices, as they are utilized today, owe their survival to the dynamic process of living. Health is a valuable commodity, and its preservation has led to the use of many rituals and practices. The Latino/Chicano folk practitioner believes the process of recognizing a disease condition and knowledge of the proper techniques of eliminating it are much more essential than a knowledge of its scientific or technical name. The folk practitioner's use of plants, herbs, prayers, and chants has proven to be successful in curing both "good" and "evil" illnesses. Consequently, the survival of folk health practices into the twentieth century can be attributed to two factors: the need for preservation of health and the success achieved in obtaining cures.

In this chapter, the authors have attempted to inform the reader of the significance of folk health among Latino/Chicano people. We have established a basis for self-assessment and understanding which will equip the nurse with a frame of reference in approaching folk health practices.

We hope to have impressed upon the reader that knowledge and respect of patient's health beliefs and practices is prerequisite to the delivery of comprehensive health care. No longer can the health provider afford to ignore cultural values or variables. The patient is demanding and deserves a nurse who is sensitive to his (her) culture. The consequence of this is the need for the development of a meaningful individualized plan for care that can be effectively operationalized.

Definition of Terms

Acculturation: 'Behavioral assimilation,' ie, the unconscious fusion of Mexican and Anglo-American attitudes, values, and beliefs. This is to be distinguished from 'structural assimilation' which is a conscious movement into identifiable groups or organizations."[42]

Barrio: A community occupied predominately by persons of Mexican birth or descent. This definition refers to a sociocultural identity, rather than a geographical identity, and therefore it may cross various city, county, or state jurisdictions, ie, East Los Angeles is a barrio made up of several sub-barrios and is situated in both city and county territories.

Chicanos: For purposes of this text, this term will refer to persons of Mexican descent — Mexican-born and Mexican Americans.

Dominant culture: The prevailing cultural beliefs, attitudes, and values of a society. In the United States, the dominant culture is represented by the white Anglo-Saxon Protestant (WASP) ethic.

Folk health: "The folk medical beliefs and practices, which are indigenous to the Chicano culture, and refers to the services provided by *curanderos* (folk healers), *sobadores* (folk chiropractors), *brujos* (witches), and *espiritualistas* (spiritualists), and the use of herbs for healing."[43]

Folk health practioners: Used interchangeably with "folk healers" and are described in the text.

Holistic Health: "The practice of viewing a person as a whole psycho-physio-socio-cultural-spiritual being in relationship with his total environment or universe. This holism, therefore, includes the teachings, philosophies, religious and social mores of health care systems used by various ethnic people.[44]

Latinos: Refers to a group of people in the United States commonly known as Hispanos, Chicanos, Boriqua, Cubanos, Mexican American, Spanish-American, and Latin American.

References

1. Castaneda C: The Teachings of Don Juan: A Yaqui Way of Knowledge. New York, Touchstone (Simon and Schuster), 1974, p 147
2. Saunders L: Cultural Differences and Medical Care: The Case of the Spanish-speaking People of the Southwest; New York, Russell Sage Foundation, 1954, pp 141–73
3. Clark M: Health in the Mexican American: A Community Study. Berkeley, University of California Press, 1959, pp 162–217
4. Cabrera AV: Emerging Faces, the Mexican Americans. San Jose, Brown, 1971, p 24
5. Idem, p 56
6. Kiev A: Curanderismo, Mexican-American Folk Psychiatry. New York, The Free Press, 1968 pp 175–77
7. Idem, p 176
8. Romano OI V: Charismatic medicine, folk-healing and folk-sainthood. Anthropol, 67: 1152, 1965
9. Kiev, op cit, pp 22–23
10. California Regional Medical Programs, Area V, University of Southern California School of Medicine, U. S. Dept. HEW: East Los Angeles Health, A Community Report, Los Angeles: A Welfare Planning Council, 1970, pp 21, 33
11. Idem, pp 54–55
12. Cabrera, op cit, p 22
13. Galarza E: Merchants of Labor, The Mexican Bracero Story. Santa Barbara, Mc Nally & Loft, 1964, pp 121–71, 183–229
14. MacWilliams C: Factories in the Field. Santa Barbara. Peregrine, 1971, pp 221–82
15. Chandler D: Huelga! New York, Simon & Schuster, 1970
16. Cabera, op cit, p 24
17. Jackson C: A study on the relationship of acculturation and age to the use of folk medicine. Los Angeles, University of Southern California (unpublished article), 1973, p 4
18. Saunders, op cit, pp 142–43
19. Clark, op cit, pp 236–39
20. Saunders, op cit, pp 93–98, 141
21. Madsen W: The Mexican Americans of South Texas. New York, Holt, Rinehart and Winston, 1964, pp 99–104
22. Idem, p 95
23. Krofcheck M, Jackson C: The Chicano experience with nativism in public administration. Public Administr Rev, 34: 535–536, 1974

24. Cabrera, op cit, p 24
25. Murillo N: The Mexican American Family. Chicanos Social and Psychological Perspectives, St. Louis, Mosby, 1971, p 102
26. Rubel AJ: Across the Tracks. Austin, University of Texas Press, 1966, p 103
27. Cabrera, op cit, p 25
28. Arias R: The Influence of Chicano Culture on Health Care In East Los Angeles Health Systems, Inc., Community Health Bulletin, Special Report No. 4, 1974
29. Nall FC, II, Speilberg J: Social and cultural factors in the responses of Mexican-Americans to medical treatment. J Health Soc Res 8: 305, 1967
30. Guzman IG: Biologia Medica. Mexico y la Cultura. Mexico, 1961, p 749
31. Kiev, op cit, pp 106—07
32. Clark, op cit, p 207
33. Jackson, op cit, p 14
34. Edgerton R, Karno M, Hernandez I: Curanderismo in the metropolis, Am J Psychother 24:11, 1970 pp 124—34
35. Madsen W: Society and health in the Lower Rio Grande Valley. Mexican-Americans in the United States, Cambridge, Mass. Schenkman, 1970, p 85
36. Jackson, op cit, p 14
37. Fabrega H Jr, Silver D: Illness and Shamanistic Curing in Zinacantan, An Ethnomedical Analysis. California, Stanford University Press, 1973, pp 5—6
38. Romano, op cit, p 1153
39. Dominquez-Ybarra A: Lecture delivered at Holistic Approaches to Health, The San Francisco Consortium Health Services/Educational Activities East West Academy of Healing Arts June 28—29, 1975
40. Cabrera LG: Plantas Curativas de Mexico, 5th ed. Mexico, p 23
41. Haley, J: Lecture delivered at Harry Stack Sullivan Society in January 1965. New York City (tape transcribed at Rutgers)
42. Jackson, op cit, p 6
43. Idem, p 14
44. Holistic Approaches to Health. The San Francisco Consortium, Health Services/Educational Activities East West Academy of Healing Arts, San Francisco, June 28—29, 1975. (Conceptual Framework for Conference-Abstract)

Bibliography

Alexander RJ: Today's Latin America, 2nd ed. New York, Anchor, (Doubleday), 1968
Amelia ———, Interviews with Curanderas. Los Angeles, May 1973 (unpublished)
Arias H, Costas F: Plantas Medicinales, Talleres Graficcos Gonzales. Mexico, Biblioteca Practica, 1955
Bernal I: Mexico Before Cortez: Art, History, Legend. New York, Dolphin, (Doubleday), 1963

Capo N: Mis Observaciones Clinicas Sobre El Ajo, El Limon, y la Cebolla, 3rd ed. Mexico, Editores Mexicanos Unidoes, 1974

Cifre P: Interviews with Consumers regarding Folk Health Practices. Los Angeles, California, 1975 (unpublished)

Hernandez MB: Interviews with "Key Family Members" regarding Folk Health Practices. Los Angeles, California, March 1972, May 1974, May 1975 (unpublished)

Hernandez MB: Interviews with Curanderas. Los Angeles, California, May 1974 (unpublished)

Martinez JH: Interviews with Consumers regarding Folk Health Practices. Los Angeles, California, May 1975 (unpublished)

McHenry JP: A Short History of Mexico. New York, Dolphin (Doubleday), 1962

Meyer C: American Folk Medicine. New York, Crowell, 1973

Moore J: Mexican Americans. Englewood Cliffs, N.J., Prentice-Hall, 1970

Pompa G: Medicamentos Indigenas. Miami, Fla., Mexico, Editorial America, S. A., 1972 (unpublished)

Rusca A: El Libro de Fray Anselmo. Mexico City, Hermanos Brothers (No year given)

Samora J (ed): La Raza: Forgetten Americans: Notre Dame, Indiana, University of Notre Dame Press, 1966

Wagner F: Remedios Caseros con Plantas Medicinales. Seminario, Mexico, Medina

4

Cultural Health Traditions: American Indian Perspectives

Jennie Joe,
Cecelia Gallerito,
and Josephine Pino

Native Americans* make up one of the smallest minority groups in this country. What once was a majority population is now so small that it often is listed in population figures under "miscellaneous" and "other." According to the 1970 United States Census report, there are 792,730 Native Americans, a figure which is disputed by some Indian sources who estimated that the census data underreported the true figure by 20 to 30 percent.[1]

Presently there are well over 200 Indian tribes left in the United States. According to the same census report, Indians reside in every one of the 50 states, but over half of them are concentrated in the western portion of the country. Oklahoma, Arizona, California, and New Mexico are the four states with the largest populations of American Indians.[2]

Native American communities range from a single family, living on one acre of land, to large land bases called reservations upon which thousands of families live. More recently, increasing numbers of American Indians have been migrating to urban centers, often in search of employment and education. The majority of those migrating take up residence in the poorer sections of town, thereby becoming invisible in the city ghettos.

What formerly were nations of people are now more commonly referred to as tribes. The ten largest tribes are listed in Table 4.1.[3]

A glance at the small population figures might cause one to wonder why such numerically "insignificant" minority groups are worth the "trouble" of specific consideration in this book for students of nursing.

American Indian, Native American, and Indian are used interchangeably.

Table 4.1

TRIBES	NUMBERS
Navajo	96,743
Cherokee	66,150
Sioux (Dakota)	47,825
Chippewa	41,946
Pueblo	30,971
Lumbee	27,520
Choctaw and Houma	23,562
Apache	22,993
Iroquois	21,473
Creek, Alabama, and Coushattal	17,004

Especially so when the chances are pretty slim that an average nursing student will have the opportunity to see a "real" Indian patient in a typical university or private nursing school in the Midwest or Eastern metropolitan areas. Even if there were a "real" Indian patient or resident within the community, chances are he would be identified with some other more "visible" minority group. To many white people, you are not an Indian unless you are wrapped in a colorful blanket, wear feathers, and say "ugh," a stereotyping which has largely been perpetuated by our mass media and classroom history books.

Contrary to the popular notion of just one model "red man" wearing buckskin and beaded headband, there are definite differences among Indian tribal groups. There is no one international language or even style of dress. The difference between an Apache and an Iroquois is comparable to the difference between a German and an Irishman. They might share a similar skin color, but they certainly do not share the same traditional language or culture.

In addition to sharing information on some basic facts in general about Native Americans, the other purpose of this discussion is to highlight some ideas or concepts of health and illness, traditional Indian health systems, and some important contributions of Native Americans to Western medicine.

As previously indicated, our educational system in its attempt to teach American history traditionally has focused only on the history of the white man and whatever mentions are made of American Indians are usually negative, except for the legend of the first "Thanksgiving." To a large extent, curricula designed for higher education are not any better and sometimes worse. Nursing education is one example. There is an underlying assumption that since nurses are in a "caring" profession, there is little need to sensitize them to ethnic needs or to create an awareness that patients come in all colors. As a result, they often bring into the nurse-patient relationship different attitudes and concepts of illness and health. Some might not even believe that there is more to nursing a patient than just carrying out a physician's order.

Another common assumption of nursing education is that if a student elects to take a social science course, such as an introductory course in cultural anthropology, this will suffice for any pertinent knowledge necessary to deal with different ethnic groups and their health concerns. Because the course is only introductory, however, it stands to reason that it will rarely get into detailed information or discussion of special areas such as health concepts and cultural attitudes towards illness and health.

Transcultural nursing is one new movement which is just in the process of developing in nursing education and seems to reflect a "rediscovery" of culture. Perhaps through this new interest and other supportive developments in nursing education, nurses will broaden their perspectives on the cultural diversity of man and eventually will become as professionally knowledgeable about people as they are about pathology and techniques.

Native Americans have not been known to purposefully impose their ways on anyone. This philosophy appears to be completely alien to the white man, who, ever since he has come into contact with the Indian, has been trying to change him and mold him into a pseudowhite image. This process of assimilation and acculturation has been accelerated primarily through compulsory education programs. Included in this change process is the increased use of western medicine and physicians. The success of the acculturation process is evident in the emerging new value placed on "getting the best medical care by the best physician specialist and in the best hospital" if one can afford it. New measurements of success emphasize economic achievement as opposed to the traditional cultural views which placed equal emphasis on all elements that contributed to a "good" life.

Historically, there has been little need for Native Americans to fully accept the health system of the white man. This was especially true when it was the Native Americans who were asked to use their native medicine and techniques to administer to the sick white patient. Vogel, in his book on American Indian Medicine, writes:

> 'One of the powerful influences brought to bear on the colonists engaged in the practice of medicine,' wrote Maurice Bear Gordon, 'was wrought by the Indians. Friend or foe, the medical practice of the red man could not help but seep into the therapeutics of the pioneers of the new world. . . .' The reasons for this, he indicated, are that the colonial medical practitioners (not always physicians), especially the native born ones, were poorly trained and equipped and were ready to receive useful information from any source. Being also in a new world and a stranger to its medical flora, it was not unnatural to accept the Natives as tutor. (From American Indian Medicine, by Virgil J. Vogel. Copyright 1970 by the University of Oklahoma Press[4])

This sharing of knowledge and expertise did not last, especially after the white men had learned all that they thought was necessary from the Indians. Then, as the frontier was made more "safe," it was easier to attract physicians and other trained white medical practitioners. The Native Americans, on the other hand, confronted a threat to survival of their whole race or nation as they came under increased pressure to give up more land space to the ever growing numbers of white people coming into their country.

As more white men moved in, more Indian people were being displaced, moving into other territorial lands that were used by other tribal groups. This brought about a new and different conflict: For the first time some tribes were at war with each other over territorial rights. Other tribes, who had little choice, were forced to retaliate against the whites. This retaliation was perhaps one of the primary factors that brought about the end of an era which saw the American Indian as a "noble red man." The most common remnant of that era is the classical once-a-year elementary school reincarnation of the first Thanksgiving.

The rest of American history brings to mind such images of the American Indian as "injun," "savage," and the typical caricature of the cigar store stoic Indian. Slogans such as "the only good injun is a dead injun" summarize the treatment of, and attitudes towards, Indians in this country. It appears that, in the white man's value system, possession, whether it be of land or the minds of people, is more important than the myth of freedom.

The possession of land came rather easy for the white man. What he could not get by stealing, he got by killing; with the use of his superior arsenal and sometimes by more indirect means such as giving smallpox-contaminated blankets to Indians. Other, more civilized methods employed were treaties and other governmental policies which actually provided some payment for the land.[5] According to one source, 450,000,000 acres of land were acquired by the United States from the Indians between 1789 and 1890 alone.[6]

Indian mortality rates mounted as a result of the continuing conflicts and rampant communicable diseases for which Indians had no immunity, since most of the diseases were carried into the country by the white man. Native Americans, who were lucky to survive, did so in smaller numbers and some were permanently crippled psychologically. One example of such crippling has been in the area of resources for dealing with illness. The decimation process also brought about the end of the cadre of health workers among many of the surviving Native Americans. Those who did survive were unable to practice freely or take on new apprentices from Indian children who were later forced to go to school miles away from home. Important medicines made from herbs and minerals also became rare, as Indians were placed on reservations and were not allowed to leave for a number of years.

As American Indians rapidly diminished in numbers, so did their land. Many, knowing there were no other alternatives for survival, ceded their land in exchange for congressional promises of federally protected land enclaves and establishment of educational and health resources. That promise of health care was probably the first prepaid health plan ever to originate in this country for any group of people.

Prior to this, the only official health care given to the Indian population was the periodic visit by the military physicians from nearby army posts: military installations that were there to prevent "injun" uprisings. According to some of the elderly Indian people who had been through the tail end of some of those struggles, the visits by physicians were mainly to insure that there was no evidence of communicable diseases which could threaten lives in nearby white settlements or military installations.

These first acts of delivery of health services to the Indian people were followed by sporadic visits by physicians employed by the various missionary groups that had moved into the different Indian communities to assist in the "civilization" process. Many of these missionaries, believing that medicine men were pagan worshippers, condemned their practice as heathen and discouraged treatment for those who used the services of medicine men or used any form of native medicine or treatment. This condescending attitude towards the "ways" of the Indian became more apparent when Indian patients had to be hospitalized.*[7-9]

The identification of Indians as pagans and members of a primitive society was not just central to the health scene, but it was primary in all educational programs. These first educational programs were initiated by missionaries who were given money by the Bureau of Indian Affairs to establish schools. The Bureau of Indian Affairs (BIA) was originally established by Congress in 1834 as the principal federal agency to help "civilize" the Indians. Ironically, this agency was established within the Department of War. However, the BIA was moved to the Department of Interior in 1849, when the department was created, and there it remains today.[10]

The BIA was responsible for providing health care to the Indian population up to 1955, when the responsibility was transferred to the Department of Health, Education and Welfare, where it has remained.

Since the change in 1955, the Indian Health Service has prided itself on

---

*For more specific examples, read Adair and Deuschle's The People's Health: Medicine and Anthropology; Cahn's "White Man's Medicine: the Indian and the Public Health Service" in Our Brother's Keeper: The Indian in White America, and Vine Deloria's chapter on "Missionaries and the Religious Vacuum" in Custer Died for Your Sins.

its progress in improving the health level of American Indians. The long-range goal of the Indian Health Service is said to be "to raise the health of Indians to the highest possible level."[11] The Indian Health Service view of the health picture of the American Indian is exemplified in reports such as this one:

> *Among the most dramatic changes in the health status of the American Indians has been the drop in deaths from tuberculosis; the rate for Indians is now about 16.2 per 100,000 population, a decrease of nearly 70 percent from 1954. Tuberculosis, which ranks as the 10th leading cause of death, was the primary cause of death in 1949. The causes of death differ substantially in rank from those among the general population. Whereas accidents ranked fourth in causes of death for the general population in 1967, they were the leading causes among Indians. Although deaths from diseases generally associated with substandard living and insanitary conditions, namely tuberculosis, gastritis, influenza, and pneumonia, have declined sharply among Indians in the past 10 years, they are still high.*
>
> *The infant death rate among Indians has dropped more than 50 percent since 1955. Even with this sharp decline, the rate in 1967 was still nearly 1 1/2 times that for the general population, in which most infant deaths occur within a few days after birth.*[12]

Mr. Crockett, in his analysis of the health improvement among American Indians, attributes the progress to the "increasing understanding and participation of the Indian people themselves as well as to the effects of increased resources."[13]

In striking contrast with this progress report is the significant statistical increase in the number of reported cases of cirrhosis (alcoholism), suicide, and homicide, all indicative of poor mental health. It seems that while illnesses that are germ-specific are being reduced or successfully contained, the symptoms of social "unhealthiness" are increasing. To some extent this is also true about the general health picture of the United States, especially since our Western health delivery system has dealt with man as if there were a split between his physical and mental being. In each case, the treatment of one rarely means concern with or treatment of the other.

This separation is unheard of among traditional Native American medicine men, who consider the health of an individual as embracing the body, mind, and the ecologic sphere of man. This concept of equilibrium is a cornerstone of most Native American traditional healing systems. The treatment process, then, is guided by the idea of treating the whole person and bringing him back in balance with his surroundings. This holistic concept is not unique to Indian medicine men or their system; it is also one of the original concepts that attended the birth of Western medicine, but it has since been lost. It is said that the Greek philosophers, who gave much to the founding of the "scientific" reasoning in medicine, built their ideas on this same concept.[14]

Although Western medicine probably is the most utilized health system among American Indians today, there are those who still use the services of their medicine men. Medicine men and the traditional native healing system, therefore, still offer a viable alternative for those who are fortunate to have it available to them. Fortunate, because these tribal groups have a culturally relevant resource to deal with some of their mental health problems.

The Native American system of healing arts varies from tribe to tribe and in degree of complexity. For example, the Navajo healing traditions consist of a complex system which includes healing specialists, herbalists, and diagnosticians. Depending on the type of symptoms or illness, the patient elects one type of healer or goes through complex healing ceremonies which bring into play a number of specialists; ie, within the Navajo culture, a series of bad dreams is given an importance equal to that of a traumatic illness such as cancer.

A Navajo patient may sometimes, after using some home remedy, approach one of the "hand tremblers" (diagnosticians) for a firm diagnosis. The hand trembler is so called because the diagnosis is made with the intervention of the deities who take over the diagnostician's hand; the trembling hand then draws a picture that interprets the cause of illness. The hand trembler then informs the patient of the diagnosis and recommends what needs to be done to correct the condition. Sometimes this recommendation may mean either a series of ceremonies or a one-time treatment by a medicine man whose specialty is the treatment of the specific illness.

The patient in either case is charged whatever he can afford or offers to pay. Payment may be with livestock or other material goods. The medicine man, when asked to perform the curing ceremonies, does so usually in the patient's own home where friends and relatives can participate.

There is very little difference in most of the modes of treatment used by Navajo medicine men as compared to those used by physicians. Oral medication (herbs) is often used in conjunction with other forms of treatment, such as sweat baths for application of heat as well as used for psychologic purification. Bedrest, isolation, diet therapy, exercise, and other common treatments used by physicians are all used by Navajo medicine men. It is also very common today for Navajo medicine men and other practitioners* to refer their patients to the hospital or clinic to see a physician.

Navajo patients, however, seem to know when to use which form of health system. For example, someone who is acutely injured in an automobile accident will immediately go to the hospital, but a patient who may

---

*Practitioners is a catch-all word used to describe the cadre of Indian people who have expertise in fixing herbs, setting bones, treating witchcraft, serving as midwives, and/or have any outstanding curing skills.

be scheduled for a delicate operation may first go to a medicine man for a treatment to insure success of the impending surgery. Some illnesses, such as those possibly caused by the supernatural or witchcraft, are considered best treated by the medicine man or other appropriate Indian healers.

A couple of recent studies done among another tribe and Indians living in an urban area of San Francisco highlight the utilization and the coexistence of the two health systems. For example, with respect to the Papagos, it has been said:

> *Diagnostic and curing rituals, then, do not compete with modern medical practices, but are coexistent procedures necessary to effect complete cure. The diagnostic procedures of the medicine men place primary emphasis on the etiology rather than the epidemiology of illness. The logic of both systems is inherent in the classification of illness allowing for both "caused" and "uncaused" ailments. The system allows for Anglo control of symptoms while the Papago practitioners maintain control of the supernatural realm. Each has control of an area not of prime concern to the other.* [15]

The other study which took into account many different tribal groups also supports the claim that there is no conflict between the use of Western medicine and traditional Indian medicine men.[16]

The reader should be cautioned that this is a very general and brief discussion of some common elements found in Native American healing systems. It is by no means complete, nor does it claim to go into detail to speak on the differences among all the different tribes of American Indians. Although the specific tribes have different healing systems, all of them have in common the need to deal with the advent of Western medicine.

Many of the positive aspects of the Native American healing systems which could contribute to Western medicine would certainly include the notion of holistic medicine and the human factor to replace the clinical coldness that transforms patients into hospital room numbers and disease entities instead of persons.

Other past contributions of American Indians to the development of Western medicine, although rarely acknowledged, have been taking place primarily in the pharmaceutical fields.

> *The Indians of North and South America used for medicinal purposes well over two hundred drugs which have been included in the official drug compendia of the United States. While the aboriginal uses of these drugs were frequently incorrect in the judgment of modern science, the examples of efficacious usage which have been cited constitute an imposing monument to the original Americans. There can be no doubt that by trial and error methods they arrived at an understanding of the properties and effects of many useful botanical medicines. Moreover, independently of Old World influence, they discovered some useful medical inventions and procedures. The surgical use of rubber and cotton, the bulbed syringe for enemata and*

medical injections, the Crede method of manipulation in parturition, trephination, and the use of anesthetics and antiseptics have all been credited to American Indians. (From American Indian Medicine, *by Virgil J. Vogel. Copyright 1970 by the University of Oklahoma Press*[17]*)*

American Indians encounter problems when dealing with the health care delivery system in this country. The problems faced by Indians are based on differences within the social systems of the Indian cultures and the American–Anglo cultures.

HEALTH MAINTENANCE

The American Indian derives health care from a line of sources. There exists within the Indian culture the traditional health care perpetuated through the years. The first recourse is a member within the extended family group who becomes the caretaker whenever someone becomes ill. Next is the specialist within the community who is known for curing certain illnesses. This person lacks the religious affiliation of a medicine man. Last is the medicine man who occupies a religious position within the tribe and displays esoteric skill that connotes a supernatural quality.

With the promise of health care, the Native American was allowed access into the nontraditional health delivery system. This nontraditional health care is the white health care system composed of clinics and hospitals. The influence of the white system on the Indian is both good and bad. While providing highly technologic care unavailable in traditional medicine, the Indian is detoured from the advantages by the insensitive and foreign manner of the white system, thereby negating the intention of assistance.

In the traditional health care that the Indian receives, it is easier for that person to accept and understand what is happening, because it fits into his world view. In subscribing to the nontraditional system, it is often difficult for the Indian to accept or understand what is happening because of the highly scientific and detached nature of the Anglo health professional. The explanation of illness is hindered by the lack of Indian words to translate certain disease processes. Also, traditional Indians interpret time in terms of a natural order. For example, they tell time by the movement of the sun and by diurnal routines. Most Indians who follow traditional life patterns are not obsessive about knowing the exact time.

HEALTH PROCUREMENT

The Indian has various ways of practicing preventative health in the traditional sense. Charms are one example of securing protection and these consist of fetishes, arrowheads, and blessed pollen that is carried in a bag. Drinking special herbal teas or rubbing the body with evergreens at certain periods during the year are other methods that are followed. Parallel to this in the nontraditional system are immunizations and preventative health education which can be a benefit if they are channeled appropriately by the health deliverer.

The reality of a clinic visit may be an unpleasant experience, especially if the patient has to wait long hours, only to have the physician lecture them about why they should have come sooner. (If the patient had, in fact, arrived earlier, chances are he would have been sent home because his symptoms were too mild to warrant an accurate medical diagnosis. Infants have been known to be sent home with meningitis!) The trip to the clinic is usually a long one due to the distances on some reservations; such long trips consume a lot of gasoline, require physical and mental stamina, and require an absence from work. If the patient does not own a car, he must pay someone to drive him to the clinic or walk 40 to 100 miles. The luxury of public transportation does not extend onto the Indian reservation, which is a handicap to people who suffer enough debit from an opulent society. Nurses have been known to be resentful and unwilling to explain treatment or even to tell a patient if he/she needs to return for follow-up. The whole ordeal becomes unpleasant, and the patient hesitates to subject himself to another experience in humiliation. Some health professionals refuse to see patients unless they have something seriously wrong; and many times, preventative health care measures such as yearly check-ups do not exist for the Indian patient. It has been acknowledged that Indian health seriously lags behind the general population. Also, Indian groups suffer from many diseases that have been eradicated in the dominant society. Even though medical facilities are available for Indian patients, many Anglo health professionals bring a condescending and "superior" attitude, and they become a blocking agent which prevents the Indian from receiving adequate health care. Anglo health professionals tend to view the Indian person as infrahuman. Consequently, the Indian finds himself in a double bind: while the Anglo professional appears to have one hand out to dispense health care, the other hand slaps away those who approach him.

TRIBES FOR DISCUSSION

Since all Indian tribes are varietal, heterogenity is a dominating factor among Indian people. The concepts discussed will only apply to two large groups of Native Americans in the Southwest, namely the Laguna Pueblo and the Mescalero Apache tribes. Since they represent the tribes of the authors, the writers feel confident in speaking about these two Indian groups. We are limiting our discussion to these tribes because it is important to respect tribal codes and to avoid generalizations about Indian people. Both of the tribes belong to large "families." The Apaches consist of five groups: the San Carlos, Kiowa, Jicarrilla, White River, and the Mescalero. Most people have the misconception that the Apaches all speak the same dialect. There are different dialects of Apache, and some are alien to other Apache groups. The Pueblo tribe is comprised of 11 different Pueblos or communities and, here again, they also show disparity in language. The Pueblos are located along the Rio Grande River Basin and each Pueblo group considers itself unique. There is a strong pride in belonging to a particular Pueblo. It is a profound insult for Indians to be viewed as identical, with uniform traits. While the white society has managed to make great strides scientifically, it has failed to develop humanely. As a result, differing social and cultural groups are punished for their uniqueness. Territorial distance has superimposed on it the other verities that separate people: negative attitudes, ignorance, and greed.

CULTURAL VARIABLE IN THE INDIAN HEALTH CONSUMER

Since the Indians' life style is predisposed by tradition, they are subjected to certain influencing variables that play a part in their health care. The variables that are significant and deserve attention are: religion, family structure, food, and grief. A summary of each variable will be stated within the context of each tribe, and the implications for the hospitalized patient will be extrapolated.

Indian View on Health as It Relates to Their Religion

As indicated in the preceding discourse, Indians are not atheistic in their practice of native religion. They have a holistic view about life, and, in that view, God is the primary giver and cause of life. Illness, then, is tied into religion and consequently, when a person becomes ill, he/she will seek a medicine man and subscribe to a religious ritual to remove the illness.

LAGUNA. The medicine man is used to interpret the cause of the disease in order to treat it. In most cases, the person who is ill does not know why he is sick. His illness is beyond the customary folk remedies, and serious physical or mental symptons are present. In Pueblo culture, the patient undergoes a four-night ceremony, during which the medicine man uses chants and herbs. Pueblo belief is that the medicine man learns through his ceremonies the source of the evil, absorbs the evil, and takes the evil away from the patient at the end of the ceremony as he departs. Pueblo religion is based upon leading a good life. The Pueblo Indian must do everything in earnest and from his heart. There is no concept, as in Christianity, of receiving any reward for leading a good life. In fact, if a reward is expected, a spirit may exact vindication of some sort on the individual. Religious ceremonies and tribal dances are an important function in Pueblo "preventive health care." During Pueblo celebrations, masked dancers convey good to the village and transport away evil. Also, the masked dancers bring blessings for the sick. Other preventive health and religious practices include the wearing of arrowheads, especially for children, and offering cornmeal to the dead spirits who roam the earth. These dead spirits are believed to be those that the living have failed to remember. New mothers are cautioned against leaving their newborn infants alone, for fear that a spirit will take its life (this belief is probably tied to the sudden infant death syndrome that occurs with infants from birth to six months. The etiology of this syndrome is still unknown.)

MESCALERO. The religious aspect is diminishing in its importance because of the increase in breakdown of customs that previously dictated the Mescalero's life style. The medicine man for one of the tribes says that he is used less and less by the people, except for the yearly tribal celebrations.[18] This medicine man believes that the younger Mescaleros are not interested in maintaining their Indian heritage and, consequently, little devotion is paid to their native religion. The Mescalero perspective has an adaptive orientation. Health is represented as maintaining balance in life. Physical or mental illness represents a disruption in the balance of life, and the ritual that is performed for ill people is designed to restore the balance that has been lost. Mescaleros believe that the Spirit (God) gives light and exists above everything and everybody. The medicine man, therefore, uses song, incense, and prayers to invoke blessings from the Spirit. The grass of the earth plays an important role in ceremonies because, according to belief, all life comes from the grass. To the Mescalero, the grass protects the earth from being destroyed and feeds the animals who in turn are used to feed man.

To become a Mescalero medicine man, an applicant must undergo four years of intensive training which is sequential. The first year is spent learning about minerals, the second year deals with herbs, the third year covers animals, and the last year is spent learning about man. Since the medicine man is taught that man must live in harmony and unity with his environment, he must understand life within the context of these four areas.

In comparing the two tribes (Laguna and Mescalero), it becomes clear that the Laguna Pueblo Indians cling to their traditional beliefs, while the Mescaleros have begun to drift away from the strictness of their religious ceremonies. Some Mescalero tribal members speculate that the cause of increasing social problems within the tribe can be directly linked to the failure to practice their traditional religion.

IMPLICATIONS FOR THE HOSPITALIZED PATIENT. There are many implications for a hospitalized Indian patient as a result of his world view and his religious and health beliefs. If a medicine man is summoned to the hospital by a patient, his visit is usually done in an unobtrusive manner. He does things in an inconspicuous way, and his prayers are usually brief. It is important that medicine men become used more openly and encouraged to visit hospitals serving Indian patients. Using medicine men would only help the Indian patient and would help to reduce some of the alienation that Indians feel when they are forced into the white health care system. Having the medicine man actively participate in curing the Indian patient would contribute to the patient's emotional and psychic well-being. If both the white health care and Native health care fail to cure the patient, at least the family has the consolation of knowing that everything possible was attempted. While whites tend to consider only things that exist in the physical arena, the Indians place equal importance within the realm of the supernatural.

Family Structure

The extended family is a crucial factor in the life style of Native Americans. Historically, tribes were based on family affiliations. Food, shelter, and survival were supported on a communal approach. Maintaining family stability was so important to Native Americans that tribes evolved social safeguards to protect against a family's disintegration as a result of death. Kinships were increased through adoption rituals that existed within tribal ceremonies. Presently, the pervasive factors that have created the nuclear family are affecting American Indians as well.

LAGUNA. Most families are still composed of three-generational family units, but the younger generation is slowly seeking homes away from their parents. Undoubtedly, the future holds single-family units in store for the Lagunas. Other customs, such as the male initiation rite, are still practiced that strengthen the extended family concept. The male goes through a ceremony where he is given "adopted" parents, whom he must respect as his natural parents throughout life. The male receives gifts from his adopted parents, as well as advice. This ceremony is strictly voluntary on the part of all concerned, and it is widely practiced by the Lagunas.

MESCALERO. The extended family has all but disappeared. Few old people are alive today. Prior to the white man's arrival, the number of old people was definitely larger. There are old family photographs which testify that longevity was common in the earlier part of the century among the Mescaleros. Progress, in the form of added housing on the reservation, has fostered the single (nuclear) family living. As a result, there are few Mescalero households that have grandparents as part of the family unit. Also, young children are now left at day care centers while both parents work. This was previously unheard of in Mescalero culture.

Rituals of adoption do not prevail within this tribal group. Although a puberty rite for adolescent girls is held yearly, a new affiliation does not occur between the Indian maiden and her sponsor.

IMPLICATIONS FOR THE HOSPITALIZED PATIENT. The extended family plays an important role in helping the patient to recover. Family members prefer to have someone close at hand in case a patient experiences a sudden decline. A family will usually agree to limit their members to two at one time. Hospital staff should allow family members to participate in the patient's care. In personal work experience, we have found that family members are willing to assist with the simple tasks of caretaking, for example, making the bed, giving the patient water, and supplying the comfort measures according to his needs.

In the Laguna tribe, since it is customary for the males to have a special rite, favoritism may be culturally defined. As a result, a male Laguna patient may expect privileges which the staff may interpret as demanding. An awareness of the position held by a male Laguna within his tribe should create a more tolerant attitude on the part of the staff.

If a patient has to be sent to an extended health facility, every effort should be made to locate one close to the family. Without the support of significant individuals to reaffirm the patient's identity, what would be the use in continuing life? Indian people, especially the senior citizens, have probably spent their lives speaking their native tongue and following specific customs. Removing them from their familiar environment into a foreign one cuts them off from meaningful communication and leaves them isolated. Placing Indians in facilities far from their homesites is difficult for their psychic well-being.

Food

Native Americans were among the first "ecologists," adapting their life-style to their environment and living on what the land provided. With some tribes, food has special significance that goes beyond its nutritional value. Food is important and has been incorporated into religious ceremonies; it possesses a social value that is an integral part of any social gathering. Good food enhances a family's reputation within the tribe.

LAGUNA. Among the local people, it is said, "Whenever anything is happening with the Pueblos, there is food." This characteristic use of food in all aspects of social and religious life is shared by all the Pueblos. The Pueblo Indians are known for their food sharing during their feasts. Even in large Pueblo families, there is always enough food for an unexpected guest. Food plays an important role in religious ceremonies among the Pueblos. It is offered to the wandering spirits in hope of warding off any possible evil, and it is also prepared as a symbol of remembrance for the dead (not unlike the Christian practice). The preparation of food in the Pueblos is much like it was a century ago, and the Indian diet is so stable that it has become a tradition in itself. It is common, for example, to see outdoor adobe ovens (hornos) among the Pueblos. These ovens are used to bake loaves of bread. Easterners have often mistaken the ovens for dog houses and marvel at the kind-heartedness of the Pueblo Indians for creating such permanent protective shelters for their pets.

MESCALERO. The Mescaleros also use food at social gatherings, but the use of food in religious ceremonies is not practiced by them. The Mescaleros were nomads, unlike the Pueblos, and their basic food diet was composed of berries, mesquite beans, dried deer meat, any small game that could be caught, and other foodstuffs that could be bartered for with the Mexican community. There are, of course, different seasons to harvest various wild foods. For example, the piñon nut is obtained every four years and the traditional Apache eagerly anticipates the piñon crop. People will go camping in very remote areas in order to spend time picking these nuts. There is also a variety of natural fruits that are gathered and dried for use during the winter months. Preparing dried food is very time consuming, but the Mescaleros store this food to serve at special functions such as a marriage, puberty rite, or any other feast. The presence of these foods adds to a family's status. Failure on the part of a family to serve these delicacies would cast a shadow on the family's reputation for hospitality.

IMPLICATIONS FOR THE HOSPITALIZED PATIENT. At some Indian hospitals, attempts have been made to adapt the hospital menus to the Indian appetite. This is a positive step that is therapeutic for the patient. Anglo food can (and usually does) taste bland and unattractive when it is served to someone who is accustomed to a variety of tasty food. An Anglo health professional was encountered who was "appalled" when an Indian patient requested green chili with his breakfast eggs. Green chili is a good source of vitamin C. Racism practiced against any ethnic group almost always included that ethnic group's preferences in food.

If an Indian suffers from diabetes, it is difficult for him to maintain his

dietary restrictions, especially during feasts, when it is socially and sometimes religiously imperative for everyone to participate in the eating. Along
with accurate dietary information, a patient needs to receive understanding
and support from family members. Counseling of immediate family members by the health professional prior to feast days may help the family to
provide the encouragement that the patient needs to stay within his dietary
limits. When a health professional needs to explain the four basic food
groups to Indians, it should be done within the context of the patient's
food resources and not within the Anglo context. For years, the government has tried to provide an adequate amount of protein in the Indian diet
by providing cheese and powdered milk as food commodities. The Indian
people would not use these foods because they were unpalatable both to
taste and to the digestive tract.

Grieving Process And Death

The grieving process, though universal, has developed into certain stereotypes when applied to Indian people. Stereotypes of Indians would have
us believe that Indians are stoic and, as a result, never show emotional
extremes of any kind. Clinical and personal experience has shown that
Indians will fully express their emotions in many circumstances if they are
in a sympathetic environment.

LAGUNA. Among the Laguna Pueblos, a grieving person finds solace
in the support of the extended family. There exists a prescribed ritual for
burying the dead. They do not permit the body to be taken to a mortuary
but perform the wrapping of the body themselves. Besides the burial ritual
for a dead person, the Pueblos believe in preparing the favorite food of the
deceased. As previously stated, food serves a religious function, and the
preparation of the favorite food is an appropriate honor for the deceased.
Another burial ritual is designed to ease the grief of the family and entreats
the deceased to depart without taking any family members with him.

MESCALERO. During the grieving process, relatives are expected to
prepare the food for the immediate family of the deceased and for the
mourners. The family is freed from the menial routines in order to grieve
properly. Mourners will recall their past association with the deceased,
highlighting the happy memories of the past. All of the dead person's be-
longings are collected in a bag and buried with the person, so that personal
possessions are accounted for, and the deceased will not need to return.
This belief has been substantiated by eerie incidents occurring when the
burial protocol inadvertently is not followed. After burial, Indian songs are
sung, intoning the dead person to rejoice with his ancestors and that

he(she) is fortunate to have entered the other world with the Great Spirit. These songs have a therapeutic effect on the family, as well as being very consoling. The evening following the burial, a short session is conducted by the family where a certain sagebrush is gathered and burned as incense. This ceremony is designed to ease the minds of the survivors and to prevent nightmares about the deceased.

IMPLICATIONS FOR HEALTH PROFESSIONALS. It is important that health professionals be aware of the burial practices of any Indian population that may receive health care at a medical facility. Family members get very upset if their traditions are violated with respect to their dead. A deviation from their cultural practices in this regard would delay their grieving process and present problems in resolving their loss. According to Lindemann's documentation on the grief process, this would be an undesirable consequence.[19] Displaying sympathy by touch and verbal condolences is as appropriate for Indians as for anyone else. People generally understand and appreciate expressions of sympathy, regardless of cultural or language differences. Family members do not expect the hospital staff to join their mourning, but they do expect certain courtesies. The health professional should strive to provide a quiet environment for the family and maintain a respectful attitude during the family's grief.

We have touched on just a few areas that health professionals, who work with Indians, should consider. There are many other points that could be explored, but any sensitivity and understanding in one area serves to greatly eliminate barriers that Indians presently encounter when entering the white health care system.

References

1. We the First Americans: U. S. Department of Commerce, Social and Economic Statistic Administration, Bureau of the Census, Government Printing Office, SN 0324–00043, 1973, p 6
2. Idem, p 9
3. Idem, p 7
4. Vogel VJ: American Indian Medicine, Norman, University of Oklahoma Press, 1970, p 111
5. Officer JE: The American Indian and federal policy. In Waddel JO and Watson OM (eds): The American Indian in Urban Society. Boston, Little, Brown, 1973, p 8
6. Idem, p 65
7. Adair J and Deuschle KW: The People's Health: Medicine and Anthropology in a Navajo Community. New York, Appleton, 1970
8. Cahn ES: Our Brother's Keeper: The Indian in White America. New York, World, 1969, pp 55–67
9. Deloria V: Custer Died for Your Sins. London, Macmillan, 1969, pp 101–24

10. Brophy WA, Aberle SD: The Indian, America's Unfinished Business. Norman, University of Oklahoma Press, 1966, p 16
11. General Accounting Office of Comptroller General of U.S.: Progress and Problems in Providing Health Services to Indians. A Report to Congress, HSA, DHEW, B−16403(2), March 1973, p 5
12. Crockett DC: Medicine Among the American Indians. Health Services & Mental Health Administration Health Reports Vol 86 No 5 May 1971, p 407
13. Idem
14. Sigerist HE: The Golden Age of Greek medicine. In History of Medicine. Oxford, Oxford University Press, 1961, Vol II, Chapter 6, p 318
15. Shaw RD: Health Concepts and Attitudes of the Papago Indians, Arizona. Health Program Systems Center, Division of Indian Health, BHS, 1968, p 9
16. Fuchs M, Bashshur R: Use of Traditional Indian Medicine Among Urban Native Americans. Research done in partial fulfillment for Ph.D. thesis, University of Michigan, p 25 (submitted for publication)
17. Vogel VJ, op cit, pp 262−63
18. Personal interview with Paul A. Ortega, Mescalero Medicine Man, 1975 (unpublished)
19. Lindemann E: Symptomatology and management of acute grief. Am J Psychiatry Vol 101, No 2, Sept 1944, pp 141−48

5
Cultural Health Traditions:
Asian Perspectives

Effie Chow

If the saying "Experiment is the mother of science" represents the thesis of the West, then the East holds to its antithesis: "Meditation is the father of science."[1]

Any attempt at probing into the nature of Asian health practices must begin with a search into the age-old philosophy from which they — and indeed all Eastern concepts of health and illness, cure, and death — evolved.[2]

For the purpose of this text, Asians are defined as primarily Chinese, Japanese, Koreans, and Filipinos. The folk medicine philosophies and theories of the various Asian groups have much in common. Because of the history of Chinese migration and integration throughout Asia, Chinese influence pervades most Asian folk health traditions. Some common concepts or areas of widespread interest are nutrition, herbology, meditation (prayer), the relationship of cosmo-universal energy to human life, and the inclusion of religion and philosophy in medical practice.

The discussion here will be focused primarily on the Chinese system. It is not possible to do justice in this limited space to all of the Asian practices, and Chinese medicine is the most prevalent in public usage. Chinese medicine is a whole system of medicine. It is completely different in concept from the Western system of medicine. The Chinese emphasizes prevention, while the Western system emphasizes crisis intervention.

Although the general public thinks that acupuncture alone constitutes Chinese medicine, it is in fact only one of many areas. Chinese medicine encompasses all of the following (in the order of their importance as preventive concepts): philosophy, meditation, nutrition, martial arts (such as kung fu and tai chi chuan), herbology, acumassage, acupressure, moxibustion, acupuncture, and even spiritual healing.

The Chinese influence on Asian medicine is best illustrated by the acupuncture derivations employed by other Asian cultures. Japanese acupuncture employs an adaptation of the Chinese system, resulting in a method called Ryodoraku acupuncture. Both the Chinese and Japanese methods diagnose and treat the condition. But unlike the Chinese system, which uses more than 1000 points all over the body, the Ryodoraku system uses only 24 major points (on both the hands and the feet). A point-finder (attached to a machine called a neurometer that measures electrical resistance) is used to locate the acupoint; then acupuncture is applied with an automatic needle applicator. Harold Saita, D.O., of Vancouver, B.C., the most renowned Ryodoraku specialist in North America, has carried out innumerable lectures and demonstrations of this system. The Koreans also have a system of acupuncture in which they utilize a great many needles in each treatment.

Another area of Chinese influence is in spiritual healing. Whereas the Chinese have "temple healers," the Filipinos through a religious group called the Espiritas, carry out ethereal (spiritual) healing by using body energy (this is the same kind of energy described in Chinese medicine and will be described later in the chapter). Ethereal healing involves the utilization of the auras and psychic energies within and surrounding the human body to heal a condition. Specially endowed Espiritas have the power of "the spirit of the material" ie, they perform psychoenergetic phemomena, such as materializing and dematerializing human blood, tissue, and organs as well as nonhuman objects. These Espiritas healers reside in the village of Luzon in the Philippines. Some of them have traveled all over the world, including the United States, to practice their art of healing. However, the practice is illegal in this country. American physicians and patients have traveled to Luzon to seek treatment and to observe these healing faculties. Many individuals have experienced this healing art. For example, Mr. Donald Westerbeke, a well-known biochemist and businessman in San Francisco, had a brain tumor diagnosed by two teams of neurosurgeons. Surgery was recommended, but prior to surgery he decided to go to the Philippines to try treatment by the spirit-of-the-material practitioners. This treatment was successful, and he is now a fully active businessman again who is also learning some of their ethereal healing techniques.[3]

Another area of Chinese influence is in massage and herbology. Whereas the Chinese have acumassage and acupressure, the Japanese have *shiatzu.* Although the Japanese and Chinese systems share the same basic operating theory of body energies, the technique of applying massage differs. Although each system has some particular herbs which are unique to it, many herbs are used in common but are called by different names, have different qualities, and are administered in different strengths. To give a popular example, the properties of ginseng vary according to growing conditions of temperature, humidity, soil, etc. One should bear in mind that the principles underlying Chinese healing practices are often shared by other Asian cultures, even though there are individual variations in the health practices of each country.

CHINESE MEDICINE

Chinese medicine, both a science and an art, is a 5000-year-old system of medicine. Its earliest records can be traced to the reign of Huang Ti, the Yellow Emperor, in the years 2697 to 2597 BC. These records are dialogues between the Emperor and his minister, Chi Po, in which the Emperor sought knowledge in the art of health and healing. The following quotation reveals the holistic nature of Chinese medicine:

> *I urge you to bring into harmony for me Nature, Heaven and Tao (which is the Right Way). There must be an end and a beginning. Heaven must be in accord with the lights of the sky, the celestial bodies, their course and periods. The earth below must reflect the four seasons, the five elements, that which is precious and that which is lowly and without value, one as well as the other. Is it not that in winter man responds to Yin (the principle of darkness and cold)? And is it not, that in summer, he responds to Yang (the principle of light and warmth). . .? I should like to be informed about Nature to the utmost degree and to include information about man, his physical form, his blood, his breath of life, his circulation and his dissolution; and I should like to know what causes his death and his life and what we can do about all of this. . . .[4]*

An 81-volume classic on the philosophy of life resulted from the lengthy answers inspired by this questioning. Only two volumes have been translated into English: the *Yellow Emperor's Classic of Internal Medicine*, by Dr. Ilza Veith of U.C. San Francisco, and the *Yellow Emperor's Book of Acupuncture*, by Henry C. Lu.[5,6] In China, this classic of living philosophy became the primary medical source book, whereas in Western medicine, philosophical texts remain separated from the special texts written for medical theory.

A great deal of in-depth documentation on Chinese medicine exists in the original language; however, very little has yet been translated into English. The available translations and texts are superficial in scope. More texts are available in other European languages, such as French, German, and Russian, because as early as the 17th and 18th centuries, returning missionaries and diplomats brought back Chinese medicine to Europe.

Chinese medicine is based on the theoretical concept of energy, a concept that makes this system of medicine entirely different from the Western system. The Western system of medicine is primarily concerned with disease and crisis intervention, whereas Chinese medicine emphasizes health, is oriented toward prevention, and attempts to understand the total man in his relationship to the universe.

The theoretical and philosophic base of Chinese medicine is derived from the Taoist religion (the Right Way), with its concept that nature maintains a balance in all things. Man is seen as a microcosm within a macrocosm; the energy in man interrelates with the energy of the universe. Chi (energy) and Jing (sexual energy) are both vital life energies. They are kept in balance by the dual polarities of Yin and Yang. Yin is described as negative, dark, cold, and feminine, and Yang is positive, light, warm, and masculine. Whatever the terminology, there must be a balance of both positive and negative polarities. This balance is illustrated in a Western context by the following example. A woman primarily produces female sex hormones, but a small proportion of male sex hormones are also produced within her system; the reverse is true in a man. The delicate balance of Yin and Yang results in health; the imbalance or disturbance of this energy balance may result in disease (dis-ease). Likewise, if the hormones are in perfect balance, the person is normal, but if there is a disturbance in this hormonal balance, dis-ease or dys-function occurs.

The theory of energy balance in Chinese medicine may also be compared with the theories of immunologic competency or incompetency in Western medicine. According to Chinese medicine, most conditions are caused by an imbalance in energy caused by a wrong diet or by strong emotional feelings; therefore, bodily functions may be brought back into harmony through the application of self-restraint and through the use of appropriate herbs. Thus, one does not take herbs to kill certain organisms that can be controlled, but uses them to maintain a balanced state, thus countering forces which result from immoderation. The balance of energy Chi (Yin and Yang) means that the immunity of the body is in a healthy condition. If there is an imbalance of the Yin or Yang, then the immunity of the body is disturbed, and the body is likely to be susceptible to disease or bacteria.

A further concept of Chinese medicine is that the universe and man are susceptible to the laws of the five elements: fire, earth, metal, water, and wood (Fig. 5.1). Body and mind are integrated; they are never separated. The five elements are reflected in the different organs and parts of the body. Every organ of the body encompasses the properties of taste, emotion, sound, odor, season, climate, power, and fortification of other structures of the body. This cycle is a destructive as well as a constructive one, with each element having some effect on the others.

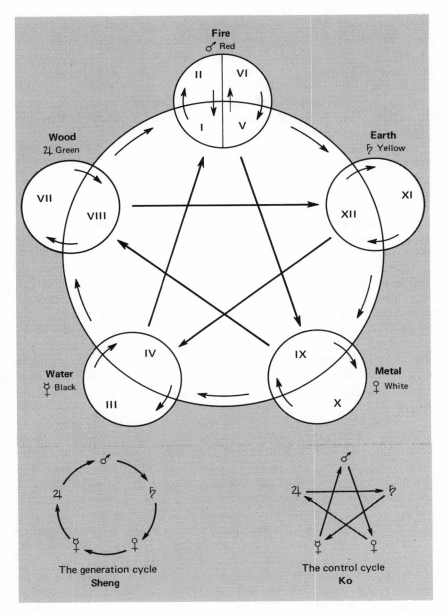

FIG. 5.1. Law of the five elements cycle (From Lawson-Wood D., Lawson-Wood J: *Five Elements of Acupuncture and Chinese Massage*, 1973. Courtesy of Health Science Press)

All the complicated details that these theories entail can be touched upon only very simply here. The most important point is that Chinese medicine is definitely a preventive process, not one of crisis intervention. In the old days, a patient went to the physician to have his energy balanced — he would get a "tune-up" to keep him well; the physician would prescribe either proper nutrition, an exercise ritual, meditation practice, herbs, or acupuncture to maintain the patient's energy balance in a healthy state. If the physician failed to keep a patient healthy, the patient ceased to pay him, and treatment was free of charge.

By examining his patient the traditional Chinese physician can determine the specific nature of an imbalance of energy through the use of the four techniques of Chinese diagnosis: (1) glossoscopy (inspection), (2) osphritics (listening and smelling), (3) anamnesis (inquiry), and (4) sphygmology (pulse diagnosis).

Glossoscopy consists of examining the general external physical state (facial expression and color) of the patient, in order to determine whether his condition is chronic or acute.

Osphritics involves listening and smelling in order to detect the condition of the patient. For example, if the patient's voice is weak and thready, then his resistance is weak. Some diagnostic value may be provided by the symptom of foul breath, or by the special odor of the feces.

Anamnesis involves making important inquiries concerning the condition of the patient in order to collect information for diagnosis: What is the location of the troubled condition? When and how did the condition first appear? What is the past history of the patient, including past treatment for any disease? What are the sleeping, eating, and bowel habits of the patient?

Sphygmology determines the balance or imbalance of the body energy *Chi* (Yin and Yang) and also the severity of the condition. Three different pairs of pulses, both superficial and deep, can be palpated at the radial pulse on each wrist. The pulses are judged according to a complex set of criteria involving strength and frequency as well as other qualities. The differences that can be felt among the various pulses are also considered. It is reported that a skilled practitioner in pulse diagnosis can achieve great accuracy in diagnosing all body functions. Traditional Chinese physicians use this method in their regular checkup of a patient to determine his well-being. This is a part of their preventive medicine.

After a Chinese physician makes his diagnosis, he discusses with his patient some aspects of his daily life (such as philosophy, nutrition, exercise, and necessary herbs) which can be used to assist the patient in keeping in harmony with nature.

Nutrition is the most important aspect of keeping in harmony with nature. The proverb "You are what you eat" holds true. The Chinese classify foods as Yin (cold) and Yang (hot); but these classifications have no relation to temperature. A balance between the two implements good health. For example, chicken is Yang food, and melon is Yin food — the two, hot and cold preparations, constitute a balanced diet. While too much of the wrong kind of food can make one sick, it is also true that certain conditions or illnesses can be cured by the proper foods. (An example of this in Western medicine is the control of diabetes and ulcers by diet.) This belief is derived from the notion that bodily disorders are also considered either Yin or Yang. Therefore, since too much Yang food may cause one to come down with a Yang illness, this Yang illness may be counteracted by Yin food.

Even colds are divided into Yin and Yang conditions according to their symptoms. In a Yin condition one feels drawn inward and suffers a cold feeling and loss of appetite; for such a condition there are certain foods that will boost energy. A Yang condition indicates an overabundance of energy; some symptoms of this are a fever, parched throat, crusty nose, and gritty eyes. Thus, a sore throat and fever (Yang) may be treated with watercress or watermelon soup (Yin). Salads should be avoided. There is no known scientific research on this subject, but the Chinese know that it works from experience. In Chinese cooking there is always a mixture of vegetables and meat; the foods to be mixed together are chosen with reference to the balancing of the Yin and the Yang composition. Moderation is the motto; extreme diets consisting of all high-protein foods, all raw fruits and vegetables, or all extremely cold or hot dishes are frowned upon.

Children are taught the value of each food that is eaten. For example, a mother giving food to her child might say, "This vegetable will give you clear skin, this meat will build up your blood for strength, this vegetable will give you better eyesight," etc. Thus the child begins to understand what value each item of food represents. The Chinese believe that ginger can counteract the toxin present in other foods. Ginger is cooked with meat to destroy the toxin in it. Garlic helps to rid the heat-producing factor in food.

There are also very "enticing" foods — like roasted beetles, rattlesnakes, and dog meat — which are good for blood-building. In old China, dogs were raised especially for eating. American society is only now beginning to realize the nutritious value of animal organs, whereas the Chinese have been eating such "soul food" for thousands of years. The entrails and the organs are the most nutritious parts of the animal. In Hong Kong there is a special beef dish called roasted testes which is supposed to be very excellent for the health. The more euphemistic name "Rocky Mountain oysters" is used here.

A perplexing problem facing Western practitioners caring for Chinese maternity patients is the postpartum diet adopted by many of the Chinese foreign-born. Because pregnancy and birth are said to weaken the body and are accompanied by loss of blood, which is a Yin condition, a Yang diet is adopted for the month following delivery. This diet consists of a variety of dishes, one of which includes rice wine, chicken, lichen, and ginger. Another dish is a soup of pigs' feet, sweet (black) vinegar, black beans, ginger, and hard-boiled eggs. Both of these special dishes require lengthy cooking. They are said to help get rid of gas, assist in the involution process of the uterus, and provide a great deal of calcium, protein, and minerals. Western physicians feel that the pigs' feet and vinegar dish may be of value because of its high mineral and protein content. An analysis of pigs' feet reveals they are primarily bone and marrow; thus one can see why they are viewed as a strengthening food.

Other preventive procedures followed by the Chinese include meditation, the martial arts (tai chi chuan and kung fu), acumassage, acupressure, and moxibustion. Meditation, a living habit with the Chinese, is currently being used in the United States for treatment of stress and diseases. Tai chi chuan and kung fu operate on the principle of the energy system, ie, the vital points in the body (locations where the energy exchange is exceptionally vital) are the foci of these disciplines. Both acumassage and acupressure utilize the acupoints in the body and the meridians in which the energy flows. Cupping is another traditional healing procedure. A bamboo cup is heated and placed on the skin; as it cools, it contracts, drawing the skin, and the energy into the cup. A modified form of cupping is applied friction, or pinching of vital spots in the body to release congestion. Often the Chinese procelain spoon is used to do this. This process reduces stress, headaches, muscles, sinus tensions, and onset of colds. When I was a public health nurse, often a teacher would come to me and say, "Oh Effie, will you take a look at Mei Ling, she's got all these bruises on her. I am sure her parents are beating her!" She would have big bruises on her temples, neck, chest, and wrists, and I would have to soothe the agitated teacher and tell her that the child had been treated with pinching treatment for respiratory congestion from the onset of a cold. I explained that this treatment was part of our cultural health system, and that it was okay.

When nutrition and other preventive methods have failed to maintain one's health, herbs are used as the next step. Herbology is the use of natural plant or animal substances to boost the body's natural energy and health. Herbalists' particular areas of specialization include conditions such as skin disease, blood disorders, and internal medical problems (particularly in relation to the gastrointestinal tract). The general classification of infectious diseases also falls within their area of competence.

While the Chinese recognize the value of Western drugs, particularly antibiotics, they continue to use their traditional cures for many of the more common ailments. Chinese herbal medicine, unlike Western medicine, is usually taken in the form of a broth. The particular ingredients prescribed by the herb specialist are boiled together, and the resulting liquid contains the therapeutic elements. Injections are not a part of this traditional practice. In many cases, patients who seek help from both Western and herb specialists will combine both types of medicine.

Ginseng is one of the most well-known herbs. It is now being sold in teas, candies, and so forth, but it is of little value in these forms, and may in fact be harmful because of the high sugar content. To be effective as a rejuvenator or as an aphrodisiac, ginseng must be prepared a certain way. It must be steamed for many hours in liquid and it is the resulting broth that is of value. Ginseng is best when grown wild in Northern China; good ginseng in extremely expensive — about $100 per ounce. There is a traditional belief that the more ginseng resembles the entire shape of a man, the more potent it is. Experience indicates that this is true. Although no scientific investigation has been made, there would clearly be some advantage in pursuing such research.

There are other interesting items such as rhinoceros horns, sea horses, shavings of bark from different kinds of trees and plants, beetles, and so forth, which have been proved valuable by experience. Many herbs look odd, and some are completely unappetizing; but there is a theory that the less palatable or appetizing it is, the better it is for you. Generally it is recommended that herbs be brewed in about three cups of water and then boiled down to one cup of tea. Then one drinks the tea.

Moxibustion is the burning of *Artemesis vulgaris (moxa)*, an herb with an aroma similar to marijuana. Moxa is wound up into pellets, which are then burned over the acupuncture points and removed when the patient feels the heat. Moxa now comes in a cigar form; it is burned and held over a particular acupoint for certain conditions to bring about the sedation or tonification of energy. That is, either to take away some of the energy or to give more energy, as the case requires. Heat application by moxibustion is considered by its practitioners to be more deeply penetrating than are the infrared treatments used in Western medicine. The herb must be nine years old. Its potency is lessened if it is younger or older.

The Chinese also consult "spiritual healers," "temple healers," or "fortune healers" who can visualize good and bad spirits, guide spirits, and reincarnations. There are still many such "fortune tellers" in the Orient and a few in the United States who can recall past history and predict the future even to the year of one's death. The author has personally seen life events of family members and friends come true according to the predictions of these spiritual healers.

Acupuncture provides the most visible demonstration of the energy system theory. It involves the insertion of fine hairlike needles into specific acupuncture points on the skin. These points are located on meridians or pathways of energy, Chi, leading to the various organs of the body. Acupuncture affects systemic energy, which in turn affects the organs and the rest of the bodily functions.

The emphasis on acupuncture in the United States has been as an analgesic (particularly in the area of arthritic pain), but there are many other very exciting uses. Conditions in which acupuncture treatment has brought about improvement or cure include deafness, gastrointestinal problems, menstrual disturbances, skin problems, allergies, asthma, appendicitis, neuralgia, fractures, trigeminal neuralgia, infections, and so forth.

In the area of acupuncture analgesia, there has been and there continues to be a great deal of research done in the People's Republic of China. It must be understood that although the interest in acupuncture analgesia is relatively new (since 1958), this is not because it is a newly derived system; acupuncture analgesia has been known since 250 AD. However, because of the Chinese belief that surgery, no matter how minute, despoils the soul and prevents the soul from entering the realms of heaven upon death, it was not used in China until Chiang Kai-shek's reign, when everything Western was being adopted. At this time traditional Chinese practitioners were forced underground when their practice became illegal, and Western medicine and surgery became prevalent in China. With the rediscovery of acupuncture analgesia, and after much research and extensive use, progress has been made in its utilization as analgesia for surgery. (It is proper to speak of analgesia and not anesthesia because the patient still has feeling, but without pain.)

The first open heart surgery performed under complete acupuncture analgesia was in China in April 1972. Acupuncture analgesia is not fully utilized in China, in part because of the newness of both surgical practice and acupuncture analgesia. Chinese physicians claim that acupuncture analgesia for surgery of the neck and head such as thyroidectomy and lobotomy is highly effective (almost 100 percent), for thoracic surgery it is moderately effective, and for abdominal surgery it is less than moderately effective. The latter two conditions almost always require use of additional Western anesthesia to complete the surgery. The Chinese are using acupuncture analgesia in dentistry with 100 percent success. Although many studies are currently being carried out, there is yet a great deal to be researched in this area.

In our discussion of acupuncture, we should examine the social-economic-political situation which has arisen in the United States because of the sensational nature in which acupuncture and Chinese medicine have been presented to the public since 1972. Chinese medicine and acupuncture have been practiced quietly in the United States since the advent of Chinese railroad and mine workers in the 19th century. It is said that the Chinese literally brought their needles with them on the railroads from coast to coast. They practiced within their own communities and nothing was thought of it. However, in 1971, with the advent of political detente between the United States and the People's Republic of China, a sudden interest developed in Chinese medicine. Even before 1971, many people in this country had adopted meditation, the martial arts, herb usage, etc.; but since the change in political atmosphere, the United States has awakened to the importance of acupuncture, the "miracle cure." This awakened interest was furthered by visits to China of well-known and outstanding physicians (Victor Sidel, Samuel Rosen, E. Grey Dimond, and the late Paul Dudley White), former President Nixon, and a noted journalist of the New York *Times,* James Reston, who wrote about his impressions of the favorable results of acupuncture treatment for postoperative pain. It is unfortunate that other members of the media have thus provided a sensationalistic view of acupuncture and Chinese medicine.

With this advent of public interest, legislation, economics, politics, and medical associations entered the scene. They imposed heavy restrictions on the use of acupuncture and other methods of Chinese medicine. Unfortunately, economics played a very heavy role. There is now in the United States a great confusion about the legal status of Chinese medicine and acupuncture. The laws are different in every state, but Nevada has taken the lead by establishing Chinese medicine as a distinctively different system from that of Western medicine. The Nevada Legislature has set up a Board of Chinese Medicine and an Advisory Council to establish and enforce standards of practice for Chinese medicine. Both physicians and non-physicians are required to take examinations before they can practice acupuncture or herbology. Most states in the United States now consider acupuncture use to be a practice of medicine. Therefore, physicians may practice acupuncture whether or not they have any training or knowledge of this art, while experts of Chinese medicine, long-time successful practitioners, are forced underground and their professions and livelihood are taken away. Many of these experts have been indicted, arrested, and forced to stop their practices, yet these very same practitioners, deemed unfit to practice by the legal system, have been invited to teach at universities and carry out research as experts.

Such practices are extremely detrimental to Chinese medicine; quick-learning quacks are debasing the art. Poor quality expensive treatment is being offered throughout the United States at an accelerated rate and poor results are obtained. Unfortunately, economic interest and political rivalry play their roles. The people who suffer in the end are the patients and the traditional practitioners. The public is demanding acupuncture, but the medical hierarchy is either unaware of the growing interest or resists it.

There are as yet no official classes on acupuncture or Chinese medicine in medical schools, but exploitative training sessions are offered by private entrepreneurs. Many quick weekend crash courses are being conducted at a cost of $495 per weekend, or $1425 for 4 1/2-day training session. Participants, both physicians and nonphysicians, come away with a certification of attendance that misrepresents them as people now qualified to practice acupuncture. During these sessions students attend a one hour class on the theory and practice of acupuncture, one hour on thoracic and visceral conditions, one hour on gastrointestinal problems, one hour on the total system of Japanese Ryodoraku, and one hour on the Korean system of acupuncture. It is then assumed that these students emerge as experts who can practice and even teach acupuncture, even though they have acquired only a superficial knowledge of the subject.

Patients, in turn, have great difficulty in finding qualified acupuncturists. One patient reported that a physician who learned acupuncture during a crash course is now charging $100 per treatment. Furthermore, a long series of treatments is frequently necessary in order to achieve successful results. Although there have been cases of miraculous relief with only one treatment (which the media enjoys emphasizing), responsible practitioners say that, generally, a series of treatments are required for proper management of most conditions to insure more permanent relief or cure.

Eventually, the practitioners of some of the modalities of Chinese medicine will most appropriately be nurses. For instance, acupressure and acumassage treatments, which could easily be relegated to nurses, are very effective ways to reduce a patient's stress and pain. Whether such treatment definitely has an effect on the energy system in the body or whether it is psychological, one thing is certain, it works. Contact healing, called the laying-on of hands, is now being taught to graduate nurses at New York University by Dolores Kreiger RN, PhD, as a means of therapeutic touch. This method follows in part the theory of Chinese medicine. It utilizes the principle of body energy in dealing with human beings. The sense of touch and the exchange of energy between people, the environment, and universe are considered conducive to the promotion of the feeling of well-being.

In discussing Chinese medicine, we cannot ignore the fact that alternative modalities of Western medicine have arisen in the last few years which have adopted many of the philosophical and theoretical concepts of Chinese medicine, such as the energy theories. *Chi* energy is not a secret power. The instruments used for EEGs and EKGs measure the same energy.

For example, biofeedback (use of a special machine to measure bioenergy and to help the patient learn relaxation) basically uses the same energy system concept. Rolfing, ESP, psychic healing, laying-on of hands, absentee healing, and faith healing are all areas in which the same system of energy is being studied and utilized. Kirlian photography, holography, and reincarnation investigations all adopt the philosophical theories of Asian health practices. Many physicians in private practice and in university research laboratories are studying the use of meditation (autogenic exercises) to relieve stress. This research is being done because it is believed that stress is a prevalent cause of disease; thus, relief of stress should prevent the development of disease. Dr. Carl Simonton of Texas is using meditation to cure terminal cancer and has much documentation of his success with this method. Dr. Erik Peper (president, 1976–77 of the Biofeedback Society and practices holistic biofeedback in Berkeley) and Kenneth Pellitier (clinical psychologist, Dept. of Psychiatry, University of California School of Medicine, San Francisco) are using biofeedback techniques to study the relief of stress conditions and to determine the relationship of meditative states and yoga states to bioenergy. Researchers in the development of holography are categorizing an energy system which they describe as plus-and-minus-energy. It may be related to Yin-Yang balance concepts.

When Mao Tse-tung came to power in the People's Republic of China, Chinese practitioners were urged to come forth and practice side by side with the Western physicians to provide a good health system for the population of over 800 million. Now "barefoot doctors" are trained to give Chinese medical care, but they also have some basic knowledge of Western medicine, and Western medical students are also taught some rudiments of Chinese medicine. The Chinese are working out a system which incorporates both medical concepts. They have determined the kinds of problems that should have treatment by Chinese medicine, those that should have treatment by Western medicine, and those that should have combined treatment.

If effective legislation is passed in the United States, perhaps we will be able to follow China's example of utilizing both systems for the benefit of the total population. Because Chinese medicine is a preventive system of medicine, however, its use may constitute a threat to the drug manufacturers and to the age-old medication practices of physicians in this country. It will be necessary to reexamine the theories and philosophy of Western medicine if Chinese medicine is to be successfully used to enhance the current system.

Chinese medicine has been discussed in this chapter as representative of other Asian health concepts. Various theories and practices have been described in the hope that the reader can become familiar with the health system that Asians are accustomed to. It should be clear that Asians see Western medicine as completely foreign in concept, terminology, theory, and attitude toward life processes: just as Chinese medicine seems strange to Americans, so Western medicine seems strange to Asians. With some mutual tolerance, education, and understanding, we can learn to use the best of both systems to our advantage.

References

1. Wallnofer H, Rottauscher AV: Chinese Folk Medicine. New York, Bell, 1972, pp viii, 1
2. Idem
3. Personal interview with Mr. Donald Westerbeke, Biochemist, San Francisco.
4. Veith I: The Yellow Emperor's Classic of Internal Medicine. Copyright 1949, reprinted by permission of University of California Press, Berkeley, 1970
5. Idem
6. Lu HC: Yellow Emperor's Book of Acupuncture

Bibliography

Austin M: Acupuncture Therapy. New York, ASI, 1972
Beau G: Chinese Medicine. New York, Avon, 1972
Chan P: Acupuncture Directory. Los Angeles, Chan's Books, 1974
_____ : Finger Acupressure. Los Angeles, Price/Stern/Sloan, 1974
Chuang Y-M: Chinese Acupuncture. Hanover. N.H., Oriental Society, 1972
Dimond EG, Grey MD: Acupuncture anesthesia: Western medicine and traditional Chinese medicine. JAMA 218:14—15, 1971
_____ : Medical education and care in the People's Republic of China. JAMA 218:14—15, 1971
_____ : Medicine in People's Republic of China: A progress report. JAMA, 222:1158—59, 1972
_____ : Ward rounds with an acupuncturist. N Engl J Med 272:575—77, 1965
Dornette WHL: Acupuncture and the law. J Leg Med, March—April 1974, pp 21—28
Duke M: Acupuncture. New York, Pyramid, 1972
Edwards WM: Acupuncture in Nevada. West J Med, 120:507—12, 1974
Elmendorf TN: A letter on acupuncture. Calif Med 117:75—76, 1972
_____ : Fringe medicine. Manch Med Gaz 49:5, 1970
Hashimoto M: Japanese Acupuncture. New York, Liveright, 1968
Hendin D: Acupuncture U.S. Style or How to Buy a Diploma. Berkeley Daily Gazette, July 16, 1974, p 9
Huard P, Ming W: Chinese Medicine. New York, McGraw-Hill, 1968

Jain KK: Glimpses of Chinese medicine, 1971: Changes after the cultural revolution. Can Med Assoc J 106:46–50, 1972

Jenerick HP: NIH Acupuncture Research Conference Proceedings. Washington, D.C., DHEW Publication No. 74–165

Joffe B: Osler revisited: Imperfect acupuncture. N Engl J Med 287:785, 1972

Kao FF: Acupuncture Therapeutics — An Introduction Text. New York, Triple Oak, 1973

Kiel FW: Forensic science in China — traditional and contemporary aspects. J Forensic Sci 15:201–34, April 1970

———: Healing "round the world." Ariz Med 28:574–75, 1971

Klass AA, Grehan JF: Glimpses of Chinese medicine. Can Med Assoc J, 108:750, 1972

Lavier J: Points of Chinese Acupuncture. New York, British Book Centre, 1965

Lawson-Wood D, Lawson-Wood J: Acupuncture Handbook. New York, British Book Centre, 1965

———: Chinese System of Healing. "Wayside" Grayshott Hindhead, Surrey, Health Science Press, 1964

———: First Aid at Your Fingertips. New York, British Book Centre, 1963

———: Lawson-Wood Multi-Lingual Atlas of Acupuncture. New York, British Book Centre, 1965

Lewin AJ: Acupuncture and its role in modern medicine. West J Med January 1974, pp. 27–32

Li FP: Traditional Chinese medicine in the United States. JAMA 220:1132–35, 1972

McGarey WA: Acupuncture and Body Energies. Phoenix, Ariz., Gabriel, 1974

Mann F: Acupuncture — The Ancient Art of Chinese Healing. London, Heinemann, 1972

———: Acupuncture Cures Many Diseases. London, Heinemann, 1971

———: Atlas of Acupuncture. London, Heinemann, 1971

———: The Meridians of Acupuncture. London, Heinemann, 1970

Namikoshi T: Shiatsu: Japanese Finger Pressure Therapy. San Francisco, Japan Publications, 1974

Nashold BS Jr: Acupuncture — fact or fiction. Nat J Dentistry 43:112–13, 1973

Palos S: The Chinese Art of Healing. New York, Bantam, 1972

Shiang E, Li FP: The Yin-Yang (cold-hot) theory of disease. JAMA 217:1108, 1971

Shute WB: East meets west: Canadians peek across the acupuncture threshold. Can Med Assoc J 107:1002–03, 1972

Sidel VW: Who helps the doctor? China's barefoot doctors. Update International, June 1974, pp 425–29

Stillings A: Acupuncture — an ancient Chinese method of healing. J Assoc Advan Med Instrument 7:16, 1973

Tan LT, Tan MYC, Veith I: Acupuncture Therapy. Philadelphia, Temple University Press, 1974

Tom, P-C: Acupuncture and Moxibustion. San Francisco, Chinese World Press, 1965

Toyama PM, Nishizawa M: The physiological basis of acupuncture and therapy. NC Med J 33:425–29, 1972
—— : Acupuncture and U.S. medicine. JAMA 223:922, 1973
Tsuei JJ: Induction of labor by acupuncture and electrical stimulates. Obstet Gynecol, July 1974, pp 337–42
Van Nghi N, Fisch G, Man PL: International Symposium on Acupuncture. St. Petersburg, Fla., Monarch Services, 1973
Watson L: The Romeo Error: A Matter of Life and Death. London, Hodder and Stoughton, 1974
Worsley JR: Is Acupuncture For You? New York, Harper, 1973
Wu, W-P: Chinese Acupuncture. New York, British Book Centre, 1974

6

Cultural Health Traditions: A Black Perspective

Gladys Jacques

Early records show that Blacks first arrived upon the North American continent in 1619, one year before the Pilgrims arrived at Plymouth Rock.[1] The first arrivals were not slaves. Between that time and 1860, however, more than four million African slaves were brought to this country. Most of them were natives from the West Coast of Africa.

The health practices brought to this country by Africans were transported by medicine men and women who served as priest—physicians to other slaves. There was little dichotomy between the physician versus nurse as curer. The physician attended to the physical, emotional, and spiritual health of the whole person. Most healing rites required participation of the patient, his family, and the community under the direction of the medicine man. Foundations of the beliefs of health and illness are grounded in the Africans' beliefs about life and the nature of being. Life was seen as a process, rather than as a state. One's nature was thought of in terms of energy force, rather than matter. All things living and dead were believed to influence each other, making one able to influence one's destiny and that of others through proper knowledge and behavior.

Religion and art were expressions of the process of living. Each event had socioreligious significance and was cause for celebration or recognition through ceremonial rites. Art was a practical expression of life, ie, a method of making what was "seen" and experienced by one visible to many. Refined expressions that allowed collective participation were highly valued. The African styles of singing and dancing were examples reflecting creative expression and served as means to enable participants to survive, to share a common experience, and to surpass in both mundane and eventful situations. Vestiges of this are seen in the call and response style of games

115

played by children in many Black communities and in the style of the traditional Black American church.

Health was viewed as being at harmony with nature; illness as a manifestation of disharmony resulting from a variety of causes. There was wide belief that illness was caused by demons or bad spirits acting on their own or on behalf of a living person or a dead one's soul. Conjure men and women or voodoo doctors were specialists in the use of magico-religious powers of manipulating spirits or demons. Good and evil were seen as natural. One's curative task was to maintain a balance between the forces of good and evil in order to attain harmony or restore health. The goal of the healer who treated a spirit- or demon-caused illness was not to destroy but to cast out or to contain the evil. Medicine dolls, created in the image of the patient, were used during certain rites. Pins were strategically placed in portions of the doll corresponding to the part of the patients' body where the bad spirit chose to manifest itself. Use of heat and cold were also methods of purging or controlling manifestations of bad spirits.

Centuries of practical experience in the mother country resulted in extensive knowledge of *materia medica*, as the use of roots, minerals, and plant concoctions in treatment. Evidence exists that a method of inoculation against smallpox was practiced. Reverend Cotton Mather, who introduced the practice to the colonies, learned the method from an African slave.[2] Knowledge of birth control and cesarean section was also known by slave midwives upon their arrival to the Western hemisphere.

Education and training of the health practitioner was through apprenticeship. Selection of trainees seems to have been in several ways — one was by descent, another, community choice at birth. The third was by divine calling as evidenced by a mystical experience that revealed to the prospective trainee his life role responsibility. The African who arrived upon this continent came from an oral culture; ie, one that transmits its historical traditions through speech and observed behavior, rather than written form. Those skills and senses necessary for the transmittal of this knowledge had to be highly developed. Sensitivity to sound, speech, touch, and behavior was necessary. Expertise in using skills of observation, listening, storytelling, mimicry, and modeling behavior were needed for survival of the group. All of these were an integral part of the African health practices. It would stand to reason that the health practitioner would have had to demonstrate even greater skills and sensitivity than the average African slave to be recognized as an effective healer. The only license for any person was success in restoring health to the patient.

The structural core of West African society was a system of many tribes in which the family was organized matrilinearly. A matrilineal culture traces its descent through the mother. Polygamy was common practice, especially among those with more wealth and status. Social life was well organized; the community as extended family seemed to be common practice. The old and young were cared for by all. There seemed to be little emphasis on the relationship of nurturing behaviors and sex roles. The elderly were honored, respected, and cared for, with deference to their endurance and knowledge of life. To live a long life was a sign of proper habits of living. Death after a fruitful life was seen as a natural process of passing into another realm of life.

There appears to be no separation of mental, emotional, and physical health in the traditional African health belief system. In fact, it adds a belief of spiritual health that seems to play a small part in traditional Western health practices. Those behaviors that most closely resemble correlations to Western diagnoses of mental illness are ones that can be described as situational. One situation is that in which bad feelings exist between two persons or tribes and a third person or tribe becomes ill as a result. A second situation is one in which the person becomes ill because he is "lost." The person is in a state of disharmony because the soul is wandering, either as a result of a sudden fright, separation from ones' cultural roots, or possession by a restless spirit.

THE IMPACT OF SLAVERY

When viewed from the African perspective, the slave trade movement would appear to be the act of demons or spirits in the form of Western white man and their African collaborators working in concert to induce illness. Once delivered to slave ports, disruption of family and tribal ties was systematically planned to reduce the possibility of slave uprisings. Since the African was thought to be chattel and the labor market required the most able-bodied laborer to be available, breeding was forced to produce special physical qualities. Special breeding places were created on some southern plantations.

Native African languages were forbidden; religious and other social customs underwent planned indoctrination or were outlawed. Special indoctrination systems were set up at many slave ports.[3] It was believed that two years was the average time needed to tame the African to be "fit" for slavery.

This form of slavery was unique to the United States. Other countries in the West such as those in South America and the Caribbean, while still oppressive, allowed the retention of family, tribal ties, and customs. The acculturation process in these countries was less marked by sudden traumatic means.

During this period, medical practices for the slave were learned as a method of survival. A slave was "ailing," or "out of sorts," when feeling badly, but only allowed to be "sick" when unable to function.

To give care to a slave whose prognosis was poor or who was too old to produce labor was inefficient business for the slave owner who was concerned about cost effectiveness.

For the most part the slave who was ailing either treated himself or was administered to by other slaves who were self-taught in survival medical practices. Older men and women who were wiser and experienced were looked to for guidance in survival.

Medical practices were a combination of knowledge brought to this country from Africa, observation when in close proximity to the white household during illnesses, and trial and error.

Review of the literature does reveal documentation of some self-trained physicians, pharmacists, and midwives in the North that were given recognition status by whites; however, prevalent discrimination prevented slave-born Blacks from participating in the rudimentary formal developing body of Western medical knowledge.[4]

Malaria, sleeping sickness, and hookworm were endemic to Africa. Smallpox, syphilis, and dysentery were brought to Africa by white slave traders. The slave was highly susceptible to smallpox, dysentery, measles, diptheria, and syphilis. This created an economic problem for the Southern slave owner. Common illnesses were taken care of by other slaves or overseers. Slave physicians' services were frequently loaned to other plantation owners during illnesses. Female slave nurses were either servants from the big house or older field hands who were no longer able to do a full day's hard labor. They were most often available to care for the plantation owners' families. The slave nurses prepared and administered medicines, along with their other care duties.

When the illness was "serious" or extraordinary, white physicians were summoned to care for sick slaves. Doctoring slaves became very profitable for some white physicians in the South. Slave hospitals were established in Savannah, Charleston, Montgomery, Natchez, and New Orleans. Where there was social contact between Blacks and Native American Indians, there is evidence that cross acculturation took place. The health belief systems of the African and the Native American were congruent. The impact of Native American medicine upon Black folk medicine is documented in some of the writings of early self-trained Black American physicians.

During slavery, trained midwives were necessary because of the strategic breeding of slaves. As costs of slaves rose, it became more necessary to keep slaves well and to insure an increase in labor force. Slave babies were very important to the slave owners' wealth. They were added to the labor force at an early age. Wet nurses were prevalent. Overseers were often judged by the health of slave children.

Puritan thought was predominant in the United States. Part of the indoctrination process was the conversion of the "pagan" African to a special version of Christianity. Where African religion had previously served as a creative expression of life, Western religion was used as a method to suppress slave uprisings by encouraging them to expect their rewards in heaven. The religion of enduring hope was created and specially interpretated by the convert, specific to the slave situation. Release from hardship of labor was only by growing old or dying. One expected to have trials and tribulations in this life and so prayed for strength to endure them.

POSTSLAVERY

Most Blacks could not afford the cost of medical care after slavery. Racial discrimination was still prevalent, and care was often inaccessible. Self-medication and home remedies from persons known to be successful healers were more readily available. These were often core family members, grandmothers and grandfathers, or some other member of the community.

The church has traditionally played a major role in the Black community. It has become one of the most enduring institutions. The styles of worship and its service to the Black person is unique with vestiges of traditional African customs adapted to Puritan Christianity. It has served as an institution of health, education, welfare, and political activity to Black persons. Missionary societies that visit and tend the sick have been organized and are administered by the older sisters. Help to the orphans and widows is seen as Christian duty. The extended family concept has been maintained by the establishing of a sense of brotherhood and sisterhood. In some rural areas, the community functions as extended family. Religious healing is still prevalent in many churches. Casting out of devils is a part of many fundamentalist conversion ceremonies. The act of fasting and praying, and solitary meditation to "get in touch with ones' soul" are practiced by some traditionalists. Prayer meetings, washing of feet, and breaking of bread are communal ceremonies during which interpersonal differences are settled. Folk health beliefs and practices can most frequently be identified in listening to older Blacks describe their experiences. Often the language used in the oral description gives the themes that are used in survival medicine.

For many, the concept of wellness remains related to being able to labor productively, sickness is related to a state of incapacitation, making work impossible. Aging is still seen as a natural process of attaining grace during which the elderly is to be paid deference and to be protected.

Death has taken on an added meaning of "crossing over to the other side," or "crossing over Jordan." Because death is considered a natural process, some families relate traditions of preparing others to accept the death of an older person by the introduction to a grieving process. Often it is initiated by the older person themselves.

Attitudes toward health practitioners reflect survival strategies. The practitioner's manner in administering care is critical. Previous success in restoring health to others is primary.

Some of the specific health practices detailed still reveal a high value for the skills of observation and sensitivity as part of the process of training and treatment.

RELEVANCE OF BLACK FOLK HEALTH PRACTICES TO HEALTH CARE

When one notes the historical development of health practices of Blacks and combines that information with observations that seem inherent to the practices of effective care-givers, one arrives at a philosophy of care. One can identify a set of beliefs and assumptions that seem common to the natural or nonacademic care-giver and the academically educated. The purpose of a philosophy is to serve as a guide to what "ought to be," rather than what exists in any given case studied.

Techniques and modalities change rapidly as new knowledge and technology is acquired. One can become stereotyped in thinking and acting if dependent on modalities and technology as the only content for practice. Practice is also process, and philosophy gives the process a direction toward life.

The following set of beliefs and assumptions are reflective of those held by health practitioners who are recognized as effective care-givers to Black persons.

VIEW OF MAN IN HEALTH AND ILLNESS

Man is a biopsychosocial, spiritual, and cultural being whose moral core is divine and human. In health, he strives to live in a state of harmony with himself and in union with other beings in the universe. Striving thus, he moves and thinks in rhythmic flow in time and space, desiring to be reunited with what he has been separated from during his harmonious existence. He exists as a being representative of a larger community which serves as an extension of himself and he of it. He has an awareness of having an extended self.

Illness is a loss of self, a sense of disharmony with one's soul, or being "the only one," "lost," and lacking communion with others. This may be expressed physically, socially, emotionally, spiritually, and/or culturally. From this perspective one's illness can be perceived as ill-at-ease — a state of dis-ease without being functionally incapacitated. Illness is not seen as individual deviancy that is measurable, but a state of being out of union, physically, emotionally, or spiritually.

Man attempts to maintain health by analyzing and choosing those resources available to him in his internal and external environment that can help him in restoring his harmony, therefore maintaining his self-esteem, sanity, and survival. Through this analysis of his resources, he is able to predict probabilities and plan alternative strategies which he can use during future events. In a state of health, he is adaptive, flexible, alert, and able to use a wide range of strategies effectively to endure and reach his optimal potential.[5] To attain this, he has a varied repertoire of effective strategies of personal assertion, containment, fight, or avoidance to choose from in situations of stress. Through appropriate use of his resources, he tends to be more active than reactive, thus able to create an energy reserve that can be called upon in times of illness so that natural healing can take place with minimal artificial supports.

Socially, he views another as a "thou" in relation to himself rather than as an object. He relates to others through affect and symbolic imagery. He prefers personal affiliations in social relations that can be viewed in terms of interpersonal harmony, rather than situations for an "either/or" competitive stance.

THE ROLE OF THE COMMUNITY

When illness does occur, the ill person is not separated from all vestiges of his familiar environment, worked upon as an object, and then returned to that environment without consideration of the disruption to his personal community. The role of the community in health and illness is essential. In health, it is one of maintenance and prevention of disability through ritualistic and interpersonal participation in acts and events that "wish one well." Acts of prolonged avoidance of responsibilities, isolation, and disharmony create sickness in individuals and may prove threatening to the health of the entire community. In illness, the role of the community is a restorative one.

The individual and the community then have an active responsibility to each other. This serves as a basis for community health care practices.

THE ROLE OF THE CARE-GIVER

All care-givers are seen as humane healers, as restorers of harmony and balance. Thus, curative powers are not only displayed by physicians and nurses. While extensive knowledge and techniques of cure are professional abilities requiring years of training and apprenticeship — healing powers are personal, nurturing abilities that are innate to the care-giver's lifestyle and nature. Certain practices, techniques, and rituals may be unique to a given profession; however, the primary healing effect seems to result from the relationship between the care-giver and the client, especially as portrayed by the care-giver's ability to create a climate in which one interacts with a person so that natural healing can occur. In curative practices, equal value is given to the manner one displays toward the client, knowledge of one's art, and technical skill. Inadequacy in any area can cause one to fail to attain the degree of harmony needed and may result in crippling effects or avoidable death for the person.

The care-giver must be qualified to be a mediator between the person and his personal community: to function as the personal community if need be; and to serve as a vigilant observer, describer, and intervener when potential disruptive internal and external forces threaten to limit the client's resources and natural abilities for maintaining or attaining health.

An essential component of the care-giver's power to restore and maintain health is reflected in his own lifestyle and conduct. A relevant concept is the one of "cool." The more "cool" one has, the more effective are one's powers to restore harmony by creating a climate in which the natural healing process can occur.

The African roots of the term "cool" have several meanings that are applicable. One meaning refers to the ability of one to engage in intense, potentially emotion-laden, heated situations with a high degree of equanimity but without the emotional detachment and lack of spontaneity that makes one interpersonally cold, frigid, or emotionally bankrupt.[6] The process calls for recognition and experiencing of feelings appropriate to one's view of reality, but it requires the development of skill in personal discipline in acting out those feelings. The latter can elevate an individual's humanity to more skillful performance and greater appreciation of the situation. How one carries oneself and conducts oneself are integral parts of effectiveness in practice and one's acceptability to the client and in the community. This requires the care-giver to strive to become an expert in interpretation of his own experiences.

One's mission, in those moments when called upon to display one's professional expertise, is to serve as an example of striving to be cool, to live in harmony with oneself, with his fellow man, and with the universe without any loss of self and integrity.

References

1. Bennett L Jr.: Before the Mayflower: A History of the Black American, 1619–1962. Chicago, Johnson, 1962, p 1
2. Morais H: The History of the Negro in Medicine. International Library of Negro Life and History Series: Association for the Study of Negro Life and History, New York, 1969, p 12
3. Wesley C: In Freedom's Footsteps. International Library of Negro Life and History Series: Association for the Study of Negro Life and History, New York, 1969, pp 45–46
4. Morais, H, op cit, pp 17–28
5. Meyers H: "Holistic Definitions and Measurement of States of Non Health" in King L, Meyers H, Cannon J, et al: African Philosophy and Paradigms for Research on Black Persons. Los Angeles, Fanon Research and Development Center, Charles Drew Postgraduate Center, 1975
6. Thompson RS: "An Esthetic of the Cool" in African Art, Autumn 1973, Vol 2 No 1, pp 40–43, 64–67

Bibliography

Abrahams WE: The Mind of Africa. Chicago, University of Chicago Press, 1962

Aptheker H (ed): A Documentary History of the Negro People. In The United States, 2 Vols. Secaucus, N.J., Citadel, 1962

Bennett L Jr: Before The Mayflower: A History of the Black American, 1619–1962. Chicago, Johnson, 1962

Billingsley A: Black Families in White America. Englewood Cliffs, N. J., Prentice-Hall, 1968

Botkin BA (ed): Lay My Burden Down. Chicago, University of Chicago Press, 1945

DuBois WEB: Black Folk: Then and Now. New York, Octagon Press, 1970 (Reprint of 1939 edition)

———: The Negro Church. Atlanta, Atlanta University Press, 1903

———: The Negro American Family. Atlanta, Atlanta University Press, 1908

Festinger L: The psychological effects of insufficient reward. Am Psychol 16: 1–11, 1961

Herskowitz ML: The Myth of the Negro Past. Boston, Beacon, 1958

Herskowitz M: The American Negro: A Study in Racial Crossing, New York, 1928

Jacques GB: Mental Health Implications of "Lord Ha Mercy": Survival Strategies of Older Black Women. Unpublished Tape Recordings

———: Steppin Out in Deep Water: Conversations With Mama. Unpublished Tape Recordings

Kardiner A, Ovesey L: The Mark of Oppression. Cleveland, World, 1951

Mays B, Nicholson JW: The Negro's Church. New York, 1932

Mbiti JS: African Religions and Philosophy. New York, Anchor, 1970

Morais H: The History of the Negro in Medicine. International Library of Negro Life and History Series. New York, Association for the Study of Negro Life and History, 1969

Nobles WW: African Philosophy: Foundations for Black Psychology. In Jones RL (ed): Black Psychology. New York, Harper, 1972
——— : Psychological research and the black self-concept: a critical review. J Soc Issues, 29:1, 1973
Noel DL: Group identification among Negroes: an empirical analysis. J Soc Issues, 20: 71–84, 1964
Thompson RF: An aesthetic of the cool. African Art 2(1):40–67, Autumn 1973
Wesley C: In Freedom's Footsteps, New York International Library of Negro Life and History Series: Association for the Study of Negro Life and History, 1969
Woodson CG: The History of the Negro Church. Washington, Negro University Press, 1945
——— : The Negro Professional Man and the Community. Washington, Negro University Press, 1934 (Reprint)
Woodward CV: The Strange Career of Jim Crow. New York, Oxford University Press, 1957

PART III

Guidelines for Safe Nursing Care

Nursing assessment and intervention has been discussed and included in nursing literature for a number of years. During the past decade, there has been increasing efforts to systematize the nursing process. One important, necessary focus, however, has been overlooked. Generally, nursing assessment has been addressed from the perspective of the "professional." Lay input has not been seen as valuable. When assessment is incomplete (only done from the professional perspective), then it follows that nursing care planned and implemented is often irrelevant to the "real" world of the client.

Included in this section of the book are guidelines for expanding the care/cure process.

The authors suggest that epidemiologic principles need to be applied to the study of health and factors which support a positive state of energy balance for the human organism. Generally speaking, when race-related diseases are cited in the literature, the pervasive tone of the presentation does not clearly state the relationships among the whole gamut of factors. Often race is not the primary predisposing factor in disease causation. Thus, ethnic people of color are often labeled as deficient by textbooks used in the education of health care professionals. The pervasiveness of deficit modeling relative to ethnic people of color impinges on the quality of care given.

Goals of nursing care is another focal area in this section of the book. Nurses, as well as other health care professionals, must take a new approach to goal-setting. The goal for the entire nursing process must become one of mutual participation. Mutual participation, as a philosophical theme, recognizes the individual worth of each person on the health team as a contributor. Of course, the patient and his significant others are included as an integral part of the health team. This inclusion should be operationalized throughout the care/cure process from assessment through evaluation.

Finally, this section of the book expands the parameters of assessment so that inclusions relevant to ethnic people of color are part and parcel of a holistic model for assessment and intervention.

Although a number of disease processes are cited as examples, it must be recognized that the basic purpose of this text is not to provide information on pathobiopsychosociology. Therefore, the reader must utilize presentations here as supplements to content presented in basic texts. Students in the health disciplines are encouraged to have standard texts as references during the reading of Chapters 7, 8, and 9.

7

Epidemiology in Health and Disease

Phyllis Perry Paxton

INTRODUCTION

Epidemiology is an applied science which focuses on the distribution and determinants of disease in man.[1] The original tools of the science were directed at sorting out the causative organisms involved in contagion. The scope of epidemiology has been expanded to include a wide variety of noninfectious diseases which plague man and which account for most of the diseases and deaths in advanced societies.

Epidemiology has had a profound effect on all health care disciplines. Millions of dollars have been spent to investigate cause—effect variables as they relate to disease processes. Health care educational systems direct the student in problem solving, which involves correlation of variables, relating predisposing factors to patient situations, developing profiles of disease processes, isolating causative organisms and factors, and planning intervention to impede the action of causative agents and to increase the human defenses against illness.

The epidemiologic approach to the study of disease has affected a number of discoveries and has provided the impetus for advanced medical technology. The pervasiveness of epidemiologic approaches to the disease dilemma has provided health care professionals with a mind set for correlating events, organisms, and a number of factors with specific diseases. Frequency of disease has been correlated with a number of factors such as age, sex, race, and socioeconomic status. Epidemiology has provided the health care professional with valuable tools for applying trends in disease occurrence to prevention, early diagnosis, and treatment.

Admittedly, the control of disease becomes more manageable when scientific principles are applied. Nevertheless, the science has produced an almost compulsive mind set in health care professionals. The danger is that frequently the health care professional, in an effort to identify the primary cause of disease, resorts to associating race or genetics as the cause of disease. This kind of problem solving is subtly encouraged by most medical and nursing texts. When disease entities are presented, a profile of persons who are most likely to be affected by the diseases is given. In most cases, the profile includes age and sex. Generally speaking, race is introduced when the disease affects members of an ethnic group of color with more frequency than its occurrence in the general population. As a result, because race is included in the profile, the health care professional may falsely believe the disease to result from genetic weakness. This author believes that a fresh look needs to be taken at disease causation. If one is able to identify the preponderance of factors related to illness, then one might be better able to identify and support factors associated with wellness. This is often cited as the primary reason for continued research into the phenomena of disease. Nevertheless, when research has identified the disease process as related to environmental or social factors, resulting intervention has not been directed at the basic fabric of the social disorder.

DISEASE

There are a number of dysfunctions which are labeled as disease. Diseases are diagnosed and labeled by the presenting signs and symptoms, and changes in function that can be identified by gross and/or discrete examination. Oftentimes the etiology is not clear. There is lack of clarity relative to the etiology of disease for a very good reason, since there is no single disease entity. By and large what we see as, measure, and label disease is the human organism's attempt to adapt to the stresses of life.[2] This adaptation may be relatively localized or generalized, but it never merely affects a single organ system. It stands to reason then that there are a number of factors interacting to effect dysfunction in the human organism.

Damon states that the epidemiologist analyzes disease rates among groups who are more homogeneous than the general society. The immediate sensitive factors of homogeneity are race, ethnicity, sex, age, geographic location, and socioeconomic status. Likewise these factors are often presenting characteristics of persons with high frequency of specific diseases.

Poverty must not be overlooked as a perpetuator of a number of diseases and injuries. Buying power is instrumental to the life style and patterns of people, just as it is instrumental to the level of health. Material goods necessary for the maintenance of human integrity are accumulated only in proportion to money available. One might hasten to add that this basic fact is applicable in a number of ways — from the purchase of food to the purchase of health care, including the ability to purchase a safe environment.

Bullough and Bullough cite a health care problem, dangerous and deadly, which never touches affluent members of this society. The problem is injury, mutilation, and/or death of children caused by rats.[3] A number of health problems affect children of the poor.

Primary malnutrition is often a poverty-perpetuated problem in children. In an era of unprecedented American prosperity, malnutrition is, paradoxically, a major health problem. The list of diseases of children in which improper diet is implicated includes rickets, mental retardation, growth retardation, dental caries, gastroenteritis, marasmus, kwashiorkor, anemia, obesity, and emaciation. Some nutritional disorders are clearly related to poverty, and the problems growing out of poverty must be viewed in this context.

Fetal wastage has been correlated with low socioeconomic status. Just as fetal deaths are associated with the status of poverty, so too is neonatal mortality and prematurity. The basis for the wastage of human potential and life is interwoven in poverty, malnutrition, and inadequate prenatal care. The former factor (poverty) plays havoc with nutritional demands and the accessibility of prenatal care.

Prenatal care and health care, in general, remains inaccessible to a significant sector of the American population. Health care only becomes accessible when people are able to utilize it. Thus, location, cost, time, attitudes of health care workers, lack of transportation, etc. may interact to prevent accessibility to health care.

Poverty is identified as a factor in disease causation. How a status of poverty influences one's level of wellness is related to the survival life style of people in poverty. A survival life style may be defined as a way of life which dictates action directed toward meeting the most basic needs for the maintenance of life. Thus, activity is centered around maintaining life, rather than fulfilling it. Energy output is oftentimes greater than intake over an extended period of time. Constant energy output threatens the integrity of the organism.

The organism's capacity for warding off potential stressors is decreased. A survival life style embraces life in an environment which, in itself, is harmful. Combining the decreased capacity for fight against illness and the increasing environmental hazards, it is no wonder that poor people have a lower level of wellness than members of the dominant society.

Poverty (lack of material resources) creates and perpetuates a survival life style. The more immediate the threat to life, the more intense is activity for survival. Thus, primary preventive health care, and early detection of disease, assumes low priority; not because good health is seen as having little value, but because health care is not accessible or affordable. The intensity of life stresses the human organism and wears the body out. This phenomenon, in part, accounts for the shortened lifespan of migrant workers of all hues, American Indians, Puerto Ricans, Chicanos, and Blacks.

Although cervical cancer is frequently cited as occurring with increased frequency in ethnic women of color, the relationships of a number of variables to cervical cancer have not been sorted out. Even though, definitive causes have not been isolated, the fact that early detection is the key to cure is well established. Early detection and treatment implies the need to have these services accessible at limited cost.

During the years from 1940 to 1963, the death rate from cervical cancer dropped from 22 per 100,000 to 16 per 100,000. Yet during the same time span, the rate dropped only one point for Blacks, from 30 per 100,000 to 29 per 100,000.[4] The questions then are raised: Why the difference in the trend? Why the difference in the death rates? Is frequency of occurrence related to race, culture, socioeconomic status, environmental, or geographical factors?

Tuberculosis may be viewed as a poverty-perpetuated disease. Although the incidence of TB has declined in this country, the incidence of the disease is increasing in large metropolitan areas or inner cities. What peoples live in the inner cities?

Infectious diarrhea is a poverty-perpetuated disease. Generally associated with lack of cleanliness, it poses a negative stereotyping on people who are affected by the disorder. Blame is often subtly or overtly placed on the patient or his family. The basic root of the problem frequently revolves around inadequate plumbing, sewage disposal, etc., as opposed to lack of motivation for cleanliness. Thus, the problem often is socio-environmental.

Racism must be addressed as a factor in disease causation. The pervasiveness of the oppression of ethnic people of color affects health. The dynamics of racist society-triggered reactions related to disease causation, although important for the understanding that racism is a public health disease, is beyond the scope of this book. Suffice it to say that racism relegates ethnic people of color to subordinate positions in the economic, educational, and political arenas. Therefore, a number of factors related to economics, education, and lack of political power interact to compromise the level of health and quality of health care.

The fact that ethnic people of color are viewed as "less than" is reflected in policies and practices which restrict entry in the professions, limit entry into institutions of higher learning, thwart entrepreneurship, sanction the degree of human experimentation, and encourage reduction of the genetic pool. This view is also reflected in the number of sterilizations done on ethnic women of color. During 1973, the median age of women sterilized in federally financed sterilization programs was 28. More than 50 percent of the total family planning population was white, but only 40 percent of the population sterilized was white. At the same time, approximately 33 percent of the family planning population was Black, but 43 percent of the sterilization population was Black.[5]

Elective hysterectomies are often performed on poor Black and Puerto Rican women in teaching hospitals in New York City. This phenomenon becomes a part of the teaching imperative of the hospital — operations are scheduled to train residents. This kind of action is by no means limited to New York City; it occurs in many public hospitals across the country.[5]

Measham, Hatcher, and Arnold cite the results of a survey of physicians in the Southeast section of the country. Of the 105 physicians surveyed in regard to their attitudes about contraception, 46 percent responded that they favored compulsory sterilization for women on welfare with three illegitimate children.[6] Since our society is structured along class and caste levels, and there is both class and caste discrimination, then one questions whether the expressed attitudes related to class are indicative of attitudes with respect to caste.

The phenomenon of selective sterilization must be viewed in its proper context — that of genocide, since this is the view of the people affected. Additionally one must note that the above practices actually decrease the genetic pools of biologically distinct groups of people.

There are a number of diseases of adaptation. Neurosis and psychosis are viewed as the human organism's attempt to adapt to the stresses in the environment. Thus, both neurotic and psychotic behavior serve to protect the organism from harm.[2] Paranoia, which is often seen as symptomatic of mental illness, serves to help the ethnic person of color screen input from health care professionals in an attempt to avoid harm in an environment which regards ethnic people of color as "less than."

The concept of symptomatic disease being healthy adaptation is vitally important. A disproportionate number of ethnic people of color are confined in mental institutions, jails, and prisons. Behaviors directly related to their isolation from society often served to maintain physical and psychologic integrity. The imperative is mediation at the basic fabric of society, which by its oppression, on the one hand, causes the unacceptable behavior, and, on the other hand, punishes those same behaviors.

Each biologically distinct group has low frequency of some diseases and high frequency of other diseases.

Although there is variation among the different Nations, American

Indians show a low frequency of duodenal ulcers, and Legg-Perthes disease, phenylketonuria, and Tay-Sach's disease. There is a high incidence of suicide, dental caries, and tuberculosis.[7]

Asians have a low incidence of leukemia and prostate cancer, but a high frequency of cancer of the gastrointestinal system.[7]

Blacks have a low incidence of dental caries, skin cancer, and central nervous system malformations. There is a high incidence of hypertension, S hemoglobin, and uterine fibroids.[7]

Chicanos have low frequency of cystoceles, prolapsed uterus, and phenylketonuria. There is a high incidence of hypertension, thalassemia, and tuberculosis.

The integrity of the skin, musculature, and connective tissue is conversely related to the hue intensity of a people. Therefore, dark skinned people experience less loss of elasticity and damage of supporting structures, ie, cracked, fissured nipples during lactation; prolapsed uterus; cystoceles; and rectoceles. However, the darker the skin, the more likely the person is to suffer from keloidosis. The reason for the above phenomenon probably relates to biologic environmental adaptation which results in genetic transmission.

Since data on the ethnic distribution of diseases are scarce, the above are cited only as examples. These examples by no means even begin to present a comprehensive picture. Although some diseases are distributed along racial lines, they also have environmental causation. One good example is sickle cell anemia. S hemoglobin was formed as an adaptation to malaria-endemic environments, yet it is transmitted genetically.

WELLNESS

Just as a number of factors interact to cause illness, a number of factors interact to facilitate wellness. The relationship of a number of variables to wellness is probably better understood than the relationships of factors to illness or disease.

Wellness is facilitated by the dynamic interaction of energy systems for the maintenance of a balanced state. Need fulfillment is a key to wellness. Biologic constitution, capacity for adaptation to stress, and physical and emotional environmental factors influence need fulfillment and, hence, wellness.

SUMMARY

Epidemiology focuses on the distribution and determinants of disease in the human organism. The complexity of the organism makes it impossible for one to identify single causes of specific diseases. This is further effected by the fact that there is no single disease entity. Epidemiologic tools have been able to determine patterns of disease occurence along a number of variables, such as age, sex, race, ethnicity, socioeconomic status, and geographic location. Nevertheless, very little is known about the relationship among the factors that are related to specific disease causation.

References

1. Damon A: Race, Ethnic Group, and Disease. Soc Biol, 16(2):69—71, 73—75, 77, 1969
2. Fadiman J: Introduction to Holistic Health. Tape No. 727, Saratoga, Calif., Cognetics, 1975
3. Bullough B, Bullough V: Poverty, Ethnic Identity, and Health Care. New York, Appleton, 1972, pp 1—4
4. Tipton D: Physiological Assessment of Black People. Paper presented March 4, 1974, University of California, San Francisco
5. Sterilization: Women Fit to Be Tied. Health PAC Bulletin, No. 62, January/February 1975, p. 4
6. Measham A, Hatcher R, Arnold C: Physicians and contraception: A study of perceptions and practices in a southeastern United States community. South Med J, 64:500, 1971
7. Damon: op cit, pp 73—77

8

Goals of Nursing Care

Florence Stroud,
Ruth Ann Terry,
and Barbara Lea Giles

INTRODUCTION

This chapter will focus on the process of establishing mutual goals for nursing practice among ethnic people of color. Such a task includes a discussion of professional behavior and action from a theoretical and empirical point of view. Equally important is a discussion about client behavior relative to health care services, as well as the influence of racism — institutional and personal — as it is manifested in health care. Finally, the authors will suggest ways in which the forces of professional dominance and racism can be attenuated so that reciprocity in the care relationship is established. While much of the literature uses the physician as the professional prototype, it is equally applicable to nurses.

The Nature of Racial Oppression

Racial oppression in the United States has been conceptualized as having two major components — personal (or individual racism) and institutional racism.

Institutional racism has been defined as the systematic subjugation, oppression, and forced dependence of a people that is developed and reinforced by institutional operating policies, priorities, values, and normative patterns. Institutional racism is operationalized by: (1) establishing and sanctioning unequal goals, objectives, and priorities for ethnic people of color; and (2) sanctioning inequality in status, as well as in access to goods and services.[1] Personal racism differs from institutional racism in that it describes behavior or acts by individuals and/or groups that are rooted in beliefs of racial superiority. Institutional racism provides the structure for individual racist acts. Personal acts of racism can thrive only if there is sanction or legitimazation of that behavior. Institutional racism provides such a framework.[2]

The need for special programs to insure that more than a token number of minority students gain entrance to nursing schools results from institutionalized racism. From the point of entry, minority students must contend with the various forms and acts of racism. During counseling, they are encouraged to enter L.P.N. programs rather than baccalaureate nursing programs. Most, if not all, registered nurses have had the experience of having physicians on the ward walk past them to give medical orders to a white subordinate on the nursing team. In one sense, the behavior is understandable. The majority of ethnic people of color are relegated to the "paraprofessional" positions in health care. Ethnic students of color have few role models; ethnic patients of color have few caretakers; white professionals and team members are unable to conceptualize or internalize the professional Black worker.

Newby has described the range of personal racist feeling in the United States. He identified three major groups: the extremists, moderates, and reformers. All three groups subscribed to racist beliefs, but in varying degrees. The extremist was characterized as the most "out front" in that he openly endorsed policies and practices that maintained white superiority. While the moderates are equally convinced of white superiority, they call for reason and understanding. The reformers advocate an extension of rights to nonwhites, as long as ultimate power and control can be maintained by whites.[3] Comer updates Newby's paradigm by adding a fourth category. He included in this group those individuals and groups who recognize racial differences without making a value judgment. They advocate equal opportunity but, on occasion, manifest racist responses as a consequence of growing up in a society that has legitimized, promoted, and transmitted racist attitudes.[4] It is critical that health care practitioners identify where, in this classification, they fall — for until they know and confront it openly and honestly, they will probably experience difficulties in working with ethnic people of color.

Those groups who have been the subject of oppression also represent a range of responses to the oppressor. On the one hand, there are those who tend to accept the values and beliefs of the dominant group without question; they tend to imitate and emulate their behavior. To the extreme opposite of this response are those who totally reject and rebel against the dominant culture. An example of the latter is an incident in which a

20-year-old Black woman was seeking an abortion. She had a 9-month-old child, had had an abortion 5 months previously, and was currently 3 months pregnant. Family planning had been broached with the family, but the father's attitude was that this was a form of genocide being perpetrated by the dominant culture on the Black community. His rejection and rebellion against the efforts of persons from the dominant culture to assist him and his mate in birth control is exemplary of the posture taken by some ethnic people of color. The aforementioned couple found it easier to behave in a way that was neither sanctioned by the dominant culture, nor by their own ethnic community. Somewhere between the parameters of imitation/emulation and rejection/rebellion are those who find that their religion, music, neighborhood groups, the family, and general way of life provide support and assistance in the development of personal competencies that can lead to a healthy self-concept. Somewhere along this continuum, health care practitioners will find ethnic patients of color. Practitioners will have to develop sensitivity to the relative place on the continuum into which the individual patient in their care falls.

Using a systems approach, Eliot Friedson describes client (patient) behavior that can significantly affect professional medical and nursing practice. He identifies two systems which he labels the professional system and the lay system.[5,6]

THE PROFESSIONAL SYSTEM

Professional practitioners maintain that their work is so mystical and complex that only their colleagues, not lay persons, can evaluate them. Their primary loyalties belong to professional associations with colleagues called the professional community. The recently organized consumer or patient groups for evaluation of care has had little visible impact on professional practices. Although the professional community does not recognize the legitimacy and value of consumers as evaluators of patient care, the professional must practice in a physical community dominated by lay people. The professional is dependent on clients for his livelihood. Since clients exercise some choice in the selection of physicians, client standards and norms are introduced into the care/selection process. Therefore, Friedson postulates that actual health care practice is contingent on the interaction of the two, sometimes conflicting, systems: the "inside" lay referral system and the "outside" professional system. He further admonishes, that if we are to understand medical practice, we must look at the client and the practitioner in one analytic system and explore the sources of strength for each.[5]

THE LAY SYSTEM

Before clients make their way to the practitioner, they go through a number of lay consultants, friends, neighbors, and relatives. Symptoms and treatments, including drugs, are discussed during these interactions. This process is called the lay referral system. Each community will have its own lay referral system. What is common to all communities is (1) the degree of incongruence between client culture and professional culture, and (2) the relative number of lay consultants between initial symptom perception and the decision to seek a professional practitioner. In this sense, Friedson's lay system may be likened to the cultural health care systems discussed in Chapters 3, 4, 5, and 6. The culture of a given community tends to determine what is within the domain of the professional referral system and what is within the lay referral system.[5]

The lay system may have its own definitions of health and illness, and these may not include professional practitioners. For instance, cultural definitions may contradict those of the professional system; therefore the lay referral process may not lead to a medical practitioner.

The lay referral system not only decides the client's choice, but sustains it, or perhaps makes the client change his or her mind. When lay prescriptions fail, the client is led to the physician, the professional practitioner, as the last consultant chosen. At this point, control is taken out of the client's hands. He may get service he does not want or understand and activity geared to change the client's mind about the "value" of treatment may not be successful. The patient now is separated from his lay support, and the patient remains unconvinced of the merit of the treatment.

In a community health nursing situation, a referral was received for a 40-year-old Black woman who was identified as depressed. The referral indicated that the woman had been seen recently by a psychiatrist. A home visit was made, and, during the visit, the community health worker gathered the following information. Five years before, the woman had had a vaginal discharge. She contacted a female neighbor who was the "giver of health advice" in the neighborhood. The patient was told by the woman that she had cancer. The fear of having cancer temporarily immobilized the patient. Then, after much thought, she decided to see a physician. According to the patient, her vagina was painted purple, and she was not instructed to return to the physician. Being dissatisfied with the care, she sought another physician and was given medicinal suppositories. Whether or not she followed the medical regimen is unknown, but the discharge continued. She continued physician shopping (she saw five in all) until she was finally referred for psychiatric care because of her preoccu-

pation with cancer and the resultant behavioral changes. During the home visit, the community health worker, after eliciting this information, contacted the last physician seen by the woman and found out the patient had a fungal infection, monilia. She explained this to the patient and discussed the transference of the disease back and forth between partners during sexual intercourse. It was the first time in five years that a health worker had given the patient any information about the infection. The woman was not perceived as depressed or manifesting abnormal behavior by the community health worker. The client managed the various aspects of her daily life in a manner that was, for lack of a better word, normal.

The above situation identifies the need for the collaboration between the professional system and the lay referral system. Moreover it vividly reflects gaps in the eliciting of client input in the care/cure process. Fanon added another dimension to Friedson's analysis when he described patient care in politically and racially oppressed Algeria during the 1950s.[7] He described the Algerian person who went to see the European physician as diffident. The Algerian client tended to answer in monosyllables, gave little information that was explanatory, and soon aroused impatience on the part of the physician. This attitude was not the same as the usual type of inhibition which patients demonstrated, giving control to the physician. Moreover, the personal approach, utilizing "acceptable" interpersonal skills did not put the Algerian patient at ease, nor did it facilitate the establishment and maintenance of rapport. Fanon's observation using a colonized versus colonial frame of reference does not precisely parallel the lay versus professional system. However, his descriptions are particularly useful, for they describe yet another layer of domination: political oppression based on beliefs of racial superiority. Patient behaviors must be analyzed within this context in order to understand their perceived realities and the decisions they make based on their current state of affairs.

Analyzed within this context enlightened professionals can gain greater understanding of the "whys" of patient behavior and perhaps in some instances an appreciation and respect for the two very different worlds of patient and practitioner. Fanon's account of the colonized Algerian's noncompliant behavior is not unlike the actions of ethnic individuals of color in the United States. Such actions, more often than not, are misunderstood or stereotyped as manifestations of apathy, ignorance, lower-class life style, and innate inferiorities, instead of purposeful behavior within the context of the patient's perceptual world. Consider the following with respect to nursing care.

The practitioner finds that his patient cannot be depended upon to take his medicine regularly, and when he does, he takes the wrong dosage.

The patient fails to appreciate the importance of periodic visits, so appointments are frequently missed or cancelled; he takes a paradoxical cavalier attitude toward the physician and a frivolous attitude toward the prescribed diet. These are some of the most striking and common peculiarities noted by the practitioner. The general impression is that the patient plays hide-and-seek with his health care source. None of the practitioners has a hold on the patient. They find that, in spite of promises and pledges, an attitude of flight — of patient disengagement — persists. All the efforts exerted by the physician and by other health personnel to modify this patient's behavior encounter evasion or withdrawal on the part of the patient.[7]

In describing conflict between the professional and lay systems, Friedson notes that the client's effort to assert his own conceptions of illness and appropriate care often takes the form of evasion.

Friedson suggests that those patients who feel helpless and at the mercy of professionals will not use care at any optimal level, ie, they are less likely to cooperate with prescribed care. Often, the behavior of these patients is misunderstood. For them, professional care represents a pragmatic compromise between a desired but unrealized goal and the realities of the present. Practical adaptation underlies their responses to health care and may manifest itself in passivity by the patient who unquestioningly accepts prescribed regimens, or it may take the form of ingratitude for interventions that are not consonant with the patient's suggestions.[6]

Friedson's study illustrates the concept that individuals act in a purposeful way to achieve goals they feel will benefit them most. When their desired choices are frustrated, they may agree to some kind of compromise, but they will not totally abandon their unrealized ideal.

Evasive behavior tends to be more prevalent in highly structured hierarchical situations. For instance, the patient who fails to keep scheduled clinic appointments may have decided that the benefits from these visits (a perfunctory examination by an inexperienced practitioner) are not commensurate with personal costs (long waiting periods and dehumanizing treatment). If the patient persists in his belief that he needs care, and his access to care is restricted, he will often devise ways to achieve his aim with the least amount of personal cost. This may take the form of increased visits to emergency rooms for care, or it may take the form of certain kinds of manipulation on the part of patients.

Roth has observed that patients in highly structured public facilities are able to exert control over their care. He believes that patients who regularly receive care in such institutions are not entirely helpless in the hands of hospital personnel. Patients use their own techniques for obtaining prompt and effective treatment. They calculate when to remain silent and when it is to their advantage to assert themselves to achieve appropriate treatment. They decide which symptoms ought to be dramatized in order to get priority, and what persons to approach for needed information.[8] An important question is, what happens, or is thought to happen, once the patient and practitioner are interacting in the care process; or stated another way, what is (or ought to be) the nature of this care relationship?

THE SZASZ–HOLLENDER MODEL

Szasz and Hollender have described three types of patient–physician interaction in terms of decision behavior. Like other human relationships, the patient–physician relationship is viewed as "embodying the activities of two interacting systems (persons)." Unlike other relationships, this one is profoundly affected by ideas about disease, treatment, and cure.[9] The authors of this chapter hasten to add that these relationships are also influenced by the race of the provider versus that of the patient, and the sex of the provider versus that of the patient.

Table 8.1
Three Models of the Nurse—Patient Relationship

MODEL	NURSE'S ROLE	PATIENT'S ROLE	CLINICAL APPLICATION
Activity—passivity	Does something to patient	Passive recipient	Anesthesia, acute trauma, coma, delirium, etc.
Guidance—cooperation	Instructs patient about the desired role	Complies with instruction	Acute disease report
Mutual participation	Assists patient to assume responsibility for his own care	Collaborates in the management of disease — uses expert help	Chronic disease, health maintenance

Adapted from: Szasz T and Hollander M: A contribution to the philosophy of medicine. Arch Intern Med. 97:586, 1956

The three models adapted to nursing are: (1) activity–passivity, (2) guidance–cooperation, and (3) mutual participation (Table 8.1). The first model views the patient as totally helpless and passive, requiring the nurse to assume complete control of care. In a real sense, this is not interaction. The relationship is based on the effect of one person upon another in such a way that the person acted upon is unable to contribute actively. The nurse is active, the patient is passive. Regardless of the patient's contribution and response, treatment is performed on the patient. It is viewed as an appropriate model for certain kinds of emergencies, and for major surgical procedures.

The second model (guidance—cooperation) refers to a situation where some cooperation on the part of the patient is required, unlike the severe emergency of the patient in the first model. The patient experiences discomfort or pain, seeks help, and is willing to cooperate with whatever guidance is offered. He is conscious, has preferences of his own, but is willing to defer to the authority of the nurse, and to follow those prescriptions indicated. According to the authors, it is this model that most closely approximates much of health care practice. The nurse guides and the patient cooperates if a cure is to be effected.

The third model (mutual participation) is reciprocal. Nurse and patient are involved in a partnership that moves toward some mutually shared goal. Both interactants are committed to the goal, but the judgements of either can actually change the goal during the treatment process. Such changes can complicate the relationship.

The models are not ranked in hierarchical form. That is, no one model is viewed as superior to another. In fact, each model may be appropriate for the same patient under differing circumstances. For example, a patient who was injured in an accident, and subsequently found to be partially paralyzed, would assume the patient role in model number one during a necessary surgical procedure, model two during the postoperative—recovery phase (advice about certain activities or exercise), and model three during the rehabilitation phase. What determines the assumption of one model versus another are medical notions of disease, treatment, and cure.

As the patient's condition changes, so should the nature of the relationship. Interpersonal problems may develop if patient and/or nurse are so inflexible that they do not permit changes in the relationship commensurate with changes in condition. Institutional racism often encourages and supports the activity—passivity model for ethnic people of color, regardless of the client's status. The belief that ethnic clients of color ought to be passive, so that they may be controlled and/or dominated is a familiar racist posture that is supported in many patient (client) interactions.

The models are prescriptive. That is, they presuppose what ought to be in such relationships. Models one and two are more clearly defined than model three. They also embody patient passivity. The authors see model three (mutual participation) as essentially foreign to health care practitioners. Such a relationship necessitates a high degree of empathy and has properties often attributed to the ideas of friendship and partnership plus the imparting of expert advice. The practitioner's gratification cannot stem from power or control of another person. Rather, satisfactions must be derived from more abstract kinds of personal mastery which are not yet clearly understood.[9]

Again, the intricacies of the influences of institutional and personal racism on patient and provider are not discussed in relationship to the models. When ethnic people of color are discussed relative to health care, a major reality that practitioner and patient must confront is the reality of racial oppression and its potential influence on the encounter.

ESTABLISHING GOALS IN NURSING CARE

Freeman makes the distinction between setting goals and then securing the compliance of others, and truly setting mutual goals.[10] Nurses working with ethnic people of color must appreciate other considerations and influences before truly mutual goals are set.

Tinkham and Voorhies discuss transposing nursing needs into realizable goals. The nurse and the patient must determine together if the needs or problems are agreed upon and acceptable to both.[11] The nurse may see as a need, eg, the inability of a family to maintain adequate nutrition. The family may see the need as not having adequate financial resources to meet the basic needs necessary for the family. Therefore, it is necessary for the two to work as a team to identify needs and problems and set goals that can realistically be met by both the nurse and the family. Goal setting and subsequent nursing care must be modified to encompass the needs, interests, and conditions of ethnic people of color. Nurses must understand the subculture of the client, ie, diet, dress, language, verbal, as well as, nonverbal modes of communication. The importance of nonverbal behavior, such as facial expressions and gestures, cannot be overstressed. Often nonverbal behavior is perceived as uncommunicative and hostile. Equally important is an understanding of the nurse's own feelings and behavior toward people of color. Banks addresses the issues in relation to psychologists and clients.[12] His cogent principles are equally applicable to nursing and other health practitioners. He believes that large numbers of Blacks have, for some time, registered amazement at how certain social scientists expect radical changes overnight in the attitudes of the ethnic people of color. However, these same scientists are unquestionably pessimistic about the potential "attitude change" in the majority group. The author supports description of behavior of ethnic people of color in context, rather than continuing to label the behaviors in negative stereotyping ways. This is an initial step for nurses in setting mutual health goals with ethnic people of color. This step is applicable to all patients.

The Nature of Goals

Goals are defined as the end toward which an action is directed. Goals are established to guide the actions of both the nurse and the client. Goal setting involves choosing certain alternatives over others. There may be constraints to achieving an ideal outcome and compromise may be necessary. Goal setting also involves making judgments. This process often evokes values. It must be agreed upon that the interactants' value systems are active factors in how goals are established and in what is done to achieve them. It must be recognized that the nurse may need to actively clarify the values as she works with the client on goal setting. Also, the norms of society influence the internalization of a value system and how one chooses to function.

Those who function in nursing are also carriers of the values and norms of their culture, and these values and norms necessarily come into operation when activities requiring goal setting, formulation of problems, or diagnosis of conditions are undertaken. If this is true, it may be difficult for nonminority nurses to work in ethnic communities because of the oppression and racism they represent to the patient and because of certain attitudes they may have acquired toward ethnic people of color. Often this aspect of the care relationship is negated, since nurses as caretakers are expected to perform adequately in whatever situation they are placed.

Mutual Goal Setting

In order to work productively with patients, prior to setting mutual goals, it is necessary for the nurse and patient to establish some rapport. Several suggestions have already been made to assist the nurse when working with ethnic people of color:

1. Awareness of one's own behavior, feelings, and value system in relation to a differing subculture is essential
2. Responding to the behavior of the patient in context without labeling is another principle
3. Recognizing that ethnic people of color manifest some behaviors as coping, adapting mechanisms in what is, for them, a hostile environment
4. Additionally, the nurse needs to be aware of, and be sensitive towards the subcultural differences when working with ethnic people of color

Banks cautions that one should not interpret all of the Black client's behavior in racial terms. The numerous interpersonal variables must be considered in determining what is really happening from the client's experiences and perceptions.[12]

In the following example, the patient manifests behaviors that result from living in a racist society. She also exhibits behavior that is reflective of problems experienced by most hospitalized mothers, regardless of ethnicity.

Information:

> *Mrs. J., a 30-year-old mother of three children: ages 3 years, 5 years, and 9 years was admitted to the hospital with a diagnosis of thrombophlebitis of the right calf. Her treatment consisted of strict bedrest.*

Problems:

> *Mrs. J. seemed depressed. She had been observed to change her nightgown two to three times each day. She frequently went to the lobby to see her children and friends. Although on "bedrest," she made constant trips to the telephone down the hall to call her children. She refused to participate in ward activities, and to stay in bed.*
>
> *What goals had been set up? By whom? Why didn't Mrs. J. follow medical and nursing advice? What might Mrs. J.'s goals be?*

New Information:

> *In a ward conference, the staff decided to take a more active part in getting Mrs. J. to comply with the order for complete bedrest. The L.V.N.* who was Black, related that she and the patient's physician had established rapport with the patient. She also observed that the white staff did not spend as much time with Mrs. J. as with white patients. Mrs. J. had told the L.V.N. that the white staff did not understand her anxieties. The L.V.N. also relayed the statement that child care had been arranged by the Social Service Department and that Mrs. J. had enough accrued sick leave and vacation to cover the absence from her job.*
>
> *With the new information, the staff decided to talk further with the patient to better understand her behavior. The questions posed were: "What might the patient's goals be?" "Why doesn't she adhere to treatment?."*
>
> *While talking with the patient, the L.V.N. was informed that Mrs. J. was not pleased with the child care that had been arranged. She was concerned about her children because she had worked hard to rear her children in a manner that would develop healthy egos and which would better enable them to deal with a world that was frequently*

*Comparable to L.P.N., dependent on geographic location within the United States.

hostile. Mrs. J.'s children represented one positive accomplishment in her life and to have them cared for by someone she didn't know was very difficult for her. Mrs. J.'s children helped to reinforce her sense of self-worth and her self-esteem.

Since it was difficult for the staff to understand Mrs. J.'s preoccupation with her job, the topic was discussed with the patient. It was found that, although Mrs. J. had successfully completed several job training programs, most of her employment had been in temporary jobs. Her current job was the first permanent position she had been able to secure, one that she enjoyed and wanted to keep. Because of her past experiences and the fact that she was Black, she feared she would be terminated, since she was the last hired.

In relation to her illness, Mrs. J. had always had a fear of having "bad veins." Her mother had worked long hours as a domestic and seasonal worker. Her mother had had a problem with varicose veins and eventually had to apply for disability. Mrs. J. correlated her mother's experience with her own episode of thrombophlebitis.

To compound these fears and anxieties, Mrs. J. hated the hospital. She felt she was being treated by the white staff as if she were invisible. In addition, she felt in a hopelessly dependent role. The staff was always doing for her and to her, never actively involving her in her own medical regime.

Questions:

Were treatment goals compatible with patient goals?
How might they be reconciled?
What might be done?
What might explain the frequent change of gowns?
What significance has it?
Why did Mrs. J. not share her concerns and anxieties with other staff?

What was done:

The head nurse met with Mrs. J.'s physician, the L.V.N., and other staff caring for the patient. The patient's physician and the L.V.N. welcomed an opportunity to address some of the cultural differences Black patients share which sometimes make it difficult for staff to manage patient care successfully. The staff decided they would: (1) explain her illness and its consequences to the patient's satisfaction; (2) call the public health nurse to assist the patient with the kind of child care that would be acceptable to her; and (3) contact her employer for information about the patient's job status. Prior to implementation, the staff validated with Mrs. J. that these plans were agreeable to her. In addition, it was decided that the ward activities (eg, needlepoint and games) were not appropriate for this patient. It was assessed that Mrs. J. enjoyed writing poetry, so supplies and encouragement were provided by staff. Ward activities were instituted that were more in line with the patient's interests.

Short-term goals:

1. *Arrange child care acceptable to patient*
2. *Clarify the patient's misconceptions about her illness*
3. *Provide ward activities in line with patient interests*

Long-term goal:

1. *Maintain patient on complete bedrest as long as medically advised*

The frequent changing of gowns was not explored further by the staff. There are a number of assumptions that can be made about this behavior. With the clarification and establishment of mutual goals, the patient began to follow through appropriately with her care plan. The frequent changing of gowns was determined to be more a staff problem than a patient problem.

The above example illustrates the manner in which professionals dominate with respect to the care of patients. Historically, in our society, we have held to the belief that medical and health care practice ought to be determined solely by providers, with their relationships to professional associations, educational and work institutions, and the government. The patient is regarded as having minimal influence and impact on what ought to happen in the care/cure process. Passive behaviors, while representing a diagnosis disease entity in psychiatry, is dictated as the professional assumes power over the patient's treatment. The patient is acted on and is expected to respond in a certain compliant way. This phenomenon is not restricted to health care, but it is also the expected norm in other professions ie, law, education, etc. This ideology tends to be an integral part of professional education and, afterwards, is reinforced in professional associations. Moore and Rosenbaum have discussed this professional posture in great detail. The assertion by academia and professional organizations is that clients are better served if the professional assumes power and control over the problems he has been asked to solve. Client passivity is not peculiar to medical and health care practice.[13] Talcott Parsons, a noted sociologist, has also conceptualized the necessity of professional dominance in the professional—patient relationship if the patient's medical problem is to be resolved.[14–16] The thinking and writings of Parsons has had a pervasive influence on medical and nursing education and practice. The naiveté of notions that power and control facilitate the care/cure process is amazing to the authors. If power and control over the client is assumed by professionals, stress is actually increased and adaptation and cure are prolonged.

Historically, the health care system has been provider oriented.

Acceptable, assessible, and available health services for ethnic people of color have not existed. Accountability to insure acceptable health services has rested with community groups, rather than with provider groups. Goals for health care services on the individual patient level, as well as on the community level, often have not been the same for the provider of service and the consumer of the service. Nursing is as much at fault as are the other health care providers. If nursing believes that health care is a right, nurses must more actively and aggressively involve patients in setting up and realizing mutually established goals of nursing care. Nursing education and administration will have to facilitate such a direction by providing the kinds of experiences which will allow such learning to occur. Moreover, nurses may have to confront traditional beliefs and customs as to who ought to set goals and to what end — the patient's or the provider's.

References

1. Stafford WW, Ladner J: Comprehensive planning and racism. J Am Inst Planners 35:68—74, March 1969
2. Stroud F, Bello T: Community nursing in racially oppressed communities. In Archer S, Fleshman R (eds): Community Health Nursing. North Satuate, Mass., Duxbury, 1975, Chapter 12
3. Newby IA: Jim Crow's Defense. Baton Rouge, La., Louisiana State Univ Press, 1965
4. Comer JP: White racism: its root, form and function. In Jones R (ed): Black Psychology. New York, Harper, 1972, pp 315—16
5. Friedson E: Client control and medical practice. Am J Sociol 65:374—82, 1969
6. Friedson E: Patient's Views of Medical Practice. New York, Russell Sage Foundation, 1961
7. Fanon F: A Dying Colonialism. New York, Grove, 1959, p 126
8. Roth J: The treatment of the sick. In Kosa J, et al (eds): Poverty and Health. Cambridge, Mass., Harvard Univ Press, 1169, p 230
9. Szasz TS, Hollender MH: A contribution to the philosophy of medicine. Arch Intern Med 97:585—92, 1956
10. Freeman RB: Community Health Nursing Practice. Philadelphia, Saunders, 1970, pp 61—71
11. Tinkham C, Voorhies E: Community Health Nursing: Evolution and Practice. New York, Appleton, 1972, pp 166—72
12. Banks WM: The black client and the helping professionals. In Jones R (ed): Black Psychology. New York, Harper, 1972, pp 205—11
13. Moore N, Rosenbaum G (eds): Professionalization. New York, 1970, Introduction
14. Parsons T: The Social System. Glencoe, Ill., Free Press, 1951, pp 428—79
15. Parsons T: Definitions of health and illness in the light of American values and social structure. In Jaco EG (ed): Patients, Physicians and Illness, 2nd ed. Glencoe, Ill., Free Press, 1972, pp 107—27
16. Parsons T: Illness and the role of the physician: A sociological perspective. Am J Orthopsychiatry 21:454—60, 1951

9

Nursing Assessment and Intervention

Phyllis Paxton,
Martina Carmen Ramirez,
and Esther Coto Walloch

THE NATURE OF MAN

Man may be viewed as a synthesis of heredity and environment into an adaptive energy system. Man is who he is genetically from time of conception, and he becomes who he is holistically through the process of adapting to the internal and external stresses of life. Holistic man is composed of a number of linked open energy systems that activate and mediate the human potential for life and living. Thus, the relationship between man and energy is coequal, and man is energy. Man does not have a limitless supply of energy. Energy stores must constantly be replenished to provide fuel for the demands of living. Each energy system is both a consumer and a provider of energy. The human organism enjoys a state of wellness when there is a balance between energy supply and demand (Fig. 9.1). Energy supplies and demands are both internal to man, and external from man. The energy systems are not arranged in hierarchical order, since all are seen as essential to life (the function of energy). Nevertheless, spiritual energy (supply and demand) is primarily external, whereas circulatory energy (supply and demand) is primarily internal.

Man strives to maintain a state of wellness by adapting to the stresses of life to create a balance between the supply of and demand for energy. Stress has been described by Hans Selye as the sum total of life's experiences that cause wear and tear on the body.[1] Stress, in itself, is not necessarily harmful or life threatening. The intensity of stress, genetic potential of the organism, capacity for adaptation, and the integrity of body energy all interact to determine whether the stresses of life will overtax the organism. When the organism is overtaxed, the energy systems

FIG. 9.1. Man and his energy systems

becomes depleted, and exhaustion occurs. Adaptation is man's mechanism for protecting the organism from exhaustion, which, if uninterrupted, leads to death.

Adaptation, according to Webster, is the process of changing (oneself) so that one's behaviors, attitudes, etc., will conform to new or changed circumstances. Adaptation may be defined as the biologic, psychologic, sociologic, and cultural responses of an individual in reaction to stress. Adaptive responses attempt to preserve or protect the human organism. The four categories of adaptive responses are not mutually exclusive. Superimposed on these overlapping categories of responses, it is noted that adaptation may also be automatic or conscious, localized or generalized, innate or learned (Fig. 9.2).

Innate responses are the natural survival defenses of the human organism. An example is the response of the reticuloendothelial system. Phagocytes formed in the bone marrow, spleen, liver, and lymph nodes act as natural defenses against bacteria, viruses, and other foreign substances.[2] Phagocytosis is innate, automatic, and initially localized. Automatic responses may be innate or learned. The psychologic defense mechanisms are examples of learned automatic responses. When transient defenses are made relative to particular threatening events, stress is reduced, and adaptation is localized. As the responses become pervasive, stress is increased by the energy required for the process of adaptation.

Jane B.'s employer gave her an assignment involving mathematical computations that was due in three days. Jane avoided math whenever it was feasible (she had had a number of traumatic experiences with her high school math courses, but managed to pass them). She labored over the assignment, but finished it the evening before it was due. Two weeks after Jane had given the completed report to her employer, she was called into his office. He voiced his frustration in discovering mathematical errors during his presentation of the report to the Board of Directors. In response to the boss's remarks, Jane stated that if she had been given the assignment sooner, she would

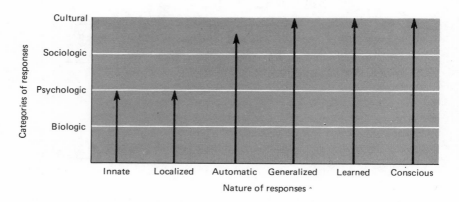

FIG. 9.2. Categories and origins of adaptive responses

have been able to recheck her figures. Jane's rationalization served to reduce anxiety and to preserve her ego. Approximately a year later, Jane's rationalization had become a pattern of life for her. She had been called on the carpet several times for the poor quality of her work, including frequent errors in reporting capital gains. Jane now daydreamed excuses for her poor performance. Prior to the completion of each assignment, she had identified several reasons why the work could not be acceptable. Finally, Jane was fired. Her rationalization become more and more pervasive. She eventually sought psychiatric help for insomnia that had its onset during the period of overuse of rationalization. Jane's rationalization as a response to the demands of her job progressed from automatic and localized to conscious and generalized. Jane's rationalization can be plotted (Fig. 9.3).

Biologic, psychologic, and sociologic adaptive responses are generally recognized and supported by health professionals. Cultural responses, though recognized by anthropologists as vital to the existence of a people, are generally either ignored or severely limited by health care delivery systems. Culture has served as an extremely potent adaptive mechanism throughout the history of man. Culture, the way of life for a people, has profound effects on the mediation of stresses on body energy. The various components of culture develop out of man's reaction to and interaction with his environment. Cultural development results in a built-in system for the elimination of behaviors that are harmful, and the development of behaviors that facilitate a relative harmonious existence for a people within a time frame. Culture is dynamic and evolves out of life experiences. If nursing is to be functional and relevant for a people, then nurses must be

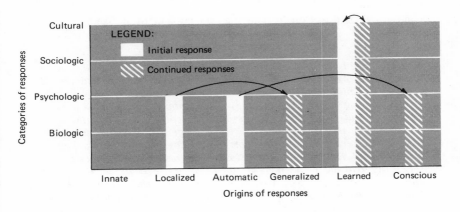

FIG. 9.3. Evolution of Jane's rationalization

able to include culture in the assessment and plan of care for each patient. This may be facilitated by a holistic nursing model.

HOLISTIC NURSING MODEL

The holistic model, and nursing models in general, may be difficult to operate unless the concept of modeling is internalized. Part of the problem with any model or approach to nursing care revolves around the human tendency to attempt to fit each patient behavior neatly into some segment of the model. In order to utilize a model effectively, the nurse must understand that a model is merely an incomplete miniaturization of the relationship of man to the environment, and of nursing to man and the environment. Realizing that the process of miniaturization deletes some of the intricacies of facts and relationships, the alert, sensitive nurse will be more able to fill in the gaps during each patient interaction. The holistic model is based on a problem-solving approach. It includes the patient and his significant others as active participants in the nursing process from assessment through evaluation. In this sense, the holistic model is akin to the mutual participation model discussed in Chapter 8. A holistic approach to nursing care recognizes the importance of the environment and prior episodes of repeated and/or intense stress on one's capacity for adaptation, and, hence on one's level of wellness. This text will focus on the points that need to be included to provide whole care (complete care) for people of color. Holism is facilitated when the nurse implements the nursing process in collaboration with the patient and his significant others. The first step in the nursing process is assessment. When assessment is done from a holistic framework, a number of individual differences in man's energy systems may be seen. Each configuration of energy supply and demand provides direction in planning and implementing health care (Fig. 9.4).

Mr. A. is a 24-year-old computer operator pursuing an M.S. degree in biostatistics. At 18, he married a high school sweetheart and vowed to give her all the nice things that her family had not been able to afford. Having heard that the key to economic success was a good education and hard work, he enrolled in college and maintained a full-time job until hospitalized with a diagnosis of duodenal ulcer. Assessment revealed excessive worry regarding debts and educational achievement. He viewed his employment as boring, tedious, and stated he had been feeling "drained" at the end of each day for approximately two years. Mr. A. was somewhat worried that he had fallen astray. Raised as a devout Catholic, he experienced conflict, between his religious beliefs and his zeal for attaining material goods. Further assessment revealed his family, basic belief in God, relatives, and social customs to be important to him as a source of comfort. Yet, he had not allowed himself to be comforted for a number of years. History, physical examination, x-ray, lab data, and GI series confirmed the diagnosis of duodenal ulcer. Support systems for restoring energy balance to the GI, chemical/fluid, circulatory, and restorative systems were identified as the family, social services, and hospital environment. With support of family and social service, he could allow himself to "rest — be restored" in the quiet hospital environment. He could assume the "sick role," which legitimized relief from the stresses of employment and school. His family, particularly his wife, assured him of his importance to her, far greater than the material goods he bestowed on her. With rest, relaxation, dietary management, and fluid/electrolyte replacement, energy balance was restored.

Mr. B., a 24-year-old musician, married with two daughters, was admitted to an acute hospital. Assessment data revealed that Mr. B. was the only son of the owner of a bakery, a family business of three generations. Mr. B. had had musical inclinations since elementary school when he first took piano lessons. Male musicians were frowned upon by his family. The culture placed high value on "hard work." Most of the men in the extended family were laborers or had family businesses, ie, garages, bakeries, shoe repair shops, etc. Although Mr. B. made a decent living, his occupation remained a source of irritation to friends and family. He avoided contact with his family because after each encounter he felt guilty for doing what he enjoyed doing. He was constantly pressured by his wife to make up with the family. Although raised as a Christian, the mention of church made him anxious. He experienced many sleepless nights debating his future. His main source of comfort and relaxation was school. There, being a good musician was esteemed and rewarded. Assessment revealed deficits in all energy systems. Only one support system was identified — the educational system. History, physical examination, x-ray and lab findings confirmed a diagnosis of duodenal ulcer. Dietary management and a plan of rest was implemented. Fluid and electrolytes were replaced. Balance was restored in the motor/sensory, fluid/chemical, circulatory, and GI systems. Mr. B. was discharged, only to return to the hospital six months later, in shock and requiring surgery.

Both Mr. A. and Mr. B. presented clinical pictures which were very similar. Holistic assessment, however, gave clues to the relative capacity for adaptation in both situations. In Mr. B.'s case, interactions should have included ego development and self-esteem building techniques. The facilitation of open communication within the family should have been attempted, since primary stresses evolved from conflicts between family expectations and Mr. B.'s personal goals. Medical management did not substantially improve Mr. B.'s level of wellness. Surgical intervention

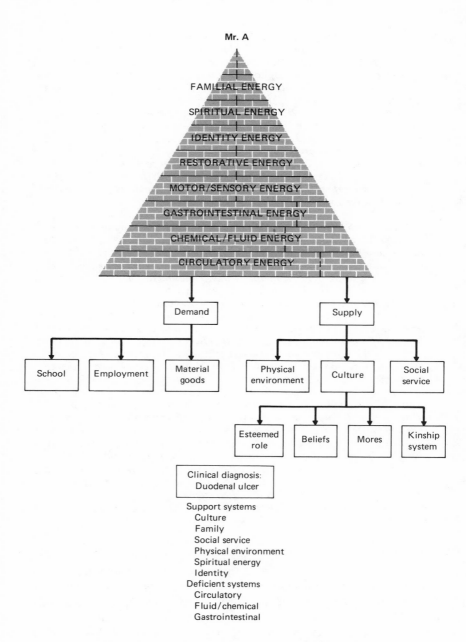

FIG. 9.4. Results of assessment from a holistic perspective

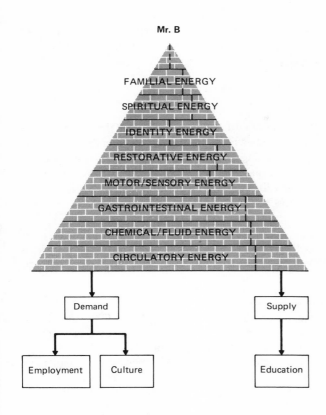

Mr. B

FAMILIAL ENERGY

SPIRITUAL ENERGY

IDENTITY ENERGY

RESTORATIVE ENERGY

MOTOR/SENSORY ENERGY

GASTROINTESTINAL ENERGY

CHEMICAL/FLUID ENERGY

CIRCULATORY ENERGY

Demand

Supply

Employment

Culture

Education

Clinical diagnosis:
Duodenal ulcer

Support systems
 Education
Deficient systems
 Culture
 Job
 Family
 Restorative
 Identity
 Spiritual
 Motor/Sensory
 Gastrointestinal
 Chemical/Fluid
 Circulatory

FIG. 9.4. (*cont.*)

(although life saving) did not deal with the primary cause of excessive energy demands. One might predict that the causes of illness would become manifest later in other organ systems.

ASSESSMENT

Assessment involves the processes of establishing a data base, collecting, ordering, and analyzing data. Assessment minimizes the chances of error in planning and implementing nursing care, and is necessary for the development of a clear picture of the patient's situation. Assessment is a function of the nurse, the patient, and his sphere of significant others. There are ten basic outcomes of cooperative assessment:

1. Diminishes errors in problem identification
2. Maintains the patient's free choice and powers of decision making
3. Provides a vehicle for planning of care that is relevant to each patient
4. Utilizes familial/affiliative support systems
5. Facilitates ego maintenance
6. Diminishes segmentation of treatment along biologic organ systems
7. Provides an atmosphere where all parties can agree and can risk disagreement on problems, priorities, and treatment
8. Provides a model of holistic assessment for members of the health team
9. Reduces the power of the nurse to act on the patient, and strengthens his/her power to act with the patient
10. Places responsibilities for care and cure on the appropriate persons, depending on each patient situation

The cooperative approach to nursing assessment may require modification due to the emergency of the situation and/or the patient's state of consciousness. When the health care professional becomes involved in singular assessment, he must be constantly alert for changes in the patient's capacity for input into the care/cure process.

The patient should be included in the process as soon as his condition allows. Assessment, without the input of the patient and his significant others, provides an incomplete data base for nursing action. The general areas for inclusion in the data base are listed in the illustration of the model (Fig. 9.5).

The data base must be complete and relevant if care plans and priorities are to reflect the true situation, and thus provide a safe approach to patient care. It is vitally important for each health care professional to recognize not only what areas need to be included in the data base, but also to recognize that the approach to gathering data must be one that is congruent with the culture of the patient. In other words, directive questioning may be appropriate for eliciting information from individuals of one ethnic group, and yet nondirective questioning may yield the best results from another ethnic group. An informal approach may communicate caring to one patient, but may communicate incompetency to another patient. Therefore, if the nurse is to develop the appropriate approach to patient care, including data collection, she/he must get direction from the authorities: patient's family, community action groups, and ethnic health care personnel.

Chief Complaint

The gathering of data on the chief complaint or reason for contact with the health care system needs to be expanded to include a number of relevant points in respect to ethnic people of color. The complaint or reason for the contact should always be from the client's perspective and should include his/her: (1) perception of the problem and/or need; (2) definition of wellness; and (3) definition of illness.

These data are important to the total situation; they may relate to other areas of need and to other factors facilitating action for improving the level of wellness.

History of Present Illness

In order to have a clear picture of the patient situation, one must recognize that ethnic people of color often rely on two systems for care and cure: the folk health system and the dominant health care system. Within the folk health care system, there are beliefs, treatment, etc., that are foreign to "professional" health care practitioners. Prior to problem solving with the patient, the health care practitioner must know what the client's beliefs and practices have been regarding the presenting situation. Data should include the client's:

1. Beliefs about the cause of the imbalance
2. Beliefs about the cure
3. Self medication
4. Self treatment
5. Treatment by family
6. Treatment by folk practitioners

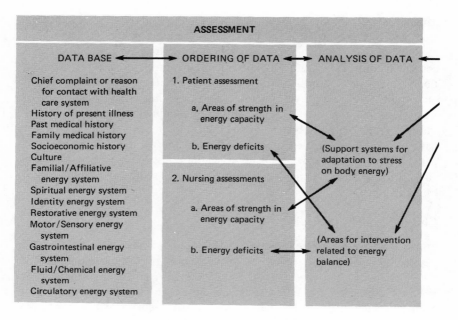

FIG. 9.5. Holistic model for nursing assessment and intervention

Past Medical History

The collection of data on past medical history should be expanded to include the aforementioned areas in relation to all prior imbalances, as well as information on previous contacts with the dominant health care system. Additional areas for inclusion are:

1. General feelings about previous experiences
2. Satisfaction with treatment
3. Assessment of whether past contact and/or treatment caused conflict
4. Assessment of whether past contact resulted in loss of status relative to family, occupation/avocation, etc.
5. Any changes in body image and/or self-esteem resulting from contact, care, and/or treatment
6. General health practices

The inclusion of the above areas will provide relevant data for the understanding of patient behavior which necessarily effects the nursing process.

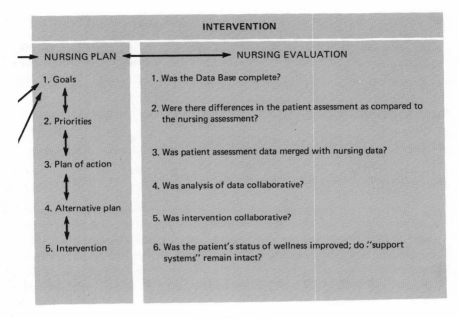

FIG. 9.5. (*cont.*)

Family History

The routine family history is geared to collect data on diseases that are familial, and on the general health status of family members. For ethnic people of color, data should also be collected relative to:

1. Family beliefs about causes of illness
2. Family beliefs about cures
3. Use of self-medication
4. Key persons in the family who assist in the care/cure process
5. Treatment of family members by folk practitioners
6. Family's definition of health
7. Family's definition of illness
8. General family health practices

Economic Status

Generally speaking, data on economic status are collected to determine whether a person qualifies for public subsidies. More often than not, data on income and resources are not related to the economic capacity of the person to afford the "hidden costs" of care, ie, transportation, baby sitting, loss of earnings, etc. Data on financial resources should be related to the client's capacity to "afford" the health care that is being sought. The nurse may need to assume the role of patient advocate to make the services affordable. As data are collected on financial resources and expenses, it is also important to ascertain:

1. Exposure to pollutants and carcinogens
2. Adequacy of housing
3. Adequacy of resources to obtain food
4. Adequacy of sanitation in the community

Poor people and ethnic people of color are frequently exposed to environmental diseases because, to meet their survival needs, they must assume hazardous occupations. Additionally, public services are often minimal in ethnic communities. Garbage collection is often less frequent; food products are often inferior; houses are often infested with insects and rodents; and codes regulating the use of lead paint, as well as general safety codes, are not enforced.

Culture

How does one elicit information on culture? Since culture is the way of life for people, if data are collected as described in the aforementioned areas, then the process has already begun. Additionally, data should be collected on the ethnicity of the client. Other areas for inclusion would be:

1. Cultural values, beliefs, and practices relative to wellness, illness, death, childbirth, child rearing, allocation of resources, male/female roles
2. Cultural preferences relative to music, food, art, recreation
3. Occupations esteemed by the culture
4. Behaviors valued by the culture
5. Cultural taboos and sanctions
6. Relative position of the client related to overall cultural systems (degree of belief and adherence)

Affiliative/Familiar Energy System

Affiliation is defined as the need to feel wanted, loved, and as a sense of belonging. This need can be met in a one-to-one relationship, by friends, or by a group that offers protection, nurturance, and support. The family is the obvious and traditional unit for fulfillment of affiliative needs, especially within the Spanish-speaking community which does not limit the choice of need fulfillment to the biologic family, but also includes any group of people perceived as providing a sense of belonging, such as the extended family, the larger community, social organizations, the church, and other groups, ie, gangs. Spanish-speaking groups seem to provide a strong sense of emotional security and sense of belonging to their members.[3] The extended family, as well as the nuclear family, play a primary role in meeting affiliative needs.

Needless to say, difficulties in communication are aggravated by the trauma of loss, injury, or illness, and become far more complicated by language barriers. The absence of meaningful verbal communication, combined with the trauma of circumstances, results in greater stress to the affiliative system. Stressors that may threaten or disrupt behavior balance are: loss of a significant relationship; unrealistic expectations from sources of need fulfillment; isolation from family and friends; perceptual distortions, ie, when the loved one doesn't perceive that he is loved, wanted, or belongs. It is painful to live without love. Living without love creates stress which manifests itself in loneliness, alienation, depression, illnesses, and it may result in suicide attempts.

Social circumstances greatly influence how one meets his or her affiliative needs, and these may be manifested both overtly and subtly. An example of this is the meeting of affiliative needs by gang members. Belonging to a gang may be the most appropriate means for fulfilling affiliative needs, especially when the family is poor and necessarily must focus its energy on obtaining basic commodities for survival, ie, food, clothing, rent, transportation, etc. Thus the role of the family in nurturing and protecting, beyond the survival level, is often superseded by the sheer demands of day-to-day life. Youths may seek alternatives for affiliative fulfillment, ie, peer allies and peer protection — especially in the streets.

Affiliative coping mechanisms may be positive for a particular environment, yet may be considered deviant by the dominant society. The failure of a nurse to understand the affiliative needs of a gang youth opens the door to countless misleading perceptions about the youth which seriously jeopardize the ability of the nurse to care adequately for the patient. Under such circumstances, a nurse may view a gang member as criminal or deviant because of his gang associations and fail to realize the necessary, vital function which the "gang family" has in the life of the youthful patient. It is, therefore, vitally important that a practitioner attempt to learn more about the many modes of meeting affiliative needs. While admittedly this may not always be an immediate possibility, an ethical practitioner must always provide humane and competent treatment and not be guided by personal prejudices or rejection of sociocultural patterns of behavior which the practitioner may consider to be personally repugnant or inferior. An immediate nursing intervention in this situation is to support the affiliative system of the patient, even though this may differ from the nurse's. A long-term intervention would be to serve as a patient and/or community advocate to facilitate the removal of barriers that hinder basic human need fulfillment. This means that a nurse must begin to assume roles that will reduce societal stressors and promote the well-being of the patient, the family, and the larger community.

It is important for the reader to understand that there are significant age, urban, rural, historical, political, and socioeconomic variables, as well as variables of acculturation and assimilation that effect affiliative behavior within each ethnic group. Nevertheless, for Chicanos and other Spanish-speaking people, the family is the most important social unit. This also seems to be true of other ethnic people of color (Asians, American Indians, and Blacks). All of the aforementioned groups and their subgroups operate within an extended family structure to a greater extent than does the dominant society.

The supportive role an extended family provides in nurturing an ill family member in a hospital setting is often viewed by the nursing staff as a nuisance. The patient, under these circumstances, is viewed as being too dependent on his or her family. Unfortunately, it is also often considered an indication of character weakness or immaturity for the patient to need or receive so much attention. As often happens, the family literally by sheer numbers surrounds the patient's bed "getting in the way" of the nurse when she is providing care. A member of a family unit needs the support of his family, especially in times of stress. The nurse can creatively explore new interventions in utilizing the patient's family or affiliative support to augment the care provided by the staff.

The nurse may need to assume an advocate role in the expansion of visiting hours and the inclusion of significant others in the care/cure process. Minimally, the nurse should provide support to the patient and his family. She should also gather information from the family that is significant in facilitating the necessary coping for health maintenance and/or healing. Simply stated, the clever, sensitive nurse would do well to understand that affiliative systems are often supporters of wellness for people of color. With this understanding, she will include the affiliative energy system in her schemata of assessment and intervention. Some points for assessment are listed below:

1. How many members are in your family? ages? occupations?

2. How often do you get a chance to be with your family for fun, relaxation?
3. Are family members a support to you when you are ill or upset?
4. When and under what circumstances do you feel lonely?
5. Are the people who are important to you too busy to be a comfort to you? If yes, what do you think will remedy this?
6. Who in your family do you worry about most? Why?
7. Do you feel you have the time or energy to love your family or friends? If no, what occupies your time?
8. Do you feel loved by family, friends?
9. Who are the people that you love? Do they know you love them?
10. When you need to come to the hospital or clinic does this interfere with your family's or friends' love for you?
11. Do you ever feel that you are a drain on your family?
12. Are you presently feeling blue? If yes, what is the cause?
13. What helps you when you feel blue?

The nurse must validate her impressions with the client. She must also be sensitive to verbal and nonverbal communications, and interactions between the patient and his family, associates, and friends. Do family, friends, associates support the patient? Does the patient derive comfort from his family? These observations and impressions necessitate validation with the patient.

Spiritual Energy System

Beliefs and values about man's relationship to man and the universe serve as a basis for both energy supply and demand. Values and mores regarding a way of life and the good of life, are embedded in religious/spiritual beliefs. Spiritual beliefs constitute an integral part of each man's existence. The pervasive concept about illness among people of color is that illness ensues when there is disharmony between the material and nonmaterial forces of life. The force of the "Spirit" is nonmaterial in nature, but it is manifested in materialism, ie, healthy body versus unhealthy body.

Man's belief system may either create or alleviate a biologic stress. Meditation has been demonstrated to decrease the basal metabolic rate (BMR) to the extent that less energy is required for the maintenance of life. The ability to utilize biofeedback mechanisms to identify and alleviate stress has been validated. Mind matter cannot be separated from body matter. Since concepts about illness and wellness are related to spiritual beliefs and practices, there are a number of questions that need to be included in patient assessment. The areas listed below may be used in initial assessment; other pertinent questions should be asked when appropriate.

1. Does the way people live have anything to do with health/illness? In what ways?
2. Have you ever felt that you were ill spiritually? Explain.
3. Do you feel that health and illness are divinely sent?
4. Does illness increase or decrease your spiritual contacts or beliefs?
5. Do your religious beliefs serve as a comfort to you?
6. Do your religious beliefs cause conflicts within you?
7. Are there religious ceremonies that are important in the prevention, treatment, and/or cure of illnesses?
8. Who are the important persons for ministering to your spiritual needs?
9. Have you ever had to go against your beliefs and values in order to get medical care?
10. Will you let us know if we suggest something to you that goes against your beliefs and/or religious practices?

Identity Energy System

In this discussion the term "identity" will be defined as one individual's personal, intimate perception of self. Identity is a dynamic state which changes or is altered according to events within the life cycle.[4] Identity encompasses one's body image, self-concept, sexuality, role achievements, and achievements in the numerous developmental tasks. The issue is not what one does, but what one feels. Does she or he feel good about herself or himself.

A person's sense of identity, whether it be realistic or unrealistic, or whether it depicts a gap between one's experience and awareness, still remains the foundation of a person's security and stability. If there is a great disparity between one's self-concept and one's "ideal" self-concept, this may result in problems of adjustment and adaptation. Incongruence between the real self and the ideal self places energy demands on the individual. The output of increasing units of energy to mediate the disparity may be disruptive to total body energy balance. How one views oneself and the world is central to the maintenance of behavioral balance. The need to value oneself positively is paramount.

Society and culture are determinants of a person's identity mediated through the family. American society fosters competition, acquisition, and a posture of individual achievement, rather than collaboration, sharing, and cooperative achievement. However, these values are not shared by all people within this society.

Ethnic people of color have their own unique values, orientations, and yardsticks of achievement, which differ from those of the dominant culture. For example, among Spanish-speaking people, a higher value is placed on experiencing one's own emotions and expressing and sharing such emotions. Great value is placed on utilizing one's full range of senses in experiencing the world. Thus, artistic and creative skills are more highly esteemed than the accomplishments of the businessman or financier.[5] The foregoing considerations have important implications for nursing care.

The expression of emotions by Spanish-speaking people is frequently viewed by the nursing staff as an indication of weakness and immaturity, or as a display of inferior traits. A point in case is the childbearing women in the labor and delivery setting. Latin women are apt to be more verbally expressive of the sensations of labor and delivery. Derogatory remarks are often made by both nurses and physicians when caring for Latin women in labor. The derogatory remarks are reflective of negative attitudes that people form about behaviors which are different or foreign to them.

It is, of course, realized that some attempts are being made within institutions to rectify these problems. Meanwhile, ethnic people of color continue to be alienated and suffer from the esteem-reducing actions and attitudes of health care professionals. Unfortunately, the self-image and self-worth of ethnic people of color is constantly being attacked and undermined.

The media, educational, judicial, health care, and other social systems do not foster positive self-images for people of color. Rather, these systems can be and generally are detrimental to the formation and maintenance of a positive self-concept for the client. Furthermore, the client often has to deal with dual discrimination in view of his poverty and ethnicity. A significant number of American Indians, Blacks, Chicanos, and Puerto Ricans still suffer the most intense conditions of poverty.[6] The state of poverty often impinges on role achievement, and how one achieves in a number of his roles has a great impact on feelings of self-worth.

Each individual operates within a number of roles simultaneously. When internalized expectations for role performance are not met, one suffers from guilt about lack of achievement. Thus, the level of achievement may reduce self-esteem. The internalization of expectations relative to role performance is influenced by what society and culture dictates to be the norm.

The societal norms for role performance may be in conflict with the cultural norms and mores. Therefore, role conflict may ensue. Role conflict may also ensue as one tries to juggle his time and energies to meet the obligations of a number of roles simultaneously.

When an individual makes contact with the health care system, it is important to ascertain what, if any, effect the care/cure process will have on role achievement and, hence feelings of self-worth. Esteem-reducing actions should be avoided.

Human beings are sexual animals. One's feelings about his/her sexuality are very basic and important to feelings of self-worth. The self-image is formed simultaneously with sexuality and sex-role identification. An important area for assessment relates to body image and hazards to maintenance of an intact body image when the patient or client is involved in the care/cure process.

Culture, mediated through the family, influences one's notions about masculinity and femininity. An example of cultural influence is seen in the Spanish-speaking people with the prescription of male roles ("macho" meaning maleness). Along with the prescription come the connotations of strength, power, and virility. This is especially true of first-and second-generation Chicanos. However, the roles of the young men and women are changing, and women are becoming more assertive in some domains that were previously relegated to the men. This change of course is not true for all Chicanas. There are age, geographic region, urban—rural, and socio-economic variables that affect the concepts of masculinity and femininity.

A first-generation Chicana from a province would most likely seek to meet her needs for achievement through her husband, children, and home. She might be modest and reserved about discussing her personal life, especially in the sexual domain. She might prefer to have her children delivered by a midwife and might be more comfortable seeing a female physician for health maintenance. Religion may be an important part of her life.

The point is that roles are tied into culture, and it is important for the nurse to understand the cultural heritage of the populations she/he serves. The nurse must furthermore understand how critical it is when a woman in the above situation loses her husband and the severity of stress she suffers. The client then needs an enormous amount of support and nurturance in the adjustment to her role loss.

Identity problems usually center on feelings of lack of achievement, lack of self-worth, and lack of a stable sense of belonging and love. It is important to note that what is considered healthy or normal must take into account the fortunes and experiences of life. In caring for people of color it is important for the nurse to understand that her patients have had to deal with societal stressors which she (the nurse) may never have experienced. The patient may respond to illness and stress in a way that the nurse may consider to be unhealthy or deviant. In fact, the patient may be using adaptive mechanisms appropriate to his or her realm of experience. Anger and the expression of anger, mistrust and hostility directed toward hospital authority figures and personnel may be a very natural response in consideration of a foreign, frightening, and mistrusted environment. The patient's life experiences may have dictated the development of the above behaviors for survival in a society which devalues him. Such patient responses usually frighten or anger the nursing staff, which results in further isolation and avoidance of the patient. It is important for the nurse to recognize that she may not be the direct target of expressed emotions. Most importantly, the nurse must support and maintain the patient's adaptive mechanisms remembering that, when patients are allowed to respond, their anxiety is lessened. Sympathy, kindness, and loving care go a long way in helping a patient's healing processes in an environment which the patient may consider as interfering with the maintenance of identity.

The major factors that are important to one's intimate perception of the self are presented in Figure 9.6.

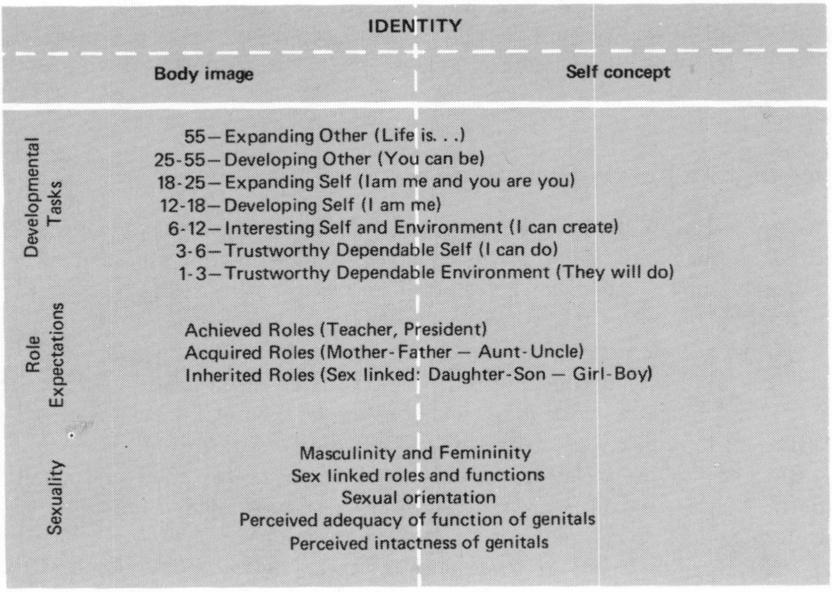

IDENTITY

| Body image | Self concept |

Developmental Tasks
- 55 — Expanding Other (Life is. . .)
- 25-55 — Developing Other (You can be)
- 18-25 — Expanding Self (I am me and you are you)
- 12-18 — Developing Self (I am me)
- 6-12 — Interesting Self and Environment (I can create)
- 3-6 — Trustworthy Dependable Self (I can do)
- 1-3 — Trustworthy Dependable Environment (They will do)

Role Expectations
- Achieved Roles (Teacher, President)
- Acquired Roles (Mother-Father — Aunt-Uncle)
- Inherited Roles (Sex linked: Daughter-Son — Girl-Boy)

Sexuality
- Masculinity and Femininity
- Sex linked roles and functions
- Sexual orientation
- Perceived adequacy of function of genitals
- Perceived intactness of genitals

FIG. 9.6: Identity formation

In order to assess the patient's perception of the self, the nurse needs to include a number of areas in her schemata. Examples of areas for assessment include

1. What kind of work do you do?
2. How do you feel about your work (satisfied, proud, dissatisfied)?
3. What are your ambitions?
4. Do you consider yourself an ambitious person?
5. Do you feel others see you as an ambitious person?
6. Do you like yourself — looks, actions, etc.?
7. What do you like most about yourself?
8. What are the things that you have done that make you feel proud?
9. As a _____ (insert various roles — mother, father, wife, teacher, patient, etc.), how do you feel about the way you function or act?
10. What things make it difficult for you to feel satisfied as a _____ (insert roles)?
11. Are you glad you are a woman (man)?
12. Do you feel pride in being a woman (man)?
13. Are your sexual relationships satisfying?
14. What would make you feel more satisfied with yourself?
15. If we suggest that you do something that you know will make you feel bad about yourself (now or in the future) will you let us know?

Restorative Energy System

"Sweet dreams" are the gentle words of good night spoken by mother to child, husband to wife, lover to lover, etc. — two words that, when sincerely spoken, engender a feeling of security, peace, and human warmth within the bosom of the would-be sleeper.

It is not necessary to refer to the extensive scientific and technical research available to conclude that a good night's sleep is both essential to one's health and indicative of such health. Our basic human experiences attest to this reality. Since sleep is a fortifier, the patient in the hospital setting has an even clearer, indeed impelling, need for good and natural sleep. A sweet dream or two, in addition to a good night's repose, is also truly beneficial to the recovery of the ill or injured person.

The Spanish words *"buenas noches"* mean "good night"; even if the Chicano or Puerto Rican patient is bilingual, it is still nice and soothing to hear the evening salutation in one's mother tongue, if the words are sincerely spoken. Old or young, male or female, the Latino patient almost always comes from a close knit family, which does its best to verbally reassure and nurture a feeling of well-being before the lights go out. This same nurturance by health care professionals would go a long way in facilitating the restorative powers of sleep.

The words *"buenos dias, tuvo sueños dulces"* means "good morning, did you have sweet dreams?" Such words and sentiments are similarly welcome to the Latino patient as the day commences. The clever and perceptive nurse will also readily understand that the quality and nature of the patient's dreams (eg, sweet dreams or nightmares) offer a very important insight into the patient's overall restorative integrity. Thus, the nurse would do well to listen and attempt to understand the patient's response. Regardless of the language of the patient, the nurse must become familiar with the basic conversational phrases and sentences related to activities of daily living. Sleep and dream patterns should be included in the assessment of the restorative energy system.

1. How many hours do you sleep a day? Have you been able to maintain this while in the hospital — or since you have not been feeling well?
2. What time do you usually go to bed and get up at home?
3. What time are you going to bed now?
4. Would you say that you are a light or heavy sleeper?
5. Have you had any problems with sleeping? If so, describe.
6. Are you presently having problems sleeping? If so, describe.
7. Do you usually dream? If so, do you have nightmares and/or recurring dreams? Describe them. Do any recurring dreams coincide with events of your conscious life? Describe the relationship of your dreams to life's events.*

Music, although perceived as loud, annoying, and disruptive by the nurse, may serve as a very important choice for facilitation of restorative need fulfillment for the ethnic patient of color. Often hospital policies require lights out, radios and televisions off at 9:00 or 10:00 P.M. For many ethnic people of color, this practice may actually hinder sleep. The patient may be accustomed to finding sweet dreams mixed in the tunes of mariachis or drums. Sleep in a quiet environment may be next to impossible. If all patients are assessed relative to what facilitates sleep, rooming can be planned so that patients with similar sleep patterns will not need to be restricted from their usual patterns of sleep, and hence rest. Additional areas for assessment are:

8. Does music help you go to sleep, if so what kind?

*These areas may be indicative of severe disruption in the restorative energy system. Sleep may actually create more stress if tainted with recurring dreams or nightmares.

9. What seems to prevent you from sleeping?
10. What can we do to help you sleep or rest?
11. What can family or friends do to help you sleep and rest?

Skin care serves a number of important therapeutic functions. It may improve circulation, facilitate elimination via the skin, and relax tense and strained muscles. Often the hospital routine dictates that the bath be given during the morning hours. This practice may be foreign to many patients, and a bath and backrub just prior to retiring may eliminate the need for the sleeping pill. The nurse should be cognizant of the fact that any forced change in activity patterns engender feelings of powerlessness and increases anxiety. Thus, energy that would be well spent on recuperation is wasted on worry.

The conscientious nurse will add the following areas to her schemata of assessment:

12. When (at what time) do you prefer to have your bath or shower?
13. Are there routines that should be done along with the washing of the body? Are there important people who should participate in the bath?*
14. Does a bath or shower help you rest?
15. Have you ever had a backrub?
16. Will you try a backrub to help you rest?

Although the bed bath is a function that is taught early in nursing school, the importance of making a general assessment of the body surfaces during the bath is often left within the doors of the classroom. The nurse should be alert to skin changes that may indicate disruption in one or more energy systems: rashes, petechiae, ecchymosis, cyanosis, jaundice, abrasions, ulcers, etc. The nurse should also understand that the epidermis is constantly shedding dead skin. The shedding skin of Black and brown patients may appear to be "dirt" to the inexperienced nurse. Black or brown flakes on a white washcloth are not indicative of the need to bathe and rebathe the patient. The nurse would do well to bathe all patients throughly, avoid overexposure, and recognize that washing removes shedding skin, which is not necessarily white.

Hair care is important for restorative, as well as identity integrity. The hair of Black patients is often neglected, because the nurse does not know how to care for Black hair. The nurse should empirically recognize that the hair of Blacks vary in texture from straight to kinky. The reason is the

---

In some cultures, the bathing of the ill person is a part of a religious curative ceremony.

differences in the structure of the protein molecules that make up the hair. The nurse should ask the patient or his family what is usually done relative to cleaning, styling, and oiling the hair. Here the nurse must become the student; the patient and his family become the teachers. Some hints for the care of kinky hair are:

Determine the usual practices for hair care

Obtain necessary materials — combs, brushes, rollers, hair oils, etc.

Shampoo and condition hair according to the patient's or family's preference and/or instructions

Use a large toothed comb, and comb hair in small sections before the hair dries

Towel dry or use a electric dryer

Comb the hair again in small sections before it is completely dry

Separate the hair in small sections, using the teeth of the comb and apply hair grooming preparation (as identified by patient or family — if specific preparation is not available, vaseline may be used in small amounts)

Comb the hair and braid, or roll the hair if indicated by gender or preference of the patient

Each patient should have his hair combed daily as a part of general grooming and hygiene. The frequency of shampooing is dictated by the patient, his family, and the severity of his dysfunction.

Folliculitis in the Black man may be caused or aggravated by shaving with an electric or hand razor. The nurse should never shave a Black man prior to determining what his usual practice is, assessing the skin for signs of folliculitis, and having him participate in deciding how the shave should be done. It may be necessary for the nurse to apply a depilatory to remove hair from the face, as opposed to the use of a razor. The nurse, using a depilatory, must avoid the eyes, nose, mouth, and ears while applying and removing the preparation. If a depilatory is usually used, and the skin shows signs of folliculitis, then the preparation should be avoided to identify possible sensitivity to chemicals in the depilatory.

Restoration or the replenishment of body energy stores is facilitated by a number of activities (from sleep to vigorous exercise). The authors have only focused on a few areas which seem to be ignored or misunderstood as nurses provide care to ethnic people of color.

Motor/Sensory Energy System

The nervous system, including the brain and musculoskeletal network, are all involved in generating energy for motor and sensory functions. This source of energy is worthy of mention in this text specifically in relation to the growth and development of children.

Each child in this country spends most of his time in the educational system during the formative years. One frequently questions the measurement of intelligence and the definition of intelligence prevalent in the educational system. Since this system has an enormous effect on the shaping of values and biases, it is important for every nurse to examine her own values and biases, as related to causes of "dullness" or problems in motor function. Concept formation is also questioned as it relates to ethnic people of color. Developmental task accomplishment is often used as a measure of mental capacity. Norms for intelligence tests, concept formation, and developmental tasks all reflect white middle-class experiences and values.

Numerous individuals have grown into adulthood with the mislabel of mental retardation. This labeling often resulted from testing with instruments that were inadequate for the measurement of intellectual capacity of ethnic people of color.

One of the authors recalls a nursing faculty conference where she heard two beautiful poems depicting life. The footnote provided by the speaker was that the poems were written by a "mentally retarded" Chicano youth. Clearly, the quality of the poetry indicated creative ability and a powerful grasp of metaphors. The poetry was clearly the work of a powerful intellect. Why then had the youth been labeled "mentally retarded?"

The ability to form concepts is only one indicator, but a very important one, of intellectual capacity. Concept formation is affected by culture – the way of life for a people. The ability to form abstract concepts has been, and still is considered to be a function of intelligence. The authors have frequently heard from educators that Blacks, Chicanos, and Puerto Ricans are not able to develop or manipulate abstractions. This remains to be a gross misunderstanding of abstract concept formation related to the aforementioned ethnic groups. Abstraction is not a problem for ethnic people of color. Abstractions different from those of the dominant society are frequently used. For example, concepts of healing are not necessarily tied to the germ theory cause – effect relationship in folk health care systems. Higher levels of abstraction have been developed. Although one cannot see the Spirit, one is able to conceptualize the power of the Spirit and/or energy forces in causing and curing of diseases. Research has validated the existence of energy forces, and documentation is available in *Psychic Discoveries Behind the Iron Curtain.*[7] Prior to documentation, ethnic people of color have defined "dis-ease" as an imbalance in body energy. Concepts about care and cure are often abstract, yet understood, and believed by ethnic people of color. There does not seem to be the need to identify a "tangible" carrier of the cause of the dis-ease. So, in this sense, abstraction is much greater than is true of the concrete disease theories of the dominant society. The point is that dominant societal tools do not measure abstract ability and concept formation for ethnic people of color. The nurse should then recognize that ethnic patients of color who have been diagnosed as mentally retarded may have been the victims of inadequate assessment.

Although we know empirically that Black children generally sit, stand, and walk at an earlier age than is true for the dominant society, there is no completed developmental scale for Blacks, Latinos, Asians, or American Indians. Therefore, the nurse must go to the experts (the family) when assessing the developmental level of ethnic children of color.

Exposure to lead is an important area of assessment when caring for poor children. Since many of the children of the poor are also American Indian, Asian, Black, or Latino, then assessment of children of color should include questions to determine exposure to lead. The greatest incidence of lead poisoning occurs in children living in old houses within the inner cities of our country. Areas for assessment include:

1. Description of the home — any chipped paint, exposed pipes?
2. Is child seen licking or chewing on wall or fixture breakages?
3. Where does child spend most of his waking hours?
4. Description of housing — any vacant lots nearby where child goes to play? If so, are there any discarded planks, pipes, etc.?
5. Has child been around newly painted buildings, houses?*

Frequent exposure to lead may produce signs and symptoms of "dullness," thus the child may be viewed as mentally deficient when he actually is the victim of a poverty-perpetuated disease.

Nutritional integrity is important for optimum functioning of the motor/sensory energy system. When caring for ethnic people of color, it is important for the nurse to do a thorough assessment of the relationship of nutrition to signs of dysfunction in all systems. Is alertness or lack of alertness related to nutritional intake or utilization (refer to assessment of gastrointestinal system — cultural food patterns — fluid/chemical system)?

Lack of visual acuity and deafness are two dysfunctions that may lead to the misdiagnosis of mental retardation. Since the problem of misdiagnosis of mental retardation is so widespread, the nurse must be aware of the common factors that influence the misdiagnosis. Areas for inclusion when patients seem "dull" are hearing and eye tests.

Motor/sensory integrity assessment cannot be done with accuracy unless the nurse recognizes that there are a number of factors that influence motor/sensory function, and that the whole notion of intelligence has greatly

Lead paint is still used for exterior painting in some locales.

decreased the objectivity of the "professional" in making diagnosis. Generally speaking, assessment of motor/sensory function has the same parameters for all people, regardless of color, one must be willing and able to place personal biases outside the parameters of assessment.

Gastrointestinal Energy System

The ability to resist and recover from energy imbalance is greatly influenced by the nutritional and eliminative integrity of an individual. As with all biologic energy systems, the gastrointestinal system both supplies energy for life and consumes energy. The maintenance of integrity is dependent on the adequacy of nutrients ingested, digested, secreted, absorbed, and eliminated. The nutritional integrity reflects the adequacy or inadequacy of a person's diet in supplying the nutrients essential for energy input, life, and well-being. From birth to death, food is a dominant factor in our lives. Food does more than just supply nutrients necessary for energy.

Food, for most, produces feelings of security and happiness. Food is used as a link to friendship, as an expression of pleasure, and as a symbol of religious beliefs. Therefore, the modes of meeting the energy input demands are related to many factors: biologic, sociologic, psychologic, cultural, regional, economic, and religious. The rituals associated with eating are deeply ingrained in patterns affected by all factors. During the assessment process, the examiner should look not only at an individual's diet, but he should consider the various factors that influence the nutritional integrity of an individual.

Problems which affect the gastrointestinal energy system vary widely and have many interrelated causes. Malnutrition is the forerunner of many of the problems. Insufficient nutrient intake is the major problem in many parts of the world, usually wherever there is poverty. Insufficient nutrition produces anemias that decrease the body's energy defense system. This lowering of the defense system increases body susceptibility to a multitude of diseases. The effects of malnutrition may be concealed for a long time. There may be little or no physical sign, and many times the symptoms are so ill-defined that the patient does not seek help. Usually people of lower socioeconomic levels have other more demanding crises that supersede a visit to the physician or clinic. Malnutrition should always be suspected when a patient presents signs and symptoms of weight loss; dry, rough, inelastic, and wrinkled skin; dry, brittle, falling, or breaking hair; fatigue and lack of energy. Generally, the cause of malnutrition in people of color is one of economics.

A 60-year-old male was admitted to an acute general hospital with signs and symptoms of excessive weight loss; weakness; fatigue; skin dry, inelastic, and wrinkled; skin pale in color. When asked by the medical team what was causing his problem, he responded that he "couldn't eat." A complete regime of studies proceeded. All the results were negative except for C.B.C. Two weeks later, an obvious improvement was noticed. He had gradually gained weight. A nurse, in doing a nursing assessment, asked him why he couldn't eat. He responded that he was broke and was unable to find any type of employment; therefore he didn't have any money to buy food. He said he was new to the city and was not aware of any other resources.

The nurse when assessing for gastrointestinal energy system dysfunction should be skilled in assessing dark-skinned individuals for any signs of jaundice. Jaundice, or icterus, is the yellowish pigmentation of the skin when bile pigments discolor the plasma, skin, and the mucous membranes with yellow coloration. Jaundice may be the first and only manifestation of a dysfunction of the gastrointestinal energy system. Jaundice is a symptom of a disease itself and may arise from various causes. It is therefore very important that early signs of jaundice be picked up by an examiner because knowledge of the cause or of the circumstances under which jaundice arises in any particular situation often gives insight into its real nature. Jaundice in the dark-skinned person may be observed in yellow discoloration of the conjunctiva. Since many dark-skinned individuals have carotene deposits in the subconjunctival fat and sclera, the hard palate may serve as an adjunct for assessment.[8] The lips and tip of the nose may be compressed with a glass slide to facilitate the assessment of jaundice. If any sign of jaundice is discovered, laboratory tests should be ordered to assist in the diagnosis.

There are some dysfunctions of the gastrointestinal energy system that are more prevalent in some cultures. Gallbladder disease is a problem commonly found in people of Spanish descent, especially in individulas of Mexican descent. Some studies and current research point to genetic etiology. Since the research in this area has been quite scanty, increased research is needed. Choledocholithiasis has been found in individuals as young as 16 years of age. Assessment should include questions related to discomfort associated with eating patterns, as well as history of gastrointestinal dysfunctions. Questions posed should be those routinely asked which are necessary for a complete data base:

1. What is the pattern of pain?
2. What is the character of pain?
3. Does pain occur after a fatty meal?
4. What are the characteristics of stool and urine?
5. Are home remedies/herbs used for relief of discomfort?

If the patient is of Mexican descent, questions posed should be in relation to *"empacho"* as discussed in Chapter 3. *"Empacho"* is a common gastrointestinal illness that is treated by the *curandero*.

When the symptoms of gallbladder disease are mild and do not necessitate further studies or surgical intervention, an accurate assessment of food patterns and diet should be carried out prior to dietary treatment. Treatment with diet should include foods available to the patient. No foreign foods should be introduced, and foods that conflict with the individual's religion, culture, and economics should not be introduced. The nurse should be skilled in working with the individual, taking into account all the various factors that affect his nutritional integrity. The incidence of gastrointestinal cancer in Asians is significant. Some current research points to the powder found in rice as an etiologic factor. This powder carries particles of asbestos, a known carcinogen. Chronic exposure is seen to increase the chances of cancer. Any signs or symptoms assessed of gastrointestinal dysfunction should be followed with the appropriate diagnostic test. To maintain or support the patient's adaptive responses, the patient should be instructed to carefully wash the rice before cooking.

Monosodium glutamate is known to cause unusual symptoms in some Filipinos. These signs and symptoms are usually described as generalized hot flashes, dizziness, and some nausea. When a patient presents these complaints, some questions to be considered are:

1. Do the symptoms occur after eating (hot flashes, dizziness, and nausea)?
2. Do they occur after eating certain foods?
3. Is monosodium glutamate added to foods during preparation?

Generally, treatments related to gastrointestinal energy system dysfunction includes dietary management. The goal of treatment may be to augment, maintain support, or restore adaptation. Problems of communication rate high in the group of obstacles encountered in dietary treatment. The breakdown in communication is often the precursor of breakdown in the treatment process. It is therefore necessary that during the assessment process, language be used that is clear, concise, and simple. The nurse should be constantly alert to behavioral indications which suggest that the message is not getting across. In many Spanish-speaking individuals, "yes" is frequently used, but only because the use of "yes" has been positively reinforced during interviews by the health personnel's verbal and nonverbal communication. In the dietary treatment of gastrointestinal dysfunction, communication, verbal or written, is a major aspect of the treatment. The following example demonstrates the fact that a breakdown in communication is a breakdown in treatment.

Mrs. S. C., a 30-year-old Mexican-American, brought her 10-month-old baby girl to the clinic because the baby was listless and not as active as her other three children had been at this age. Upon immediate visualization of the infant, it was obvious that the infant was extremely anemic. The color of the infant's skin was pale. Upon applying pressure to skin and nail beds for capillary filling, no noticeable differences were noted after the pressure was applied. The hemoglobin was 2.9 g. She was admitted to the hospital for treatment. Upon questioning the mother, the nurse learned that the family members were farm workers. This infant was the first baby that the mother had not been able to breast feed. When discharged from the hospital, the mother had been given thorough instruction on preparing the baby's formula. The mother had been told not to feed the child any other foods. No follow-up clinic visit had been made, and the family had moved to the next crop farm. The baby had been fed the 2:1 water–milk ratio formula for 10 months.

In augmenting, supporting, maintaining, or restoring the gastrointestinal energy system by dietary means, the psychologic value of food should be highly considered. Food acceptance is greatly determined by psychologic, sociologic, and cultural factors. As frequently documented, food is the focus of emotional associations, a mechanism for interpersonal relations, and is used in the communication of love and affection. This is especially true for people of color. Food practices among ethnic people of color play an important role in their lives. Attempting to change food preferences is likened to attempting to change the individual. It is extremely important for nurses to recognize food preferences for therapeutic dietary management. The data base for ethnic people of color should be expanded to include the following questions:

1. What times during the day do you usually eat?
2. Do you prefer eating with someone else?
3. Are there any circumstances that make you want to eat?
4. What takes your appetite away?
5. What foods do you like most?
6. What food do you like least?
7. What foods are neutral?
8. What seasonings do you use regularly in preparing your food?

A diet history is an extremely valuable adjunct to the above questions. The nurse should ask the client to list all of the foods eaten for a one-week period. Notation should also be made of the time of each meal. These data may serve as a point of comparison for other data. Discrepancy between what the desired foods are and the foods actually ingested should be noted. The question is: Why aren't desired foods ingested? Are there problems of economics, time, etc.? Are desired foods inaccessible for other reasons?

Each health care facility should have a list of therapeutic diets adapted to the major ethnic groups of the locale. When additional dietary modification is necessary because of the extent of the dysfunction or distinctiveness of the patient's "usual" dietary pattern and/or intake, a dietician should be consulted without hesitation.

Fluid/Chemical Energy System

Body fluid is the homeostatic agent that is most important for energy integrity. The fluids of the body serve to transport other important regulators of body function. The life of the human organism is dependent on the adequate performance of body fluids for the transportation of nutrients, temperature regulation, chemical regulation, and the excretion of the products of metabolism.[9]

The kidneys, skin, endocrine glands, gastrointestinal system, and lungs are the chief fluid regulatory systems. These systems are closely related, and dynamic interaction among them is important for maintaining a balance between total body energy supply and demand.[9]

Relative to ethnic people of color, there are a number of signs, symptoms, and disease processes that warrant discussion. Dehydration is always a sign of impairment of total body function, since fluid is necessary for cellular processes.[9] Dehydration in the infant is frequently seen as a result of gastroenteritis. Inadequate garbage disposal, plumbing (mixing of sewage with water used for drinking and cooking), and facilities for handwashing are factors that frequently produce gastroenteritis. Assessment generally includes the evaluation of serum electrolytes, weight loss, inspection of the skin and mucous membranes; however, data related to constant exposure to pathogens in the environment are rarely collected. When data are collected, one can easily see that primary prevention takes on a social flavor. The nurse must be able to serve as patient advocate to remove the constant threat of infection.

Diabetes mellitus may pose a special problem to American Indians, Blacks, and Latinos. Their basic diets are generally high in carbohydrates, and the diabetic diet is often bland and unappealing. Since dietary teaching is a function that is often the nurse's responsibility, he/she should have available a comprehensive nutrition text for reference. When foods identified by the patient as his usual or desired intake are not included in the text, a dietician should be consulted. Some dieticians may be reluctant to make recommended adjustments in the patient's diet because of their own lack of knowledge about the nutritional value of foods foreign to them. As requests for therapeutic diets based on food preferences increase, most dieticians will recognize their own deficiencies and seek the information needed to be effective in their professional role. Therefore, it is incumbent upon nurses to require accountability of dieticians to the patient population and the larger community.

It is extremely important for the nurse to not only assess the presence of glucose and ketones in the urine of the diabetic patient, but an evaluation of "hidden cost" of this chronic progressive dysfunction is also important. For low income people, absence from work usually means a real loss in dollars and cents. Poor people are most often likely to be employed without compensations such as paid sick leave or annual leave. Loss of productivity of one family member generally adversely affects all other family members; the stress of survival becomes distributed among fewer persons. This is not to say that all ethnic people of color with diabetes have economic problems superimposed on the disease process. Nevertheless, the majority of ethnic people of color are poor.

Pruritis associated with diabetes often leads to scratching and skin ulcerations. The intensity of skin tone of ethnic people of color may obscure lesions of the groin and axillae. The diabetic patient should be asked to identify sites of itching. Inspection in a well-lighted room should be combined with palpation for surface lesions. The patient should be asked whether he has observed any changes in the skin color or texture. Finally, the patient should be encouraged to inspect daily the body surfaces including the groin and axillae to detect the early development of skin lesions. Since modesty is esteemed in some cultures, the nurse must first assess how comfortable it is for the patient to purposefully inspect the genitals.

Myxedema, although not generally discussed in the context of ethnicity or poverty, bears mentioning in this text. Adult hypothyroidism (myxedema) is often tentatively diagnosed by the general appearance of the patient coupled with history data. Overt signs and symptoms of the dysfunction are overlooked, especially in Blacks. The characteristic broadening of features of the patient with myxedema may be obscured by the nurse's or physician's notions about characteristic features of Blacks. Complaints of weight gain, fatigue, and shortness of breath may be correlated with other stereotyped notions about Blacks. One of the authors personally knows of four cases where myxedema was not diagnosed and treated until the patients were examined by Black physicians. The overall frequency of misdiagnosis is not known.

Rickets, a deficiency in vitamin D which interferes with calcium and phosphorus absorption, occurs most frequently in inner-city children. The diets of poor children are frequently deficient in vitamin D, calcium, and phosphorus. Additionally, exposure to sunlight (for the formation of vitamin D) may be limited because of parental fears about allowing the children out of doors to play in the streets or vacant lots. Here again, one may visually be able to pick up clues related to the dysfunction. One of the characteristic signs of rickets is bowed legs. Dietary history may also reveal lack of ingestion of foods containing sufficient amounts of vitamin D, calcium, and phosphorus.

Reproductive disorders, whether related to dysfunction of hormone secretion, structural disorders, or psychogenic dysfunction may pose a special problem for ethnic people of color. Motherhood and the ability to conceive is still highly valued by the traditional dominant society. The status associated with motherhood is valued even more by ethnic people of color. Concepts of femininity are closely linked with the ability to procreate. Any treatment that involves cessation of the male or female hormones, or changes in structure or function of the reproductive system should be thoroughly discussed with the client prior to intervention.

With some degree of regularity, women have been known to appear at a clinic or physician's office seeking a birth control method. The pelvic examination reveals that there is no uterus. The question then becomes: when, under what circumstances, and why?

The term "partial hysterectomy" is sometimes used by physicians and nurses in explaining a surgical procedure that is a "hystero" (uterus) "ectomy" (removal of). A patient may give consent to a partial hysterectomy, not understanding that sterility results. The term partial hysterectomy has been used by the medical profession to describe the surgical procedure of removing the body of the uterus and leaving the cervix intact. This term may not connote "sterility" to patients giving consent for the surgery.

The words "tubal ligation" are often used to refer to tubal sterilization. Ligation (the act of tying) implies the ability to untie. Language differences among ethnic people of color dictate that the procedures be explained fully in terms of sterility if "informed" consent is to be given. Complete thorough explanation is also very important, for ethnic people of color are at a greater risk of genocide than the dominant society. The procedure (tubal ligation) would be more accurately described as a bilateral partial salpingectomy. In lay terms, this means the removal of a portion of both fallopian tubes and closing the ends by burning or tying.

Cholasma, the mask of pregnancy, is often missed in ethnic people of color, since the health care professional is unaware of the "normal" degree of melanization in the patient. The pregnant patient and the patient receiving steroid therapy, including oral contraceptives, should be asked if she has noticed skin changes. Explanation should be given concerning the temporary nature of the skin changes (in relationship to therapy) since the patient may be worried that the changes are permanent.

Circulatory Energy System

The basic functions of the circulatory system are to provide adequate oxygen and nutrients for the cells, remove the waste products of cell metabolism, and to defend the cells against invading organisms. The integrity of the circulatory energy system is dependent on adequacy of structure and function of passageways (capillaries, arterioles, venules, etc.) and passengers (white blood cells, oxygen, sodium, potassium, etc.). The integrity of both passengers and passageways is determined by assessment.

In order to carry out an appropriate assessment, the environment where the assessment takes place should be prepared with adequate lighting. Inadequate lighting often interferes with accurate assessment of all individuals, dark skin or not. When light is inadequate, color changes that could be easily assessed, regardless of heavy pigmentation, will be missed. If the individual is admitted to the hospital at night, he should be reexamined in the morning in bright nonglare daylight. Examination must be done in daylight to permit proper inspection of the body surfaces. When an examination in daylight is not possible, the individual should be taken to an examination room which is equipped with lights that simulate sunlight. Lighting in hospital patients' rooms is generally totally inadequate. If examination rooms are not available, or if the patient's condition is such that he cannot be moved, a 60-watt bulb may provide the most satisfactory option.[8]

The position of the individual is also another factor to consider when carrying out an assessment. The individual should be placed in the position where the best lighting is upon the patient and not blocked by the examiner. The extremities, upon examination should not only be placed in correct light reflection, but consideration should be given to the effect of gravity. These factors are vital in conditions of vasomotor changes. Improper position may give an incorrect color change and may produce an incorrect assessment of early pathology. Accurate assessment of color changes warrants not only good understanding of pathophysiology, but careful consideration of the relationship between color and position.[8]

The temperature of the environment should also be considered when carrying out an assessment. Cold, air-conditioned rooms may mask color changes and can create temporary but misleading cyanosis. An overheated room, on the other hand, may cause vasodilatation and create a flushed appearance.[8]

Iron-deficiency anemia occurs in a relatively high proportion of low-income populations. Anemia, deficiency in the oxygen-carrying capacity of blood, often results in disturbances in the functions of many organs and tissues. The signs and symptoms vary from patient to patient. Generally, many patients may have moderately severe anemia without any obvious signs. Pallor is usually the first sign that is noticed. Many patients seek medical attention because relatives and friends comment on their color changes. Pallor, although observable by relatives and friends of the patient, may be missed by the nurse or physician. The appearance of pallor varies with the skin tones of the individual. Dark skin loses the normal underlying red tones, so that the patient with brown skin will appear yellow-brown, and the black skinned person will appear ashen gray.[8]

A basic function of the circulatory energy system is transmission of adequate supply of oxygen. Oxygen is the energy substance required by all cells for maintenance of life and activity. Accurate assessment of this function is critical for survival because anything that interferes with either local or general transmission or the supply of this energy constitutes an immediate threat to life. In carrying out an assessment to determine adequate transmission of this energy supply, the respiratory movement of the chest is observed and the skin examined for cyanosis. Cyanosis still remains the most difficult clinical sign to observe in people of color. Cyanotic changes in people of color are best observed where pigmentation from melanin is the least, ie, the sclera, conjunctiva, buccal mucosa, tongue, lips, nailbeds, palms, and soles. In these areas, the arterial blood flow and capillary perfusion are comparatively great, with a corresponding abundance of hemoglobin and oxygen. Observation of the nailbeds must always be supplemented with additional observations, especially in Blacks. The nails may be thick, colored, and lined. These characteristics may either mask cyanosis or give a false picture of cyanosis.

A staff nurse in the labor/delivery area of a large teaching hospital rushed up to the Black nursing instructor on the postpartum unit. The staff nurse requested the instructor to follow her to the delivery room. As the instructor walked into the delivery room, she observed a Black female lying on the delivery room table with a fearful look on her face. In the corner of the delivery room, two physicians and a nurse were preparing to insert an endotracheal tube into the infant. The infant was already receiving oxygen. The instructor immediately assessed the infant. There was no evidence of respiratory distress. She then questioned the physicians about their management, and was told that the infant was cyanotic and had an

Apgar of six. The instructor then told the physicians that the infant was not cyanotic. She suggested that the physicians compare the baby's color with the mother's, after removing some of the vernix. The physicians then looked embarrassed and agreed that the infant was not cyanotic, but Black.

In the above situation, the delivery room staff had utilized a scale for assessment that is biased. According to the Apgar scale, a "pink" skin color is one of the characteristics of an infant who has made a healthy adaptation to extrauterine life. At the time the instructor made her assessment, the other indicators of the Apgar scale were within normal limits. Although it remained unclear what the initial status of the infant was, the fact that the status quo was not accurately assessed is significant.

Other areas for assessment of circulatory integrity that the examiner should be aware of are those already commonly found in nursing literature: changes in behavior, level of consciousness, etc. In ambulatory patients, changes in breathing patterns, easy fatigability, edema, etc., should be noted.

Edema, an accumulation of fluid in the extracellular spaces causing the area to increase in size, is a sign of impaired function of the circulatory energy system; the etiology of this dysfunction is multiple. Therefore, awareness of the presence or absence of edema is essential to accurate assessment of color changes. Edema of the skin masks intensity of skin color because the distance between the skin surface and the pigmented and vascular layers is increased. This increase in distance causes the darkly pigmented skin to become lighter. Pathologic changes in color, such as pallor of anemia, may be obscured.[8]

When there is an acute impairment in the circulatory supply of energy, as in hemorrhage, this supply must be augmented. One of the most common methods used, yet still a dangerous procedure, is blood transfusion. When a blood transfusion is indicated, it should be given during the day. If this is not possible, the environment should be prepared with adequate lighting. If the patient is conscious he should be instructed to report the usual transfusion reactions: itching, chilling, etc. When the patient is too critical to do this, he should be watched more closely. Continuous and close observation of the skin should be made. The body surfaces should be exposed for better observation. Areas of the skin to be assessed for transfusion reactions are those areas where melanin pigmentation is the least: mucous membranes, conjunctiva, palms, etc. The nurse should use her skills of palpation to assess for changes in skin temperature. She should also observe for increased diaphoresis, especially on the forehead, upper lip, and palms. Diaphoresis of these areas may signify impending shock.

Mr. J.K., a 55-year-old Black male was admitted to an acute general hospital with a diagnosis of acute gastric bleeding. On admission to the Intensive Critical Unit, he was conscious and alert, skin cold and clammy, nauseated and vomiting bright red blood. His vital signs were: BP, 150/90; pulse, 132; respirations, 28. An IV infusion was started with five percent glucose and water, 0_2 6 liters/nasal cannula. A nasogastric tube was inserted and connected to low suction, and he was also given an antiemetic. Soon after treatment he began to quiet down, and vital signs began to stabilize. His Hgb on admission was 4.5 g, and the physician ordered a fresh unit of blood to be given when available. In order not to disturb other patients on the unit who were stable, Mr. J.K.'s bed was moved to a corner area of the unit, and the lights were dimmed. Close to midnight, the unit of blood was started. The routine ICU assessments were carried out: vital signs, patency of tubes, etc. After one half of the unit of blood had infused, Mr. J.K. became restless. The nurses attributed the restlessness to his hypovolemia and decreased oxygenation. He later became incontinent of urine. Better lighting was established when the nurses began to change his bed linen and gown. When Mr. J.K. was moved and turned, one of the nurses noticed some large hives on the buttocks and back of the thighs. The blood was immediately discontinued, but by this time he was dyspneic and shivering. He was assessed as being in shock. The house officer was called, and immediate emergency treatment for shock and transfusion reaction was initiated.

The preceding patient situation was a situation where the transfusion reaction might have been noticed earlier if the nurses had been skilled in assessment of people of color.

During augmentation by transfusion, the transfusion sites should be watched carefully for early signs of inflammation. Infusion sites constitute a major cause of inflammation in the hospitalized patient. When inflammation is suspected, the nurse should rely on her assessment skill of palpation. When palpating, the nurse should use the dorsal surfaces of the fingers, which are more sensitive than the palmar. She should feel for increased warmth of skin, comparing one extremity to the other for differences in temperature. She should also check the skin for edema and for hardening of deep tissues or blood vessels. When palpating the skin, the nurse should observe for any verbal or nonverbal responses to pain, which could also be indicative of an inflammatory process.

When an inflammatory process occurs, such as phlebitis, treatment may include the application of hot, moist compresses. When applied, the skin should be observed for adverse reactions. Techniques for assessment of adverse reaction are those just discussed for observation of an inflammatory process.

Sickle cell anemia is a disease which has been widely documented as occurring primarily in Blacks and people of Mediterranean descent. In the acute crisis of this disease, there are problems in the supply and transmission of oxygen. There is hypoxia resulting from lower oxygen tension, and an elevated blood viscosity resulting from an increased concentration of sickled cells. Caring for a patient with this disease necessitates that the nurse be proficient in her assessment skills in order to render safe, quality care. She should be able to pick up early signs of cyanosis, both peripheral and central cyanosis.

Hypertension in another dysfunction related to the circulatory energy system that has a high incidence in Blacks and in Asians who are recent immigrants to the United States. Therefore, a thorough examination of the vascular system in the eyes should be carried out on all routine physical examinations. The examiner should be cognizant of this when examining the young adult as well as the older adult A significant number of individuals are hypertensive prior to 20 years of age.

There are a number of systemic disease processess that are manifested by petechiae, ecchymosis, and rashes. Petechiae may be obscured in dark-skinned individuals. Nevertheless, the nurse who has developed her skills of observation and inspection may find it easy to identify petechiae. Although the buccal mucosa may have patches of melanin, usually petechiae can be observed as red pinpoints between the patches of melanin. Regardless of the etiologic factor, petechiae usually are present on the conjunctiva. The nurse should include the conjunctiva in her assessment.

Ecchymosis, when occurring as a result of a systemic disorder, can usually be observed on the buccal mucosa. Often ecchymosis results from local injury. Whenever a dark-skinned patient has been involved in physical trauma, ie, automobile accident, fall, etc., the entire body surface should be inspected using appropriate lighting. Palpation should be joined with inspection to assess areas of tenderness and/or pain.

It is not uncommon that various skin rashes are entirely missed in dark-skinned people. Again, care taken in lighting and looking may facilitate assessment. Often rashes are accompanied by itching (pruritus). Whenever a patient is observed scratching frequently, the nurse should assess for a rash. The fingers should be lightly moved over the skin surface to detect changes in skin texture and surface elevations. Visual inspection should accompany the tactile inspection.

The previously discussed data base, with suggested inclusions for assessment, should serve as a guide for the collection of data. Areas that need to be broached in eliciting data about the patient situation have been described.

Ordering of data is a necessary part of the assessment process. With each patient contact, order must be given to the collection of data, utilization of data for analysis, and, hence, decisionmaking. The nurse begins by collecting history data, unless the situation is life-threatening. In emergency situations, history data are deferred until the threat to life has been resolved. The following case study illustrates this point.

As a nurse got off the elevator on the GYN unit in a small urban hospital, she was approached by a nursing assistant who stated that Mrs. K. looked "funny" and she (the nursing assistant) was having difficulty taking the patient's blood pressure. The nurse followed the nursing assistant to the patient's room and observed Mrs. K. to be perspiring, profusely, cold and clammy, with a weak pulse. The patient's abdomen was tense. The nurse immediately pressed the call button, placed the patient in Trendelenberg position, and started oxygen at 6 liters per minute by face mask. By this time, the head nurse answered the call and was instructed to get I.V. equipment and nasogastric equipment. The patient's physician was phoned and told of the emergency situation. The operating room team was summoned after initial treatment for shock, and the patient was prepared for surgery. The nurse ascertained that Mrs. K. had been admitted to the hospital that morning for diagnosis and treatment of what was described by the patient as "female trouble." Mrs. K. was taken to surgery. She had a ruptured ectopic (tubal) pregnancy. After reversing the patient's state of shock, and, prior to the surgery, the nurse reviewed the medical records, discovering incomplete data. In approximately 10 minutes, the history was completed. Data were collected on the menstrual history, obstetric history, and the history of the onset of present symptoms. In this situation, the emergency dictated initial assessment of indicators of shock and decreased mental alertness. This was accomplished by observation, palpation, and measurement of the blood pressure. History data were deferred.

Once data are collected and ordered, then analysis begins. Analysis must also be ordered. Webster defines analysis as the process of looking at the whole in relationship to its parts to determine the nature and functions of the relationships. Analysis involves the examination of the relationships of variables for problem-solving. The accuracy of analysis is dependent on the completeness and accuracy of the data base.

Late one night a nurse was phoned by a friend who was complaining of pain in the abdomen and back. Mrs. D. was advised to see a physician and that the nurse would accompany her to the emergency room of a large urban medical center. They arrived at the hospital and Mrs. D. was asked to complete some forms and wait for the physician to call her name. After approximately 45 minutes, Mrs. D.'s name was called by a physician standing at the registration desk. As Mrs. D. got up to walk across the emergency room, the physician was *overheard by Mrs. D.'s friend saying to one of the nurses: "Put her up for a pelvic, I can diagnose that PID* by her walk." Mrs. D.'s friend (the nurse) approached the physician and cautioned him about making diagnosis on incomplete data. He had made a tentative diagnosis solely on the patient's "walk." His only mode of assessment was observation. Subsequently, the physician apologized for his impropriety, examined the patient, made a diagnosis of kidney infection, and prescribed treatment in the form of antibiotic therapy.*

Obviously, the initial diagnosis was made on incomplete data. The factors influencing the diagnosis were probably related to the physician's past experiences, his personal values and ethics (his nonverbal behavior and the tone of his voice were indicative of disgust), and negative stereotyping of Black women.

Analysis of assessment data can be approached by asking and formulating answers to a number of questions. What are the goals of each energy system? Are the goals being met? Are the goals being met to the detriment of other energy systems? What action is needed to support, maintain, augment, and/or restore adaption within each system and among the systems? How do the chief complaint or reason for contact with the health care system, history of present illness, past medical history, family medical history, economics, and culture relate to the integrity or lack of integrity of the energy systems? What facilitates adaptation, and stresses to adaptation?

INTERVENTION AND EVALUATION

Prior to intervention, the nurse must identify goals relative to areas of strength identified by the patient, his significant others, and the nurse. Goals must also be identified in relation to deficient areas identified by the patient, his significant others, and the nurse. Areas of conflict between nursing assessment and patient assessment must be mediated. Support systems (agreed upon areas of strength) should be utilized to facilitate the movement of deficient areas toward a balanced state. Priorities should be established in relationship to the significance of the intervention to the maintenance of life. In life-threatening adaptive deficiencies (severe circulatory, gastrointestinal, and/or fluid/chemical imbalances), immediate priority intervention has the goal of restoring the adaptive capacity of the vital energy systems so that the human organism can continue to live. Once relative restoration of adaptive capacity is restored, then adaptive functions

*Abbreviation for pelvic inflammatory disease which is frequently caused by gonorrhea.

may be purposefully augmented by support systems. This is to say that agreement between patient and nurse, although important in a holistic approach to patient care, may be deferred until the life-threatening nature of the situation is removed. The nurse then must be constantly alert to early indicators that the time is right for the beginning of cooperative assessment and mutual goal-setting. Nursing intervention then becomes the shared responsibility of patient, his significant others, and the nurse. The patient then is not acted on, but acted with. When relative homeostasis is accomplished, the goal of nursing care is to maintain adaptation. Support of adaptation becomes the primary goal when there is balance. The nursing goal of supporting and the nursing measures that support adaptation should not be confused with what is identified as support systems. The term "support systems" is used to refer to the collection of past experiences, coping mechanisms, economic resources, family, folk health care practices and beliefs, medical arts and sciences, natural immunity, and biologic constitution, etc., that are predicated to have value in the restoration of energy balance — hence restoration of the status of wellness. Support systems, if overtaxed, lose their value as facilitators of adaptation and become stressors to adaptation.

Ms. P, a 28-year-old Black female was admitted to a large urban medical center in the Southeastern United States at 38 weeks' gestation. She was immediately taken to the labor/delivery suite. Her family was told that they should wait in the hospital lobby. Approximately 10 hours after admission, the family asked the receptionist again to check on the patient's progress. The receptionist informed the family that the patient was in surgery. No one had indicated to the family that a cesarean section was planned or indicated. The family was told that they would be informed when the patient was moved from the operating room to the recovery room. Some four hours later, the receptionist was again asked to check the status of the patient. Ms. P was then in the recovery room, and the family was told that she was "doing fine." The receptionist told the family that two persons could go up to see the patient once she was admitted to the ward. Another couple of hours passed without any word from the medical or nursing staff. One family member decided that she would risk disapproval of hospital staff and then proceeded to demand to see her sister. When she reached the ward, she was told that she could not see the patient, since it was not "visiting hours." She then told the nurse that no family member had seen Ms. P since her admission and that they had been told several times that visitation would be allowed later. . . . The nurse then insisted that Ms. P could not have visitors until visiting hours. The sister sought out the medical director to voice her complaints and again express the family's desire to see the patient. Permission was finally granted. Ms. P's mother and sister arrived on the ward to find an empty I.V.

bottle hanging unclamped with the needle remaining in the vein; the patient's bladder was distended; she was lying in a pool of blood, and she was crying. The mother determined the reason for the tears. The patient voiced concern that she had no way of knowing what condition her baby girl was in. Ms. P was having pain, and felt she had no one who was concerned enough to help her. She imagined that her baby was actually dead, deformed, or seriously ill. She did not trust the statements of the nurses when told that her baby was doing fine. She felt that the only possible reason that she had not seen her family was restrictions of the hospital. If the nurses and physicians could not see her need for comfort by family, how then could they be trusted to be truthful about her baby's condition? They were not decreasing her discomfort, nor were they allowing her to help herself. Ms. P experienced anxiety and a frustrating feeling of helplessness.

Suppose the holistic model had been used in providing care for this patient. The process might have been as follows.

PERTINENT ASSESSMENT DATA: Uneventful pregnancy; estimated date of confinement two weeks from admission date. In active labor, contractions strong; cephalopelvic disproportion; vital signs stable; past medical history and family history negative. Predicted stay in the hospital covered by insurance. Patient expects to return to job as a teacher in two months. Breast-feeding and close contact with children esteemed by culture. Unmarried status accepted, though not approved of by family. Believes illness to be punishment for "bad" deeds. Family viewed as a comfort when ill; family desires to participate in the patient's care — two sisters are registered nurses.

ORDERING OF DATA COLLECTION: Collect vital physical exam data first, since the patient is or seems to be in labor; review medical records for pertinent obstetrical and medical data.

ANALYSIS OF DATA COLLECTED: Cephalopelvic disproportion is an indicator for termination of the pregnancy by C section. What effect will this have on patient and family? Are resources available for the added cost of care? What about "hidden cost:" possible loss of earning power for a longer period? Will this increase patient's anxiety? Will worry impinge upon the care/cure process? All babies delivered by C section are sent to the Special Care Nursery. Will the isolation of mother from baby cause added concern and stress on the patient? Does the patient view her complication as punishment for conceiving out of wedlock? If so, will guilt stress the adaptive capacity of the patient? How can the family assist in the care/cure process?

MEDICAL AND NURSING INTERVENTION: Termination of pregnancy by C section, thereby reducing the stress of contractions on fetus and mother, since pelvis is not wide enough for a normal delivery. Reduce the patient's anxiety, by explaining the need for surgical delivery, and assuring the patient that her family will be kept informed of her condition. Include two sisters who are nurses in the postoperative care of the patient. Utilize family to assure the patient that loss of time from work will not be a burden to the family.

If the above approach had been used, the patient would have been able to restore herself immediately after delivery. Family members would have provided the necessary assurance that the baby was normal and well. Family members could have participated in the care. Since she had two nurse sisters, the I.V. would have been monitored appropriately, she would have been assisted in urinating before the bladder became painfully distended, and hence the possibility of uterine atony and bleeding would have been decreased. Also, the comfort by family members would have facilitated rest and sleep, which was badly needed by the patient.

Evaluation of the nursing process begins with the collection of data and continues through each proceeding step. The emphasis for evaluation in the holistic model is related to continual appraisal of the relevance of the entire nursing process to the patient. Evaluation must encompass a critical look at whether or not nursing actions facilitate adaptation, or serve as added stress to adaptation. The nurse must realize that patients cannot be separated from their past experiences, values, beliefs, and life style if care is to be relevant and cure is to be effected.

SUMMARY

Man is composed of a number of linked open energy systems which serve both as suppliers of energy and demanders of energy (the fuel of life).

Stress initiates the adaptive responses of man. These responses are broadly categorized as biologic, psychologic, sociologic, and cultural. The nature or origin of adaptive responses may be innate, localized, generalized, learned, and/or conscious.

A holistic approach to health care recognizes the nature of man and the dynamics of stress and adaptation. Caring for the whole man necessitates the inclusion of the patient in the care/cure process from assessment through evaluation. The holistic approach encourages the adaptation of approaches for each patient contact so that the approach is congruent with the needs of the patient. When the approach to care is congruent with the patient's needs, quality care is facilitated.

Within each energy system, there are areas for inclusion to supplement the usual parameters for assessment. These areas of inclusion are important if safe nursing care is to be afforded to ethnic people of color. When the data base for assessment is incomplete, the accuracy of care/cure regimes becomes questionable.

Once the assessment process is relatively complete, mutual goals should be established to reflect areas of strength (support systems) and deficient areas (areas for intervention). Care plans should be developed, implemented, and evaluated in concert with the patient and his significant others.

Although evaluation is generally considered the endpoint of the nursing process, the holistic model includes evaluation from assessment onward. Evaluation during assessment is directed at criticizing the approach to gathering data and the completeness of the data base. Evaluation includes not only a look at changes in patient behaviors and level of wellness, but it also focuses on the process, tools, and modes of gathering, sorting, and analyzing data. Evaluation seeks to define the relative worth of the nurse—patient interaction in the facilitation of the care/cure process. Thus, the holistic model encourages self-analysis, clarification of values, and cooperative care/cure activities. The responsibility for care and cure is shared by the patient, his significant others, and members of the health team.

References

1. Selye H: The Stress of Life. New York, McGraw-Hill, 1956, p 254
2. Guyton A: Textbook of Medical Physiology, Philadelphia, Saunders, 1971, p 108
3. Murillo N: The Mexican American family. In Wagner N, Haug MJ (eds): Chicanos Social Psychological Perspectives, St. Louis, Mosby, 1972, p 100
4. Stein J: Neurosis in Contemporary Society. Belmont, Calif., Brooks-Cole, 1970, p 69
5. Murillo, op cit, p 100
6. Harrington M: The Other American. New York, MacMillan, 1963, p 185
7. Ostrander S, Schroeder L: Psychic Discoveries Behind the Iron Curtain. New York, Prentice-Hall, 1970
8. Roach L: Color changes in dark skins. Nursing 72:19—25, November 1972
9. MacBryde CM, Blacklow RS: Signs and Symptoms. Philadelphia, Lippincott, 1970, pp 746—47

PART IV

Curricula Supplements

10
Conceptual Framework

Teresa A. Bello
and Diane N. Adams

In the philosophy of nursing, there exists commonality of purpose for the nurse's existence and the serving of all mankind to the best of her ability, with scientific knowledge as a base. However, in practice, one finds inconsistency as to who constitutes all of mankind and who receives the best of the nurse's ability, and whether the knowledge is scientific. It appears that today nursing education chooses to focus on the development of a sound theoretical base that ignores the needs of ethnic clients of color, ethnic nurses of color, ethnic students of color, and the white nursing student's need to learn these things in order to deliver quality care to all of mankind.

In the history of nursing, the care of human beings is paramount. Criticism that nursing was not a profession because it lacked a scientific body of knowledge caused nursing to shift to the development of professionalism, rather than continue to develop quality care standards for all patients.

The failure to provide quality nursing care for everyone is particularly evident when one sees who is not receiving the best nursing care: — ethnic people of color. Comparative statistics show that ethnic people of color continue to suffer from preventable diseases while heart transplants are a relatively frequent occurrence. The United States is continually embarrassed by its high maternal/infant mortality figures, as compared to some European countries. Those high figures reflect the inner—city populations of large metropolitan areas where large numbers of ethnic people of color live.

While one cannot deny the importance of a strong theoretical base whose foundations rest in valid research, the exclusion of a strong commitment to provide quality care to ethnic people of color based upon valid research must be questioned. Most schools of nursing continue to resist creative admission requirements which would recognize the other strengths of students of color. "Lowering our standards" was the old battlecry; today, it is reverse discrimination; tomorrow it will be something else. However, the void in quality nursing care continues as people of color continue to receive inadequate nursing care, and nursing continues to shirk its responsibility. There is resistance to "lowering standards" for admission, and resistance to raising the standards of care for people of color. The question thus becomes: If the schools do not admit students of color and do not teach nurses how to care for people of color, whose responsibility is it?

As the push toward more active consumer participation becomes a reality, perhaps schools of nursing will recognize their accountability, or consumers will develop new ways to meet their own health care needs. Consumers will actively exclude the professionals who are not prepared to recognize and attend to their needs by developing clinics that are staffed by lay people etc.

Also, one finds more socially conscious student nurses, both white and nonwhite, who are concerned about learning how to care for all people. They are also less inclined to accept as fact everything a nursing instructor says about a particular ethnic group. They know what they want from their education and do not hesitate to tell nursing faculty what their educational needs are.

The ethnic people of color in need of quality health care are American Indians, Asians, Blacks, and Latinos. Quality health care includes health professionals from their ethnic groups, and clinics or hospitals that are sensitive to their needs and that are easily accessible.

Although there is a growing trend in the United States to develop health care facilities in the communities of people of color, there still exists a glaring lack of adequate facilities of easy access to this particular population. Facilities such as clinics and hospitals need to be located in geographic areas that are accessible to the population. These health care facilities need their services to be geared to the actual health needs of the community people and not only to what the staff perceives as health care needs. This covers the range of adapting care practices to include the community's cultural health practices, diets, and the consideration of family inclusion as basic to well-being and respect for the community residents. However, in order for the health facilities to be relevant to the needs of the community, there should be health professionals of the same ethnic group as the community residents. These health professionals would understand the particular health practices and beliefs of the residents. Health care professionals from the same ethnic group would also be aware of the different ways of expressing needs particular to their community.

Nursing schools can meet the challenge of being the first health profession to develop curricula that would produce behavior change conducive to providing safe nursing care to ethnic people of color. Such a curriculum might have as its overall goal to produce nurses whose practice includes quality care to ethnic people of color. It could be constructed with the following primary models:

1. Cultural and racial diversity
2. Humanistic attitudes
3. Patient advocate

Before one can benefit from the primary models, however, one should conceptualize the formation of need states and the cultural variants to behavior.

Every human being has common human needs, such as shelter, food, love, etc. Every human being is born with the capability of learning how to express those common needs. The learning process is influenced by many factors. Consequently, the manner in which a human being meets those needs varies from person to person. One individual may choose to live in an apartment or another may choose to live at the YMCA. However, both are meeting their need for either shelter or isolation. Similarly, one may choose to eat meat at every meal, whereas another chooses to eat only vegetables. Likewise, the expression of those needs and perception of and response to them varies from person to person. For example, if a person is observed to be continually eating (expression), one may perceive it to be an indication of an endocrine problem; another may perceive it to be a need for love through oral gratification; and another may perceive it to be the behavior of a freeloader. One person may respond by suggesting a physical examination; one may suggest a psychiatrist; and another may suggest a quick exit from the kitchen! Although all of the above explanations and responses may be appropriate, it must be determined from the person who is exhibiting the need behavior what need he is expressing. Therefore, within the commonality of human needs, there is variation as to their expression, perception, and response. The variation exists because of what we call culture.

Every human being has a culture. The features of culture are illustrated in Figure 10.1. Factors that influence culture are society and its norms, economics, education, experience, and values. These factors also influence people's perception of need expression and their choices for action.

The diagram shown in Figure 10.2 begins with A — a human being whose brain signals "something." This something passes through B where it is sifted through the factors that influence the definition of that something

FIG. 10.1. Components of culture

into a need. The now self-defined need is again sifted through the factors (D) that influence how that need will be expressed (E). The self-defined expressed need is sifted through factors (F) that will influence the perception of that need (G), ie, its nature and strength. The perceived need again is sifted through factors that will influence the choice of responses to satisfy the need (H). Because of the numerous choices available, the thinking process for the selection of the choice must be sifted again (I,J). In K, the human being made a choice that is in concert with his learning experiences, formal education, economic situation, environment, etc.

Let us take an example from our schemata. Economics is an important influencing factor that can have a disastrous (poverty) or marvelous (wealth) effect on a person's life and the choices to meet a need. In our diagram, if that something signaled is hunger and the effect of the variable,

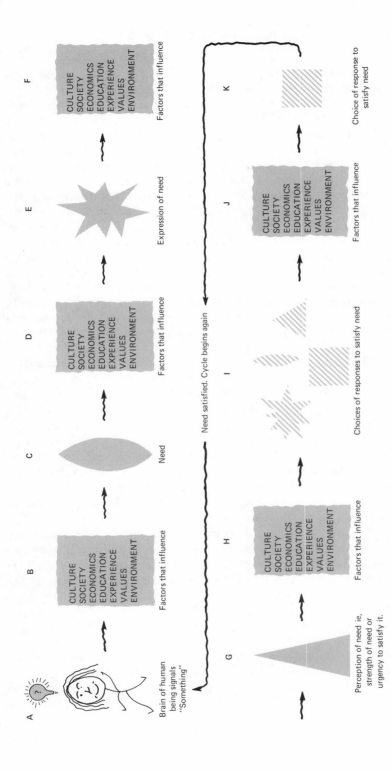

FIG. 10.2. Perception and expression of need

199

economics (poverty), is present, the hungry human being will probably not enter an exclusive restaurant and order a lavish meal. On the other hand, he may enter a fast order hamburger joint or a greasy spoon restaurant. That choice would depend on the variable, economics, and his experience as to whether a fast order or a "greasy spoon" special would satisfy his hunger. If in his previous experience these types of eating places caused illness, he would avoid them. If he is from an area where this type of restaurant was not within walking distance, his experience may dictate that he seek food at home or at the homes of friends and neighbors. The influencing factor would be environment. Let us say that, although the need perceived is hunger, there is a desire (appetite) for a particular food. That would be influenced by culture, experience, and environment. One human being may have an appetite for ham hocks, beans, and rice; another for *carnitas, frijoles, con queso,* and *tortillas de maize*; another for fried bread; another for pansit, rice, lumpia, etc. In every case, the hunger may be satisfied with a hamburger, but the particular appetite may remain until satisfied. The individual will try to remember who cooked the desired food the best. Mothers usually win the "best cook" award, and foods similar to those cooked in the home are sought.

In looking at quality health care delivery, the breakdown occurs at D — the expression of need. Here the need is expressed, and the health care professional decodes the expression, based on his experience, education, etc. Understanding the expressed need is influenced by the same variables that influenced the client's expression of the need state. Often, action will be taken that does not satisfy the expressed needs of the client, and no action is taken to investigate the true need. One big factor is that the health professional's education does not teach him to think in the manner we are proposing. He is taught to look at disease processes, but not to regard the psychologic, cultural, and spiritual being. Even in the field of psychology there is much to learn in this area.

Consider the following true example. A Latino nurse was suddenly stricken with a rash, swollen lips and tongue, and difficulty in breathing after eating seafood. She was rushed to a local emergency hospital where she was given oxygen. She told the white attending physician that she had an allergic reaction to seafood. (She did not tell the physician she was a nurse because it did not seem important). He denied that it was an allergic reaction. Shocked, the Latino nurse's response was that her lips and tongue were swollen and that she had a rash. The white physician's response was that the lips and tongue were not swollen and that they were of normal size for her. He went so far as to diagnose the condition as hysteria! In desperation, the Latino nurse — feeling ill and fearful that no antihistamine would be given — removed her clothing and showed the physician the rash on the lighter skin of her breast areas. Somewhat chagrined, but ever haughty, he ordered 50 mg of benadryl, a 1-hour stay in the emergency room, and advised the Latino nurse not to be so hysterical.

In this example, an ethnic person of color expressed a need (allergic reaction). The definition of the need was influenced by education (nurses' training and experience). The Latino nurse perceived the need to be serious, whereas the physician perceived it as hysterical. The choice of the Latino nurse to satisfy the need was to remove her clothing. The choice was influenced by experience, knowing that the physician would remain skeptical as long as she was alert and could not show proof of a rash, swollen lips and tongue. The Latino nurse's other choice was to leave the hospital with the serious need being unmet. The physician lacked the education and experience to assess a rash on brown skin. He did not know what "normal" lip and tongue size was for this particular client; therefore, his assessment of normalcy was probably based on some stereotyped notion of the physical characteristics of Latinos. Despite being in a metropolitan area composed of a large multiracial community, this physician remained ignorant, probably through his own choice influenced by racism. If one multiplies this type of occurrence common to ethnic clients of color who are less familiar with signs and symptoms than the Latino nurse, one begins to see the magnitude of the problem. Figure 10.3 illustrates the example.

In taking our example and discussing what was lacking, the question becomes: How can this type of situation be prevented? Despite the obvious deficiency in the physician's education and experience, there are safeguards that can be applied, despite ignorance and racism. To begin with, incorporation of probing questions that might aid in the initial examination would be a step in the right direction. That is already what is done by physicians; however, their intense data gathering does not usually elicit cultural data. It is not offensive to ask the race of a client in a matter-of-fact manner. Secondly, if the client is alert (as in our example), and there is some doubt as to the physical symptoms, the physician could ask to see a recent picture or a driver's license. If the client is with a family member, one could look at the family member's features or ask if the family member notices any difference. Using a bright light to inspect the skin, the lighter areas in particular, would aid in the examination of the skin.

Unfortunately, health care professionals often make decisions based upon assumptions. They are brave enough to ask about and advise about birth control; however, they seem reluctant to ascertain the normal behavior or appearance of an ethnic person of color during an emergency. Also, in our example, the physician was not a psychiatrist, yet he felt no hesitancy in diagnosing the client as hysterical.

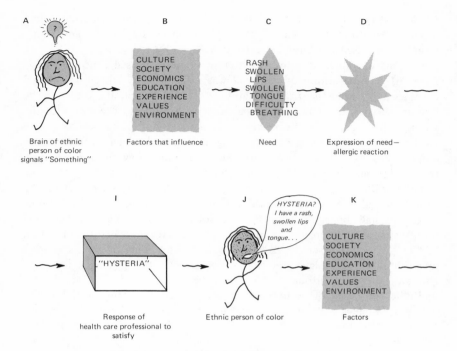

FIG. 10.3. The dilemma of seeking quality health care

In the area of life and death, health care professionals have the responsibility of gathering ethnic and cultural data that will make a difference in the well-being of the client.

Through our analysis, one can identify the breakdown in the system of health care delivery. Ideally, society's thinking should change. Since this has not yet become a reality, we can begin by recognizing the importance of providing ethnic people of color the best possible care, developing the knowledge needed for provision of that care, placing this information into the vast compendium of medical and nursing knowledge, developing an information processing system such as proposed here, choosing appropriate clinical experiences where this knowledge can be tested and applied humanely, providing feedback as to the proper application, and evaluating the results.

In summary, there are a number of paradoxes in our health care delivery system beginning with the pledge of both nurses and physicians to provide the best care possible to people; often they do not carry out this pledge to cover ethnic people of color. The education of health profes-

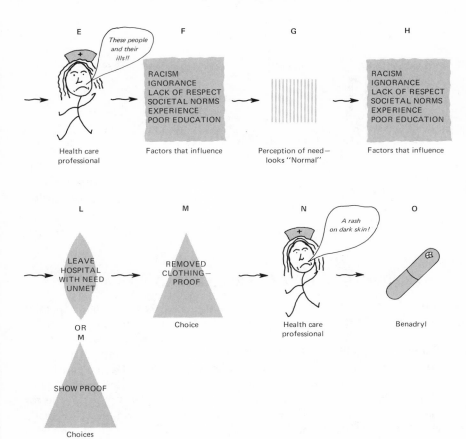

FIG. 10.3. (*cont.*)

sionals lacks content related to the health care of ethnic people of color. Society's attitude toward ethnic people of color has been one of pressing for assimilation.

Developing a conceptual framework that views human beings (patients, clients, and professionals) as individuals with a particular culture that influences behavior will serve to decrease the tendency to place value (negative or positive) upon behavior that is different. This framework should be based upon the assumption that the health professional's behavioral self-awareness will make him/her recognize that behavior in others is not necessarily a result of a personality deficiency, but of the human needs and cultural factors that affect us all.

11

Models for the Curriculum

Diane Adams,
Teresa Bello,
Effie Chow,
and Laura Martinez

INTRODUCTION TO THE PRIMARY MODELS

Throughout this book, the need for quality health care of ethnic people of color is documented. The fact that nurses and other health care professionals do not have the knowledge for providing this care is also shown. Content that will fill this knowledge gap is offered within these pages; however, this is insufficient. The concepts and knowledge presented here must be integrated within the foundations of nursing education, the curriculum, in order to teach behavior that will lead to quality nursing care for ethnic people of color. Underlying these behaviors should be a systematic classification of the knowledge necessary for delivering quality nursing care to ethnic people of color. We developed three primary models which we think will systematize that knowledge into a useable form. These primary models are:

1. Cultural and racial diversity
2. Humanistic
3. Patient advocate

Inherent within these primary models are clinical nursing skills particular to ethnic people of color, such as the assessment of dark skins for rashes, jaundice, and cyanosis; communication skills; etc. The specific skills are covered elsewhere within this book.

We have included course and behavioral objectives and have proposed teaching strategies to aid nurse educators in facilitating the learning of the students.

CULTURAL AND RACIAL DIVERSITY MODEL

The cultural and racial diversity model will identify those areas of cultural and racial diversity in American society that are appropriate for inclusion in curricula of schools of nursing. The areas identified are not intended to be inclusive of the rich variety of cultural experiences of ethnic people of color in the United States. Nor are the areas presented inclusive of all the implications of racial diversity to nursing care. Other chapters within the book present, in detail, the content and nursing processes relative to cultural and racial diversity. The content areas presented in this model are intended as a guide for the identification and organization of the content which needs to be included in nursing curricula for teaching cultural and racial diversity. The model will suggest goals for directing the organization of content areas identified in the curriculum; teaching—learning strategies and tools to accomplish the goals of the curriculum; and course and instructional objectives.

The philosophy guiding the cultural and racial diversity model is a modified concept of cultural pluralism, ie, a sociologic notion which advocates the recognition of cultural diversity in American society and its acceptance and preservation. The philosophy proposes designs for social and political participation in general American society by ethnic groups which would be directed toward minimizing interethnic conflict and maximizing cross-cultural understanding and appreciation. Cultural pluralism is a reality, since cultural and racial diversity exists; however, the dream of cross-cultural understanding, appreciation, and interethnic harmony does not yet exist. The concept of cultural pluralism providing a philosophic or guiding framework for this model is that of the reality of cultural diversity in American society. Racial diversity has special implications for nursing care because of the physiologic and anatomic differences that effect the delivery of nursing care.

The cultural and racial diversity present in American society is either ignored in nursing curricula or, when recognized, is presented as a deviance from the norm. The norm is the white middle-class American. Growth and development theories, pertaining to family structure and function, personality development and even physiologic and anatomic characteristics guiding nursing care, are based on this white middle-class norm.

The roots of this situation lie in the myth pervading the educational system that the United States is a homogeneous society. This myth is known as the melting pot theory or the theory of assimilation. According to this theory, the various European people who immigrated to the United

FIG. 11.1. Myth of the melting pot

States were absorbed into the mainstream of American life. This process of assimilation required that the particular European ethnic group relinquish those aspects of culture, ie, language and dress, that did not fit in with the culture into which they were being absorbed. The end product of assimilation, thus, was the evolution of a distinct American society (Fig. 11.1). Like most myths, there is some truth to the melting pot theory. Many religious and national groups, eg, along with their cultures, were assimilated. It is an idealism which historians seem reluctant to give up that this assimilation process was smooth and free of conflict. Actually, most new immigrant groups were oppressed and discriminated against. Assimilation, the giving up of their own cultural values and norms, was a necessity for survival and acceptance in the new country.[1,2]

Those groups that were not assimilated are ethnic people of color: Asians, Blacks, American Indians, and Latinos. Ethnic people of color were never assimilated into American society for a variety of reasons. The history of their introduction to American society differs from those of the immigrants. They are physically distinct from other immigrant groups and are subjected to racism. Ethnic people of color form separate enclaves within American society (Fig. 11.2).

The racial distinctiveness of ethnic people of color is more easily acknowledged than their cultural distinctiveness. It is seemingly more diffi-

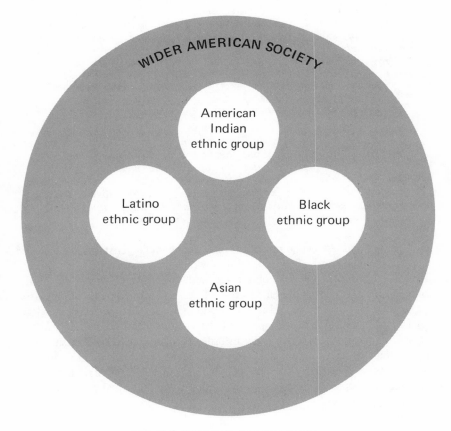

FIG. 11.2. Enclaves in American society

cult for ethnic people of color to be accepted as distinct groups with a sense of ethnic identity and with cultural values and behaviors which differ from those of other Americans. Most nursing curricula continue to ignore racial distinction by not providing learning experiences which incorporate differences.

Ethnic people of color as separate groups fit well into Milton Gordon's definition of ethnicity. In *Assimilation in American Life*, he defines an ethnic group as a "relatively large configuration of people with a shared feeling of peoplehood."[3] He further described some attributes of an ethnic group and the sense of ethnic identity. A sense of ethnic identity

> *is the social–psychological element of a special sense of both ancestral and future-oriented identification with the group. These are the "people" of my ancestors, therefore, they are my people, and will be the people of my children and their children. With members of other groups, I may share political participation, occupational relationships, common civic enterprises, perhaps even an occasional warm friendship, but in a very special way which history has decreed, I share a sense of indissoluble and intimate identity with this group and not that group within the larger society and the world.*[4]

Two definitions of culture are:

> *... Culture is a group's design for living, a shared set of socially transmitted assumptions, about the nature of the physical and social world, the goals of life and the appropriate means of achieving them.*[5]
> *... The culture of a particular people or other social body is everything that one must learn to behave in ways that are recognizable, predictable and understandable to those people.*[6]

Clearly, culture encompasses language, beliefs, customs, diet, and patterns of behavior, all of the things which make up a person's way of life. Most ethnic people of color share with other Americans some of the same cultural values and behaviors, such as a desire for education, affluence, security of home and family, and a desire for personal freedom. Figure 11.3 identifies those aspects of the culture of ethnic people of color of which the nurse needs to know in order to plan and deliver nursing care. These areas of culture can also serve as guidelines for the identification of content areas which need to be included in nursing curricula which teach cultural and racial diversity. However, the areas identified in Figure 11.3 are not all inclusive.

> Diet
> Language
> Inter and Intragroup social patterns
> Values
> Concepts of health and illness

FIG. 11.3. Guidelines for identification of culturally diverse content for nursing curricula

Diet

Diet is a function of culture. Everyone must eat. But the foods that you eat, what food means to you, how you prepare food, the frequency of eating, time of day that you eat, and the utensils you use to eat with, are all culturally determined. If told to close your eyes and imagine a good, home-cooked meal, one person might close his eyes and visualize roast beef, mashed potatoes, and green peas. Another person might see fried chicken, rice and gravy, sweet potatoes, collard greens, and corn muffins. The foods that give us the most pleasure and satisfaction in a physical and psychologic sense are the foods that we are most familiar with. These foods have formed the basis of our diet throughout our life. These foods usually carry with them fond memories of good experiences at home, ie, our favorite Sunday dinner, mother's or grandmother's specialty dish. One of the pleasures of returning home after you have grown up is to have all your favorite foods cooked for you.

This is not to say that because you are Black, "soul food" forms your complete diet, or because you are Latino or Asian you eat only Mexican or Chinese food. Blacks may eat spaghetti, or pizza, or chow mein. Latinos may eat mashed potatoes and roast beef. Whites may eat collard greens and candied yams. However, there are certain foods that are apt to be more common in the daily diet of a Black person than foods that form the major part of a white person's diet, or an Asian's, or a Latino's, and vice versa.

Language and Communication

Language is the basic communication modality for man. The fact that all men do not speak the same language is obvious. Some people speak variations of Spanish, such as "pocho Spanish." Some speak Chinese, Tagalog, English, or variations of English, such as "Black English."

It is not practical to expect health professionals to be fluent in several languages. The admission of greater numbers of bilingual ethnic students of color into schools of nursing would help the problem. Schools of nursing need to offer content in the use of interpreters and strategies for communication with non-English-speaking clients.

Content should also be offered in the verbal and nonverbal language of racism. Examples of the verbal language of racism are the use of certain impact phrases such as, "gal," "boy," or "you people." An example of the nonverbal language of racism is the message communicated by such behavior as watching carefully where you sit when you enter the home of a client which appears disorderly and messy.

Techniques of communication with and interviewing ethnic clients of color need to be included in curricula — such as, what are the most effective approaches for eliciting information from an Asian, American Indian, Black, and Latino client?

Intergroup Social Patterns

Curricula should include content areas which explain and describe the ways in which different groups meet the functions of a family. Different styles of child-rearing, as the use of discipline and rewards, expectations and responsibilities of children are content areas to be included. The use of family or friends as support systems in ethnic groups of color is another content area to be included in curricula.

Concept of Health and Illness

The ways in which individuals define the state of health and illness are culturally determined. What it means to be sick or to be well to an individual is culturally determined. To one parent, the child who is running a slight temperature with a sore throat and a cold is "sick" and should be routinely taken to the physician. To another mother, a cold is not a sign of "illness," but, rather, a normal manifestation of childhood that is treated by rubbing Vicks VapoRub on the child's chest and by giving a cup of sassafras tea along with a lot of tender loving care. The first parent is more likely to be urban or suburban, middle-class, and white. The other parent is more likely to be rural and Black. To one person, illness may be the occurrence of a rational, cause-effect circumstance, the presence of a germ or virus, the absence of a certain hormone or chemical from the body. For another person, illness may be explained by the presence of evil spirits, an imbalance of hot and cold (in Chinese culture, Yin and Yang), or a disequilibrium between nature and man.

In middle-class American culture, illness is usually considered the presence of pain or discomfort, as compared to a feeling of well-being or state of health. For many Blacks and Latinos, illness is defined as a major disruption of the daily activities of living, and minor discomforts, back-aches, upset stomachs, or headaches are ignored until they reach such proportions that they interfere with the conducting of the business of living. Therefore "illness" in the Black patient may not come to the attention of a physician until it has reached serious proportions.

The Chinese mother, after delivery, may refuse to drink any water because ice water is usually provided in the hospital. She may believe that childbirth instigates a condition of imbalance of the cold forces in her body and should therefore be counteracted by taking into her body substances such as hot soup to counteract this condition. The person who believes that evil spirits is a cause of his (her) illness, a common belief among some segments of the Latino community, will be more concerned with the exorcising of the evil spirit than with another form of treatment. Particularly with the Asian, American Indian, and Latin patient, the nurse should be aware that the patient may simultaneously be receiving treatment from a traditional practicner, herbalist, a *curandero*, or a medicine man.

The following are preliminary curriculum goals for teaching cultural and racial diversity to nursing students:

1. The curriculum should produce a nurse who recognizes the existence of racial and cultural diversity in American society
2. The curriculum should produce a nurse who is knowledgeable of the ways in which culture influences the health beliefs and health practices of ethnic people of color
3. The curriculum should produce a nurse who recognizes the influence on the nursing process of culturally determined values and behaviors of the nurse and the patient
4. The curriculum should produce a nurse whose nursing practices maintains and fosters the ethnic identity and cultural practices of her patients
5. The curriculum should produce a nurse who is able to make nursing assessments and interventions appropriate to the culture of the client

The Curriculum Should Produce a Nurse Who Recognizes the Existence of Racial and Cultural Diversity in American Society

Although most baccalaureate nursing programs require an introductory course in sociology as a prerequisite for admission, these courses usually identify differences in American society as deviant. When this knowledge is transferred to patients, the deviant or deficit perspective is also transferred. Therefore, students assess ethnic families of color comparatively, ie, from a white middle-class norm, rather than describe the ways in which different groups meet the functions of a family. Because the majority of nursing faculty are white, they, too, use the comparative deficit model in relationship to ethnic patients of color and ethnic students of color.

When nursing curricula recognize the existence of cultural diversity, the usual practice is to present this information in one seminar, lecture, or panel discussion. There is no integration of the content throughout the curriculum. Instead, it is served up as a side dish.

The teaching of racial and cultural diversity as a fact of American society should be introduced early in the nursing curriculum and remain there throughout. For example, in the fundamentals of nursing course or its equivalent, patient hygiene is taught eg, hair care, oral hygiene, bed bathing, skin care, etc. As part of this course, hair care of the Black patient, skin care of dark-skinned patients, and normal coloration of mucous membranes in the mouth should be taught. The fact that this information is presented as part of the basic knowledge required for nursing gives it validity in the eyes of the student.

Concomitantly, theories which have been written by ethnic people of color about their own people should be presented along with other theories. As an example, when theories of families, written about by white authors such as Duvall[7] and Bell,[8] are presented, other theorist views about ethnic people of color[7] by Huang,[9] Staples,[10] Hill,[11] Billingsley,[12] and Scanzoni[13] should also be presented.

The Curriculum Should Produce a Nurse Who is Knowledgeable of How Culture Influences the Health Beliefs and Health Practices of People of Color

As previously stated, the ways in which individuals define the state of health and illness are culturally determined. Nursing students enter school with well-defined concepts of health and illness based on their own cultural backgrounds and beliefs. Curricula in schools of nursing tend to foster these beliefs and define health in terms of prevention and maintenance. Usually, the curriculum does not take into account views of health and illness which are divergent from the white middle-class norms. Therefore, when the student encounters an ethnic patient of color who has sought medical help only after his illness has reached emergency proportions, she may assume he lacks the proper concern for his health. Because she does not know that there are different conceptions about the state of health and illness, she is unable to assess the patient's health care from the patient's perspective. She has allowed her own culturally determined values to influence her assessment of the patient's behavior. If she had been taught other concepts of health and illness, she would be able to view this patient's behavior within the context of his frame of reference. This would prepare her to focus her energies on ascertaining how the patient handled his illness before he appeared for treatment. For instance, did he apply home remedies? Did he feel his illness was not sufficiently incapacitating to warrant treatment? Did economic and practical considerations such as transportation and medical bills influence his decision to wait? Because the student has a broader concept of health and illness, she is able to maximize her nursing skills to include teaching and referral to community resources.

The Curriculum Should Produce a Nurse who Recognizes the Influence of the Culturally Determined Values and Behaviors of the Nurse and the Patient on the Nursing Process

As mentioned earlier, family concepts of ethnic people of color should be integrated into the curriculum. This would also include patterns of inter-actions such as childrearing practices and ways of relating to others. Again, this becomes important in the nursing process. The student nurse, when interacting with clients of color, may not understand certain behaviors. The student should be taught to examine the patient's behavior within the context of that patient's culture.

For example, the Asian patient who is hospitalized may never voice a complaint to the nurse and may nod his head in affirmation of everything she says, whether he understands her instructions or not, whether he is uncomfortable or in distress, or not. His cultural experiences and learned way of interacting with someone who represents authority denotes respect, and compliance dictates his reaction. The degree to which his life experiences and his cultural background has been influenced by traditional Asian values and codes of behavior will determine his behavior. If his background and upbringing have been traditional, he is more likely to behave in the manner described than if his upbringing and background were nontraditional.

The student who is unaware that this patient's seemingly complaint and respectful behavior may be an expression of his cultural background may be unable to accurately evaluate or interpret his behavior in relationship to his nursing care needs. If the nurse interprets the patient's behavior within the context of the meaning such behavior has to her from her cultural frame of reference she may accept the behavior at face value. It is only when the student interprets the patient's behavior from the framework of the latter's cultural experience that she is likely to interpret his behavior correctly and move toward an effective intervention.

Most nursing curricula profess to teach students nonjudgmental attitudes and behavior. However, the culturally bound attitudes of the students and the faculty are rarely exposed and examined. Culturally bound attitudes are seldom acknowledged as the motivation for much of nursing assessment and intervention.

For example, some nursing students who make a home visit to a family on welfare are unable, in the nursing process, to move beyond the feelings inspired in them by the fact that the family has a color television set. The color TV has such a negative impact on the student's sense of value that it is impossible for any in depth nursing intervention to occur. This incident is not unusual, and it reflects the impact that the culturally determined values of the nurse can have on the nursing process.

Nursing schools should offer courses that involve students in values' clarification exercises. There are "games" on the market which allow the players to experience the "minority" role by providing simulated life experiences of poor, ethnic people of color and the choices open to them to obtain monetary and educational advantages. Schools should also offer and require attendance at seminars designed to discuss racial tensions. In this manner, students will learn to recognize their own cultural values and behaviors in a "safe" environment.

The Curriculum Should Produce a Nurse Whose Nursing Practice Maintains and Fosters the Ethnic Identity and Cultural Practices of Patients

Although there is common knowledge of the existence of Mexican food, Chinese food, soul food, etc, nursing faculty only teach about the middle-class diet and its nutritive values. The different kinds of foods eaten by ethnic groups and the nutritive value of those foods are not taught. Nurses are not taught to consider the influence of culture on diet or to consider this influence when teaching diet. Everyone may receive the same low sodium, bland, or diabetic diet, regardless of food preference, eating habits, or styles. The nurse who is helping an Asian patient with a diabetic diet should be prepared to include in her teaching whether or not — or how much — soybean, soybean milk, or bamboo shoots the patient can eat — how much cornstarch can be used in the preparation of food — whether or not the diet can include squid or eel. When foods that constitute the usual diet are included in the therapeutic diet regimen, the patient is more likely to adhere to the prescribed diet.

Diet teaching is a traditional function of nursing care. In carrying out diet teaching with ethnic people of color, the nurse should avoid assuming that ethnic people of color eat only foods particular to their culture. For example, the nurse who approaches a Black patient with the assumption that this patient only eats soul food may find this approach offensive to the patient. The nurse who is able to provide care from an awareness and knowledge of cultural diversity would approach the individual patient with the knowledge that, because the patient is Black or Latino, his diet may reflect his cultural heritage; however, he may prefer a variety of foods.

The nurse's approach to the patient would be to determine with the patient what foods form a daily part of his diet. The nurse, the patient, and/or nutritionist should plan the prescribed diet with as little variance as possible from the patient's preference for food choice and preparation.

Very often, nursing curricula describe folk or home remedies as having little or no medicinal value. The result is that nursing students do not consider folk or home remedies as treatment. As previously mentioned, integration of this topic area in the curricula will give it similar respectability as enjoyed by other treatment modalities. For example, the use of anise teas to "settle" bowel discomfort could be taught while the student is learning about medications prescribed for abdominal ailments. By teaching students the value of health practices of ethnic people of color, such as folk remedies, the student begins to value those practices. What is seen as having value is fostered and preserved.

It has been pointed out how the theory of assimilation pervades the thinking of our society. The desire that the minority alter their culture to conform to the majority can be seen even in nursing. For example, many Latino patients have long names which should be pronounced according to the Spanish vowels. What we find is an attempt by nurses to shorten the name, slaughter its pronunciation, or ridicule the name because they cannot remember the name in its entirety or cannot pronounce it. This behavior may also be exhibited toward African names which Black parents choose for their newborns.

The Curriculum Should Produce a Nurse Who is Able to Make Nursing Assessments and Interventions Appropriate to the Culture

Although many nursing schools profess to teach health promotion and maintenance, one sees, in practice, an emphasis on problem identification. Whether it is called a potential problem or an actual problem, problem identification per se is at odds with a framework for cultural and racial diversity for quality care for people of color. In problem identification, the "norm" is a well-adjusted, normal person with no problems. Then, the student encounters a poor client with all the health-related problems of the poor, and the cycle begins. As long as the "norm" continues to be the white middle-class standard, poor clients and clients of color will continue to be identified with the many discouraging problems that may have more to do with poverty and our health care system than an inherent neglect of health.

The alternative is to teach from a strength identification framework which would:

1. Aid the white middle-class nursing student in gaining an appreciation for the survival modalities of those below her income level or outside of her experience
2. Aid the student of color who comes from a financially disadvantaged background to continue to use and appreciate the survival mechanisms learned, and provide support for like clients
3. Aid the client in appreciating his strengths so that he does not fall prey to the discouragement and degradation of our current system

For example, a white nursing student was assigned to a Spanish-surnamed family. The 28-year-old mother was pregnant with her third child. The children's ages were two and four. The father was a migrant farm laborer who earned $4000 per year. They lived in a rented three-room shack which the mother kept neat and adequately furnished. Mother and children seemed content and healthy.

The nursing student's assessment looked like this:

Problems	Action
1) Birth control	1) Counsel mother about birth control; bring birth control kit

2) Inadequate income	2) Refer to social services for food stamps
3) Lack of space and privacy	3) Call housing authority to find other housing; ask social worker for resources
4) (Potential) malnutrition	4) Counsel about diet
5) (Potential) immunization booster may be due	5) Take immunization history

While this may be a good initial assessment based on the data given, there is no indication of family strengths. For example, it is a strength for a family of four to live on $4000 per year without major health or emotional problems. It is a strength to live in a shelter labeled as a shack and keep it neat and adequately furnished. The strength of the parents to cope with this situation is not touched upon. The assumption that birth control is a problem would need to be checked out with the mother. The action for this "problem" does not include mention of needing more data and consideration for the husband's thoughts. Another strength to look for in this situation is the strong family component within the primary group and extended family group.

The strength-identification assessment would look like this:

Strengths	**Objective(s)**
1) Family of four surviving on $4000/year without major emotional/physical health problems	1) Gather more data re: a) potential financial/space problems with family addition b) family counseling on birth control c) nutrition d) immunizations
2) Although shelter is a shack-type structure, it is adequately furnished and neatly kept	
3) Despite economic poverty, there is contentment and health within family	
4) (Potential) strong intra- and interfamily ties	
5) No evidence of malnutrition	

As the student gathers more data, she can move into problem identification based upon facts and consensus from the family. Part of her data would be to ascertain how the family would like to handle problems mutually agreed upon. These are also dimensions of a strength-identification framework: mutuality of problem identification and utilization of family problem-solving skills.

The following course and instructional objectives in Table 11.1 are intended only as guidelines for nurse educators. It is hoped that the nurse educator will develop them further in combination with her own courses, instructional objectives, teaching strategies, and modes of evaluation. These objectives are purposely loose, to allow for flexibility and creativity in utilization.

HUMANISTIC MODEL

Humane is defined by Webster's dictionary as "marked by compassion, sympathy, or consideration for other human beings or animals." Humanitarianism is "a philosophy that asserts the dignity and worth of man and his capacity for self-realization through reason." These definitions support our explanation that holistic, loving, or humanistic health is the practice of (1) seeing a human being as a total entity of body, mind, and spirit, (2) maintaining the assumption that man has the inherent capacity to be responsible for himself, to exercise his will toward his own fulfillment and well-being — capacities which are important to the healing process, and 3) viewing the patient as a person is greater than any model of disease or psychology.

Holistic, loving, or humanistic health care is thus reflected in the manner in which a patient is regarded: he is a holistic human being with an interrelationship of mind/body/spirit, and he is more than a disease; the health care provider is more than a trained technician. Interaction between patients and health care providers as whole human beings involves a communicative potential which by far exceeds the treatment of the disease. The teaching of health and health maintenance is of great importance, and the receptiveness of the patient depends upon the harmony of his whole person. In helping the patient attain or keep this harmony, one must consider the enormous complexity of his past, present, and possible future experiences and reactions and his spiritual and material goals. He must be treated as more than a simplistic model of disease or psychology. The health care provider should guide the patient in making conscious choices regarding his own health because each individual has the capacity to define himself, to be responsible for himself, and to exercise his will for his own well-being and fulfillment. A patient's mental attitude should be viewed as having a great influence upon his being well or being ill. Conditions such as pain, disease, aging, suffering, and death should not necessarily be looked upon as frightening crises; they may often be understood as meaningful evolutions in life that are to be treated with a high degree of dignity. To deny, relieve, or eliminate the physical problem alone is not an adequate method of dealing with human emotions and the realities of life.

If the above factors were considered in every aspect of health care, a humanistic system would evolve. However, there are a number of other factors which preclude the health system's acceptance of the reality of man as a holistic being. The humanistic approach has been negated by the steady development of science and technology, which has increased impersonalization, bureaucratization, and insensitivity in contemporary life. Attention is now being drawn to the increasing dehumanization of major institutions, including those of health care.

The Dehumanization of Health Care Systems

Our health care system has become dehumanized by a variety of causes. For one, care is fragmented due to specialization. Medical specialists, technicians, and other members of the health profession prescribe and care for the patient with inadequate intercommunication. Specialization in health services and facilities forces the juggling of patients from one department, building, or specialist to another. The patient is seen as a segment of a body, and he lacks identification as an individual whole person. This, along with authoritarian attitudes on the part of health personnel, leads to a lack of meaning and interpersonal caring and even to despair. The compartmentalization of health care succeeds in defining the patient and disease only through technologic and scientific measures. It strips away the patient's ability to assert responsibility for his condition and compels him to become reliant upon the health care provider as an authority figure who will tell him what to do and even do it for him.

Humanistic concepts are minimally present in educational curricula, design of facilities, program and health care planning, implementation of health care, policies and standards affecting health care practices, interchange between professionals and patients, design of evaluative processes, actual evaluation of services, and even attitudes of many professionals. Most planning, implementation, and evaluation is carried out primarily at the convenience of the health care personnel.

The training of nurses and other health care providers is geared toward developing proficiency in technical skills, thus leaving them ill-equipped to make qualitative decisions. For example, the nurse is well-trained in

Table 11.1
Objectives for Cultural and Racial Diversity Model

COURSE OBJECTIVE	BEHAVIORAL OBJECTIVE	TEACHING STRATEGY	EVALUATION
1) To teach the student to assess physical needs of patients/clients from various and different racial and ethnic backgrounds.	Collects data from clients about physical needs through interview and patient's chart.	Assign relevant readings. Show relevant films/slides.	Establish criterion for the demonstration of behavioral objective, eg, 80% accuracy, six out of nine behaviors demonstrated.
	Observes skin of people of color and discerns if there are rashes, bruises, swelling, dryness.	Provide experience for the inspection of normal variations of the skin of people of color.	If student does not satisfactorily demonstrate behaviors according to criterion established provide more experience and reading and reevaluate after a period of time.
	Observes a Black person's hair and scalp and determines need for washing or conditioning.	Utilize agencies that serve ethnic people of color in a reciprocal relationship.	
	Determines Black male's need for shaving.	Utilize ethnic people of color as a resource.	
	Describes the parts of the body which should be observed for accurate assessment of cyanosis and jaundice in dark-skinned patients.	Provide relevant communication theory and experience of collecting oral data. Provide guidance and experience in reading charts.	
	Identifies jaundice and cyanosis in patients by using skills of observation.		

2) To teach the student to meet physical needs of patients/clients from various and different racial and ethnic backgrounds.

Demonstrates the ability to use observation and touch in assessing body temperature.

Identifies the normal variations of the oral cavity of a Black person.

Seeks resources if unable to assess other physical needs.

Demonstrates the ability to wash a Black person's hair.

Demonstrates the ability to comb a Black person's hair.

Demonstrates the ability to braid long hair.

Applies lotion to dry skin after washing.

Demonstrates the ability to apply depilatory as alternative to razor shaving of Black male's face.

Asks patient/client if there are special routines, lotions, etc., that he needs.

Assign relevant readings.

Show relevant films/slides, ie, care of Black hair, protein of kinky vs. straight hair.

Provide experience in hair braiding, washing, etc.

Utilize relevant agencies.

Utilize resource people.

Establish level of accuracy for demonstration of behavioral objective.

Patient satisfaction survey.

Table 11.1 (cont.)

COURSE OBJECTIVE	BEHAVIORAL OBJECTIVE	TEACHING STRATEGY	EVALUATION
3) To teach the student to recognize effects of nurse's values and attitudes on clients from various and different racial and ethnic backgrounds.	Uses Mr., Mrs., Miss, or Ms. when addressing patient.	Require attendance at seminars related to discussing racial tensions.	Feedback from students/staff/patients regarding demonstration of desired behaviors.
	Does not gossip about patients with peers/staff.	Assign relevant valid readings.	Establish criterion for acceptable level and frequency of required behaviors.
	Investigates negative feelings about people of color.	Provide feedback to student found to be demeaning toward client/staff/peer.	
	Seeks appropriate resources for clients if nurse cannot communicate.	Provide resource people to aid student work through feelings.	
	Seeks information/resources.	Involve student in values clarification exercises.	
		Use field assignment to place student in "stronger" role — "minority" role — discuss feelings.	
4) To teach the student to recognize and identify cultural health practices of clients from various racial and ethnic backgrounds.	Collects data from patients/clients relative to their cultural health beliefs and practices.	Assign relevant and valid reading, films.	Establish criterion for demonstration of behaviors, ie, desired behaviors demonstrated in 80% of patient assignments.

5) To teach the student to integrate knowledge of cultural health practices into the nursing process.

Encourages the use of home remedies if not harmful.

Encourages family to bring patient food to hospital when this is desired by family and/or patients.

Seeks information and resource people.

Demonstrates the ability to accurately plan a basic diet for various racial and ethnic groups.

During conference, relates other pertinent cultural points to consider in the care plan.

Demonstrates understanding of the importance of family visiting the hospitalized patient by encouraging family visitation.

Schedules appointments that are convenient for the patient/client.

Provide clinical experience that is relevant.

Assign relevant and valid reading and films.

Provide resource people.

Feedback from students/staff/patients as to success.

Student demonstrates desired behaviors by performing at an established level on written, oral, and clinical examination.

Feedback from student/staff/patients as to student's demonstration of behaviors.

Table 11.1 (cont.)

COURSE OBJECTIVE	BEHAVIORAL OBJECTIVE	TEACHING STRATEGY	EVALUATION
	Respects modesty of patient/client and drapes appropriately.		
6) To teach the student to understand the influence of politics and the economy on health care delivery.	Describes the nursing implications of selected legislation.	Provide information.	Student demonstrates desired behavior by performing at an established level on oral, written, and clinical examination.
		Provide resource people and material.	
	Demonstrates political awareness by active participation in at least one political organization.	Provide experience.	
	Informs patients/clients of their legal rights as consumers of health care.		
7) To teach the student to consider sphere of nursing outside the boundaries of the health care setting.	Volunteers for planning agencies, professional organizations.	Provide relevant readings.	Student demonstrates desired behavior within acceptable levels of participation established.
	Attends community meetings.		

measuring body functions by machine, but lacks in-depth training in coping with important emotional and personal problems of the patient, which may be crucial to his recovery. In light of the type of training that is generally given to health care providers, it is not surprising that the quality of health care is measured by the quantity and distribution of patients, rather than by whether or not the health care prescribed is relevant or acceptable to the patient and his family.

The dehumanization of the health care system affects everyone adversely, but, for ethnic people of color, there are additional difficulties. For example, those who speak no English find it a hundredfold more discouraging and troublesome to go from health provider to health provider because of the fragmentation of services. Very often, ethnic people of color do not complain or fight about the poor service of the system, but instead they prefer to "drop out" and salvage what is left of their dignity. Ms. B. Bloch, R.N. (administrator and coordinator of the Moffitt Hospital Nursing Service, University of California in San Francisco, and a member of the Bay Area Black Nurses Association) noted the following: "There are countless physiological, psychological, and cultural factors which make health care different for the Black patient. . . . Professionals sometimes forget that certain things can be more important than adequate health care. When Black people are forced to choose between losing their dignity and respect, or omitting health care altogether, many will choose the latter."[14] For those ethnic people of color who are poor, the additional costs for transportation, baby-sitting and, sometimes, the hiring of an interpreter make it impossible to follow through with services needed.

Possible Solutions to Dehumanized Health Care

We will examine two aspects of solving the problem of dehumanized health care: (1) the establishment of a service environment which considers the patient's individual needs; (2) the establishment of curricula which would have loving and humanistic care of the patient as a primary goal and which would include special communication techniques.

ESTABLISHMENT OF HUMANISTIC SERVICE ENVIRONMENT. In order for these approaches to be successful, there must be a flexible administrative structure which is adaptable to new ideas and responsive to changes necessary to create a more humanistic system. The training curricula should develop the kind of person who will have capability, responsibility, authority, and accountability for planning goals and rendering care to patients. The nurse, because she is more frequently in contact with the patient, is the most appropriate member of the health care team to establish an atmosphere of trust and identification with the patient. However, she needs to use innovation and creativity in establishing better communication channels and an environment more conducive to considering the patient as a total human being. She must be free to use her judgment and creativity in establishing a plan of care according to the needs of the individual patient. She must be capable of giving emotional support to the patient.

ESTABLISHMENT OF HUMANISTIC EDUCATION CURRICULUM: REQUIRED ATTITUDES, SKILLS, AND ENVIRONMENT TO DEVELOP A HUMANISTIC NURSE. In order to promote the teaching of humanistic behavior in the curriculum for nursing, many things need to be considered. For example, what attitudes, skills, or environment would assist a person in becoming a humanistic nurse?

BASIC CONCERN FOR THE PATIENT AS A PERSON. First of all, it is important for the student nurse to have a basic concern for the patient as a person. It is possible to encourage such sensitivity, awareness, and concern by providing the opportunity for open discussions about human values. If the student has had limited exposure to people from various walks of life or cultures, then experiences in differing communities and life styles should be arranged. By widening her base of experience and becoming familiar with living patterns dissimilar to her own, the student nurse would be made more capable of sensing and feeling the patient's individual needs as a human being. She can then visualize the person as a part of a family, and community, rather than just as "patient X, gall bladder case in bed Y." This experience in different communities would, in fact, help develop her ability to recognize the situations in which patients are depersonalized in the health care setting.

In order for this experience to be optimally beneficial, the student could, at the same time, be shown films and be given readings relative to the communities and lifestyles of the people she is visiting. However, she must recognize that the films and readings have deficiencies which must be taken into consideration. Classes or experiences in personal growth and special communication skills to enhance her capability to relate to these people would be helpful. These could include sessions on clarification of values; cross-cultural understanding; medical, cultural, and social anthropology; sensitivity and awareness skills; communication skills (both verbal and nonverbal); and alternative lifestyles and health care practices. Expert guidance in each area is imperative. If the student is an ethnic person of color, she should be encouraged to be more aware of her personal identity, the strengths and uniquenesses of her own community group, and to explore her feelings regarding her own ethnicity and that of other groups.

With a better understanding of her own identity and feelings, with a broader view of society, and with additional communication skills and sensitivity, the student would be aware of and would be able to analyze what it is in the health care environment that places people into a box or mold, thus causing a loss of identity and dignity.

ROLE MODEL OF BEHAVIOR BY INSTRUCTOR. Second, in order for the student to learn and to perform the role of a humanistic nurse, she must be able to envision and experience the humanistic approach herself, as demonstrated by her instructor. Therefore, it is essential that the teacher have training similar to that recommended for the student nurse — self-exploration, community experience, instruction in special communication skills, and so forth. Only from such personal experience can the teacher exemplify an appropriate role model for the student.

Along with having basic concerns for the patient as a human being and the ability to recognize dehumanizing situations, the student should also have a personal commitment for change. Of course, the teacher must also feel such a commitment and provide a role model for the student. Otherwise, the student's commitment is at a dead end, for she is not in a position to carry out any action without the teacher's cooperation. Both parties should understand that change involves risk, resistance from the traditional hierarchy, and often times doubt and confusion.

Because of these difficulties, it is especially important that a humanistic atmosphere of trust, respect, and desire to share good intercommunications and repeated honest exchanges be developed between the student and the teacher in order for change to occur. Again, the development of communication skills and the clarification of values will assist both the student and teacher in creating and maintaining this kind of atmosphere.

INVOLVEMENT OF STUDENT IN PLANNING PROCESS. Third, another way to encourage the student to become a humanistic nurse and to be fearless of changes is to involve her in the design and implementation of goals for her own professional and personal growth and for a nursing care plan for the patient. This would foster in her a sense of personal satisfaction in contributing to the new message in nursing care — humanistic health care. Besides human values, organizational skills are needed to accomplish planning. Classes on theoretical planning and repeated clinical experience should be provided for the student.

In assisting the student with this, great patience is required of the teacher because concepts of human values and organizational skills for efficiency are in conflict. When implemented in a clinical setting, plans made with special humanistic considerations may create frustration for the student, the patient, the teacher, and other staff members. For example, the student who plans to give a patient and his family the needed emotional support may find that this obstructs her other goals of efficiency: finishing all the bed baths, getting all the dirty linen out, and having the rooms in order by the time lunch trays come out. The student feels, though, that she has done a superb job of patient care — she has comforted the family in spite of all their anxieties, and her bedridden patient is resting well for the first time. The head nurse, however, is furious and severely reprimands her in front of everyone because the beds of two ambulatory patients in the same room are not made and the room itself is still in disorder. The student nurse is upset because she does not understand the reaction of the head nurse. This highly unpleasant confrontation with the head nurse, particularly if the student is quiet, shy, or timid (which is typical of many ethnic students of color) may have other repercussions. The confrontation may override the pleasure she has gained by comforting the patient and his family. This traumatic experience could cause the student to acquire a distaste for nursing, resulting in withdrawal from school if she sees the head nurse as typical of others in nursing. Or the student may remember the pleasure of patient contact, but, in the future, she may become "afraid to rock the boat." If this continues, her pleasure in patient contact may diminish because of her strict adherence to the efficiency code, and she may forget the humanistic aspects of patient care. The student graduates, becomes an R.N., and continues nursing — for that is her only source of livelihood. In time, she may impose her inhumane organizational efficiency on other staff and students. A vicious cycle continues.

This cycle can be interrupted if the instructor has skill in helping the student and can keep her from becoming disillusioned. Ideally, the teacher would: (1) have an open discussion with the student to encourage her to explore her feelings about herself, the head nurse, the situation, the nursing care plan, and what the student felt was right or wrong; (2) discuss goals and priorities with the head nurse to be sure that there is a common understanding; (3) promote intercommunication or short conferences between the student, head nurse, and herself for better understanding; and (4) help the student (and maybe the head nurse) with replanning nursing goals and health care plans. By helping the student in this supportive way, the instructor encourages the student's further participation in planning for humanistic nursing: the instructor has shown herself to be a humanistic role model.

Functions, Attitudes, and Skills Relevant to Patient–Nurse Relationship in Humanistic Model Nursing Care

We have discussed the supportive circumstances which would aid the student in learning about and carrying out humanistic concepts of nursing. Now, what are some of the functions, attitudes, and skills that are directly relevant to patient—nurse relationships and that are inherent in a humanistic model of nursing care?

1. Patient—nurse communication
2. Accessibility
3. Equality, trust, and ethics
4. Holistic insight
5. Responsibility and respect
6. Sensitivity
7. Genuine caring

Included in the discussion are some suggested questions which may serve as an evaluation tool to ascertain the effectiveness and quality of humane nursing care.

PATIENT—NURSE COMMUNICATION. Communication, both spoken and unspoken, should occur continuously as part of every action. Ideally, clear messages are sent and received every time. In order to understand meanings, one should need only acute perception. This goal may sound simple, but it is, in fact, very difficult. It is accomplished only through extensive use of teaching, reading, and audiovisual aids in theoretical concepts of communications skills, combined with repeated experiences and experiments with real clinical and personal situations. After experiences and classes, an opportunity for open discussion for evaluation of what one has learned or not learned is essential.

Some new techniques of communication such as Gestalt, special awareness and sensitivity training, encounter groups, meditation, massage, biofeedback, etc., can be explored and utilized in delivering the new nursing care message of humanism. Again, expert guidance in each area is imperative.

Open, sensitive communication between patient and nurse is desirable. Through body awareness the student may learn to read unspoken messages of fear, anger, etc., relayed between herself and the patient through posture, gestures, faces, etc. For example, many ethnic patients of color, because of their lack of English, do not try to speak, and often they are so timid and unfamiliar with routines and surroundings that they even disguise their nonverbal expressions of fear, hostility, pain, etc., with smiles and pleasantness. Unless the nurse is very alert to pretense, these patients are often ignored, and their progress chartings record them as "good patients progressing well," when in reality they have been hiding symptoms of distress.

Another communication skill is massage and touch, which is a message of caring and acceptance. Massage, touch, and body awareness provide a beautiful means of patient—nurse communication. This message of caring and acceptance is transmitted to the patient and helps to alleviate the feelings of rejection he may experience because of his condition or disease. One must be careful, however, because not all patients are used to touch or like to be touched. The nurse should use her skills to sense this and respect the patient's feelings. However, he may enjoy backrubs, and this is an acceptable method of touch.

In further relating to the patient, the nurse should explain in clear, understandable terms, all that she intends to do, what his health care entails, what she expects of him, what she is learning about him, how she feels about it, what it all means, and what the options are for further nursing care, therapy, and rehabilitation. In return, she should try to elicit from the patient his true opinions, feelings, and expectations in relation to his present condition. Her ability to develop such a rapport depends upon the degree of her skill in communication techniques.

Evaluative Questions

Does the nurse listen and is she able to communicate well?

Is the patient, as much as possible, given complete information about his condition?

Is a prompt explanation of the results or meanings of tests, examinations, or nursing care procedures given?

Is there a discussion of alternative treatment methods and their pros and cons? Is full information given about the purpose and possible risks of any prescribed medication or treatment modality?

Does the nurse encourage feedback by asking the patient for his opinions, feelings, and expectations, and does she allow for questions?

ACCESSIBILITY. The nurse should give the patient a sense of security that she is available when needed, while also helping him develop a sense of participation rather than of complete dependence. The nurse should be especially aware of patients who are quiet and nondemanding. For example, language barriers may make the patient hesitant to call the nurse.

Evaluative Questions

When the patient calls the nurse, does she come promptly?

Does the nurse spend adequate time with the patient?

Do the patient's concerns and anxieties seem to be quickly and adequately attended to?

Does the nurse make herself available as needed?

Does the nurse seek to elicit all the information possible that may have bearing on the patient's needs and expectations?

EQUALITY, TRUST, AND ETHICS. The nurse—patient relationship should not evolve in an authoritarian atmosphere but should be one between essentially equal human beings who share a joint responsibility for the patient's health. The nurse should not perceive herself as anything more than an available person who has certain knowledge and skills to offer in the patient's search to meet his own needs. The patient alone will choose whether or not he will accept the offer of care. However, the patient can choose wisely only if he is equipped with the knowledge of alternatives. The nurse must seriously weigh the ethical consequences of her decisions.

Evaluative Questions

Does the nurse trust the patient to share in the responsibility of his illness, care, and rehabilitation?

Does the nurse treat the patient as a peer, with prerogatives equal to her own?

Does the nurse relate to the patient as another human being and not as a problem or pathologic process?

HOLISTIC INSIGHT. The patient should be treated as a whole, complex, multifaceted human being having physical, psychologic, social, cultural, and spiritual components that interact with and are affected by many external and internal variables, in addition to a specific pathologic condition.

Evaluative Questions

Is the patient treated as a whole and complex person?

Does the nurse consider the psychologic origin of the patient's symptom or complaint?

Does the nurse speak with or is she familiar with the family of the patient and their effect on his illness?

RESPONSIBILITY AND RESPECT. The patient should be helped to be responsible for his own therapy and for assuming responsibility for self-care as soon as possible. The patient should not give himself up to someone else's control.

Evaluative Questions

Does the patient participate in his own care?

Does the patient have a voice in the decisions that affect him?

Is there respect for the patient's right to know about the particular therapy and care he is receiving?

Is the patient taught preventive care and ways in which he can take care of himself?

SENSITIVITY. The nurse should have an awareness of the uniqueness of the patient and his differing sociocultural, economic, and personal value systems. The nurse should be able to adapt to the possible spectrum of responses in appropriate ways. She must be aware of where the patient is in his particular spectrum of feelings and responses at any particular time.

Evaluative Questions

Does the nurse consider possible sociocultural aspects of the patient's illness?

Does the nurse seem to be aware of differences in value systems, methods, and capacities between herself and her patient?

Does the nurse seem tolerant and adaptable?

GENUINE CARING. The nurse should be in touch with her own feelings and should not avoid them. She should be genuine, open, and willing to share herself with the patient. She should be interested in and concerned about the patient so that he is able to perceive her caring. The patient should feel that the ultimate intentions of the nurse can only benefit him.

Evaluative Questions

Does the nurse seem to be genuine in her response?

Does the nurse say how she feels?

Does the nurse try to understand the patient?

Does there seem to be genuine concern for the patient?

The above are some functions, attitudes, and skills which are components of humanistic nursing, along with some recommended evaluative questions.

Evaluation

Most of these questions, and others of this nature which have not been listed, can be judged only subjectively and by their very nature must remain in the subjective sphere. We should also consider whether the care process itself is altered when the student is observed by the instructor. To augment this, student narrative and feedback methods of evaluation may also be used.

Concurrent with the observation process in evaluation, direct patient feedback is valuable in assessing his reaction to the humanistic aspects of the nursing care received. The same questions as the above may be reworded and posed to the patient.

A third process of evaluation involves reviewing the patient's record. The nurse's notes can reveal whether she is concerned with the whole person — his social, cultural, and psychologic milieu — or just with his pathologic condition. The completeness of the nurse's notes can reveal how much information she has solicited from the patient and how effective the time spent with him has been.

To measure subjective substance is extremely difficult, and objectified measurements have to be developed where possible. Along with this, there must be a new respect for the validity of intuitive, experimental, and subjective forms of knowledge and judgment. Denying this form of knowledge severely limits the scope of any human activity, and, in particular, nonmechanistic activities such as the humanistic aspects of nursing care that we are concerned with here. We must consider these questions: What sort of person is doing the evaluation? Who is being evaluated? How are judgments made, and, if observation is used, how will the observations be made? Can these judgments be trusted as valid and impartial, and can any conclusions and statistics be derived from them?

The ultimate product of a humanistic nursing curriculum should be the personal growth of the nurse and the development of holistic and loving patient care with special emphasis on the sociocultural aspects of the patient. Table 11.2 showing objectives, desired behaviors, teaching strategies, and evaluation, concludes our model of a humanistic nursing curriculum.

Table 11.2

Objectives for a Humanistic Model

COURSE OBJECTIVE	BEHAVIORAL OBJECTIVE	TEACHING STRATEGY	EVALUATION
1) To develop the student as a feeling, concerned person.	The student treats people in general with natural warmth and sympathy.	Expose the student to emotional situations through films, field trips, etc. Encourage student to actively think about each emotion felt, and put the feeling into words.	Observe for display of emotions in emotionally laden situations.
2) To help the student consider a person as a whole body—mind entity.	The student considers the patient's condition from both a physical and psychologic point of view.	Assign readings (especially anthropology-related subjects and special, well-tended case studies).	The student demonstrates knowledge of multifactors of physio-psycho-cultural-socio-spiritual-philosophic needs of patients.
	The student demonstrates understanding that social and cultural factors are important aspects of a patient's illness by assessing and intervening to facilitate the natural cultural and social adaptive responses.	Use films and other audiovisual devices showing relevant subjects.	The student's behavior with the patient demonstrates knowledge and understanding of the patient in regard to all aspects.

Demonstrates the ability to plan and implement care relevant to the religious philosophic beliefs of the patient.	Expose the student to different life styles and ethnic groups by utilizing people as expert resources for teaching.	Charting shows that the student is aware of the total needs of the patient and not just the physical disease condition.
The student demonstrates the realization of the importance of the family in the care of the patient by including the family in the total nursing process.	Place the student in agencies and communities which are conducive to her understanding of the various factors that make a whole person.	The student relates well to the patient's family.
	Provide opportunity for the student to openly discuss and question her readings, film, and placement observations.	
3) To involve the student as an integral part of the planning process of her own learning situation.	Establish a good, respectful relationship between instructor and student.	The faculty demonstrates flexibility and encourages the student to participate in planning her course of study and to pursue special interests.
The student demonstrates responsibility for her own education and learning process by her involvement in seeking out and planning learning experiences to facilitate her professional growth.	Include the student in the evaluation of her own learning.	
The student shows initiative, creativity, and motivation in learning.	Encourage participation of the student in planning her courses and pursuing special interests.	The student demonstrates initiative and responsibility when given the opportunity.

Table 11.2 (cont.)

COURSE OBJECTIVE	BEHAVIORAL OBJECTIVE	TEACHING STRATEGY	EVALUATION
		Flexibility of staff faculty and administration to creativity and initiative.	
		Counseling of quality is available to the student when needed.	
		Provide good counseling for the student.	A good relationship exists between the faculty and the student.
		Offer open discussions.	
4) To provide the student with knowledge of alternative systems of healing; eg, curanderismo, shamanism, acupuncture, Chinese medicine, psychic healing, laying on of hands, nutritional beliefs, herbology, voodooism, hoodooism, root medicine, absent healing, naturopathic medicine, homeopathic medicine, etc.	The student respects the fact that people of different backgrounds may have preferences for alternative healing practices.	Assign relevant readings, films, audiovisual material.	The student accepts concepts discussed or preferred by patients, and she does not scoff at concepts and intimidate patients.
		Offer open and frank discussions regarding alternate systems of healing.	
	The student demonstrates knowledge of alternative healing practices.	Place the student with agencies or individuals who use alternate systems of healing.	The student provides an opportunity for the patient and family to approach her with their beliefs.
		Utilize experts in these fields as resource people in lectures, discussions, and placement of students.	The student demonstrates knowledge of the different healing arts.

Objective	Student Behavior	Teaching Methods	Evaluation
5) To help the student to recognize the importance of prevention and health over disease, and to understand that this is one's own responsibility.	Student demonstrates appreciation of prevention of disease by seeking care at early signs of imbalance and by her own utilization of preventive health services, ie, dental hygiene, annual physical exams, etc.	Utilize patients who have had successful treatment as resource people. Have teachers act as role models. Assign readings, films, audiovisual material relevant to health and health maintenance. Offer opportunities for open discussion.	Establish criteria and methods of evaluation that include written tests, observation of clinical application. Observe student's own health practice.
	Student includes education in the plan of patient care, as appropriate; teaching the importance of well-being and staying well.	Place students with public health groups and with other agencies having health maintenance foci.	Audit charts for evidence of patient education. Give written tests and observe for application in face to face teaching opportunities.
6) To develop within the student special communication skills to cope with the range of emotions and crisis situations.	The student demonstrates the ability to deal with the emotional problems of the patients, as well as with their physical problems.	Assign relevant readings, films, audiovisual material on communication techniques and opportunity for open discussion.	The student demonstrates knowledge of communication skills.
	The student provides opportunities for patients to express their emotional needs.	Have teachers act as role models by coping with both the emotional and physical needs of the student.	Charting demonstrates student's awareness of the emotional needs of the patient.

Table 11.2 (cont.)

COURSE OBJECTIVE	BEHAVIORAL OBJECTIVE	TEACHING STRATEGY	EVALUATION
	The student reinforces the positive aspects of a patient's condition, eg., events that are generally interpreted as calamities, such as aging, dying, disease, etc., may be viewed as a necessary process of living.	The faculty exemplifies role models.	The student participates in communication sessions.
		Give seminars on communication techniques with faculty who are experts in this field.	
		Give special sensitivity and awareness sessions with experts in this field.	
		Provide repeated opportunity for the student to utilize the skills learned.	The student provides an opportunity for the patient to express his emotional needs.
		Have experts teach special communicative techniques such as Gestalt, massage, consciousness-raising skills, relaxation methods, biofeedback, etc.	When the patient does express his emotions and needs, the student is able to cope with them.
		Use of role play as a teaching tool.	
		Clinical placement of students in communication centers or agencies and individuals who are experts and do utilize these special communication skills.	When a crisis situation arises, the student intervenes appropriately and calls for assistance if needed; she does not become frantic.

These course and instructional objectives are intended only as guidelines for nurse educators. It is hoped that the nurse educator will develop them further, in combination with her own course and instructional objectives, teaching strategies, and mode of evaluation. These objectives are purposely structured loosely to allow for flexibility and creativity in their utilization by individuals.

PATIENT ADVOCATE MODEL

Advocacy is defined by Webster as the act or process of defending or promoting a cause and the subsequent pleading of that cause. The advocate may serve as a partisan in a social conflict, and frequently utilizes his expertise or mobilizes other experts to meet his client's or group of clients' interests. He may argue for, defend, maintain, or recommend a cause or a proposal.

The degrading, impersonalized, and imperious behavior often exhibited by physicians and nurses toward poor and ethnic patients of color can cause them to feel powerless and degraded. They cannot exercise control or provide input into decisions made concerning them. In such a situation, they need an advocate.

To be a patient advocate, the nurse should have a basic respect and concern for the well-being of all her patients. She should also be able and willing to:

1. Interpret to the patients their rights
2. Provide the necessary information for the patient to intercede for himself
3. Intercede for the patient in appropriate situations
4. Accept the consequences of being a patient advocate
5. Teach the patient and his family to be advocates for themselves and others

The nurse places the needs and welfare of the patient first and represents the patient and presents his or her concerns to physicians, other nurses, and administrators. Because of this, the nurse may find herself in the uncomfortable position of confronting other health care professional and service agencies.

In the name of patient advocacy, a nurse may over-intercede for a patient, rather than teach the patient to intercede for himself in this and other situations outside the health care setting. It is sometimes necessary to act for a patient because he may be too internally weak to cope with the situation, or is not knowledgeable of the processes involved in changing a situation. Nevertheless, the ultimate goal of patient advocacy is to allow the patient to become more independent.

The Patient Bill of Rights

The following Bill of Rights for patients was developed by the American Hospital Association and is self-explanatory.

BILL OF RIGHTS FOR PATIENTS*

Patients have the right to:

> *Get complete, current information on their diagnosis, treatment, and prognosis – in language they can understand.*

> *Refuse treatment and be informed of the medical consequences of their action.*

> *Confidentiality of all records and communications concerning their care.*

> *"Considerate and respectful" care.*

> *Be consulted if a hospital wishes to involve them in experimental drugs or treatments – and not be subjected to experimentation without their express permission.*

> *Have their voice heard on hospital management and control – eg, via representation on hospital boards.*

> *Have their complaints and questions concerning hospital care and costs heard and acted upon – via a specially appointed advocate, ombudsman, or the like.*

> *Continuity of care (follow-up) after they leave the hospital – for instance, by consultation with the physician on treatment and other measures following their discharge.*

In order for a patient to have personal power, he must know his rights. By informing the patient of these rights, the nurse increases his personal power and protects him from real or possible infringement of those rights. Because the nurse knows the patient's rights, she may assume responsibility for preventing possible abuse of those rights.

Developed by the American Hospital Association and printed in the San Francisco Chronicle *on December 27, 1974.*

Since the nurse is only one member of the health team and is account-able to others, she should know where the sources of reward and possible retribution will arise if she consistently acts as a patient advocate. This knowledge will aid her in planning how to effect change with the least amount of resistance.

Organizational Theory

To know this, she should be informed of the formal and informal structure of the organization. Usually, the motivation for action takes place in the informal structure. This is where the policy decisions are made or adjusted.

Also, knowledge of the influence of community-based organizations upon institutional policies provides leverage for the patient advocate to function. Staff in community-based organizations usually are sensitive to people's needs and do not hesitate to openly support those needs.

Confrontation Techniques

The ability to resolve conflict on a one-to-one basis or within a system is another skill needed to be a patient advocate. Underlying this skill is the intestinal fortitude developed to face someone whose behavior toward a patient does not seem to be in the patient's best interest.

This intestinal fortitude requires role-modeling and skillfully guided experience. Often, the patient lacks the courage to express his dismay over the care he is receiving. Thus, the nurse should be prepared to intercede forcefully, rather then feebly declaring, "I'll tell the doctor."

Interpersonal Skills

In order to be an effective patient advocate, the nurse needs well-developed communication skills. She must be able to listen to the needs of the patient, which are not always expressed directly, and be able to interpret or assist the patient in expressing these needs to others. She must not only hear what patients or other health professionals are saying, but she must understand the context of what she hears and the motivation behind it. The patient advocate needs to understand the dynamics of group inter-action, where grievances and problems are discussed. She will be able to appropriately and effectively provide input and feedback about patient situations.

Teaching Learning Principles

By knowing teaching/learning principles, the patient advocate is able to apply those principles and teach the patient, his family, and other staff members how to advocate for themselves or other patients, ie, getting through the health care system, or finding out what their rights are, etc. The nurse's behavior as patient advocate will serve as role model to the patient and to others. The patient advocate also will teach about health, the patient's illness, medications, lab tests, etc. This information adds to the patient's personal power and knowledge about himself, should it become necessary for him to make a decision about a procedure.

Resources

The patient advocate should familiarize herself with resources within and without the institutional setting. The fragmentation of services in our health care delivery system makes it necessary for the patient advocate to bridge the gap for the patient. It may sometimes be necessary for her to initiate contact with resource people on behalf of the patient.

Teaching the Patient Advocate Role

Many opportunities arise in the clinical setting to teach nursing students the advocate role. Often, these opportunities are not capitalized on by the clinical instructor. Students, in what is sometimes referred to as their idealism or naiveté, are often acutely attuned to the needs and rights of patients and are outraged by what they see as violations of those needs and rights.

The immediate response of these students is to seek validation from their clinical instructor. Should the instructor minimize the effect of the situation, the nursing student learns that being concerned about patients offers no reward from the instructor. If the student is outraged enough, her concern will not decrease, but she will feel powerless to act alone. As a student, she is in a position of powerlessness vis à vis her instructor and the staff.

Appropriate behavior in this instance would be for the faculty member to sit down with the student and listen to her concerns. Then, he or she should tell the student that he(she) will seek more information about the situation. The faculty member and student should discuss the situation together, on a one-to-one level. If the concern is valid, the instructor should assist the student to follow through toward resolution. The result of this process is that the student learns to problem-solve in a positive manner and finds that it is acceptable to express concern about a patient situation. Hopefully, she will probably continue to function as a patient advocate throughout her career.

Clinical Example

The following is a clinical example which afforded an opportunity to be a patient advocate: Ms. S., a student nurse, first came into contact with the patient, Ms. W., when she was assigned to the diabetic clinic in a large university outpatient clinic. During the time she was assigned to the clinic, Ms. S. and a social worker worked with Ms. W. in coordinating her care. This required a tremendous effort, as multiple problems were recognized.

During that time, some of the ways in which the student assisted Ms. W. were:

1. Securing cab vouchers for transportation to and from clinic visits when community service was not available
2. Making appointments for the various clinics involved in her health care
3. Explaining rescheduled appointments and subsequent appointment slips for clinic visits canceled by a particular clinic physician
4. Securing prescription renewals for depleted medicines between clinic visits
5. Aiding her in simplifying complications due to multiple clinic appointments so that she might prearrange for community transportation with a clear understanding of what clinic she was to visit, and what time she should arrive

In many instances, the student assumed the role of an advocate in caring for Ms. W. by assisting her in the clinics which are complex and confusing, and by informing her of available resources, ie, cab vouchers, and assisting her in obtaining those resources.

At the end of the school quarter, the student began a new clinical rotation. She was still assigned to the outpatient clinic department, but no longer to the diabetic clinic. Technically, she was no longer Ms. W.'s "student nurse." Ms. W., however, remembered the relationship that she had with "her" student nurse.

Ms. W. sought out Ms. S. (who was in a new clinic) on several occasions — complaining of pain, expressing fear over unusual "worms" in her stool, and stating she could not "get help at the clinics." Every time she called, she was put on hold and either cut off or was not able to make the recipient of her call understand her problem.

Consequently, the student independently decided to make a "friendly" visit and was shocked at the general status of Ms. W. Her health had deteriorated, and her attitude toward her medical care was negative — not at all like the "optimistic" individual the student knew.

Ms. W. expressed disappointment with the type of care she was receiving. She stated: "They don't care about me, they just run me all over the place — first one desk, then another, first one place then another, I feel worse when I leave than I did when I came. I call and I can't get nobody to help me, I run out of medicine, I still can't get no help. If it wasn't for the social worker, I don't know what I'd do."

Ms. W. expressed declining interest in herself and her health. "I keep going to first one clinic, then another, and I still don't get no better. I gets worse. I just wish I could have one doctor — I gets tired and just confused. At times I just gives up."

The student contacted her nursing instructor, who seemed concerned but directed her to the public health nurse, who also seemed concerned but could offer no viable suggestions. The student returned to her instructor, who was still concerned but who thought it was the responsibility of the public health nurse involved with the patient. The student turned to the patient's social worker with whom she had worked.

With the help of the social worker, the patient was transferred to the comprehensive clinic. The student prepared a case history and presented it to the chief of the medical staff. Here the student was at a loss because her contact with the patient was concerned mainly with only one aspect of her health status, namely diabetes. Again, it was the social worker who advised her to write her nurse's evaluation as she had assessed the patient initially versus the patient's present condition.

In this instance, neither the nursing instructors nor the nursing staff provided the student with the support and guidance needed for her to carry out an advocacy role. This particular student possessed the necessary concern and intestinal fortitude to pursue the problem without this support.

Consider the following example as one whereby an ethnic faculty of color functions as a patient advocate and acts as a role model for the students.

A Filipino patient, after 6 weeks of hospitalization, began to awaken in the middle of the night and wander around the halls in search of her family, calling their names and bothering the other patients to see if they knew where her family was. After a couple of such nights, the health care personnel decided in staff conference that her behavior probably had a cultural base, and since no one knew anything about the Filipino culture, decided to call a psychiatric consultant. The psychiatrist decided that the patient was isolated from her life style and needed someone to talk to. Who and when were the questions the staff did not bother to answer. On the third morning of this behavior, the patient was identified by the nursing instructor on the unit and assigned to a student nurse. After listening to the night report and reading the nurse's notes, the student became concerned. She went to her instructor, who was sitting in on another team report, and told her the situation. The instructor was of Filipino descent and decided to talk to the patient after listening to the student and reading the chart.

Together, the instructor and student went to talk with the patient. They discovered that:

1. *The patient was told she would only be in the hospital 1 week for tests — she had been there for 6 weeks*
2. *She was never told what disease was suspected, and when she asked, she was told that more tests needed to be completed*
3. *She was placed on a special diet and did not know why*
4. *Her family lived 60 miles away, and she missed them*
5. *Because of all the mystery, she was convinced she had cancer and was going to die soon and wanted her family to be with her before she died in a hospital room.*

The instructor and student went to the attending resident and asked why the patient was not kept informed as to the lab tests and diagnosis. "She wouldn't understand," he replied. "There is a language barrier. I did not tell her she had lupus erythematosis, because she wouldn't have understood the explanation of it. It would confuse her more." The nursing staff's reply was similar, except the lack of time to pursue her problem was mentioned.

The nursing instructor sat down with the student and asked her what the care plan should be. At this point, the nursing student was pleased that she and her instructor were working together to resolve a problem. Together, they developed a teaching plan and visual aides about lupus. They constructed a Filipino diet that would conform to the medical regime.

The patient's bizarre behavior ceased, the staff seemed relieved and was surprised at the simplicity of dealing with such a situation. The student delighted in telling her peers about this during clinical conference.

In this case study, we find an ethnic faculty of color acting as an advocate for an ethnic patient of color. She gathered data from the patient and staff to ascertain where the breakdown in care occurred. She was able to discuss this with the staff, and together with the student they came up with interventions that met everyone's needs. The staff will probably think twice the next time a similar situation presents itself. The student participated in most of the action, thereby learning how to problem-solve on behalf of a patient, and learning that acting in this manner is rewarding to all concerned, including the student.

Community Advocacy

The nurse, in promoting the health of an underprivileged class of her clients, will need to act as the advocate for a community. The health practitioner who does this must possess a unique understanding and empathy for that community. For the minority nurse, it may be easier to possess these characteristics because they are derived from the life experience and cultural roots that make it possible for her (or him) to avoid being either paternalistic or insensitive toward the community. She is accountable first to the clientele of the community, and she fully realizes that her primary loyalty and responsibility is to this community, rather than to any specific agency which may employ her. The student in a professional field may be in a similar position with respect to the school, and may find times in which her primary loyalty to the minority community conflicts with the policies and subtle aims of nursing schools or other professional schools.

Herein lies the dilemma, as well as the challenge, for the professional nurse or the student in a professional field. It may also become part of this type of advocacy to work toward an alteration of school or agency policy in order to gain just recognition of the needs and goals of the community.

Community Needs Versus Agency Wants

The following example illustrates how a community's physical and mental health was not only maintained, but was improved dramatically through advocacy.

A New Mexico barrio was faced with extinction as a social and cultural entity by Urban Renewal, an agency which ostensibly was created to rehabilitate inner cities across the country. In many instances, including this one, the agency was actually an adversary of the community. The agency worked for the obliteration of a natural minority community in the interest of the establishment.

This barrio was predominantly comprised of Chicanos. Most of the families within the barrio had known each other many years. The Urban Renewal Agency's decision to relocate all the families in the barrio was reached without ever consulting the community. The basis of conflict was the programming of the agency, which failed to perceive or solicit the barrio's needs and viewpoints. The barrio reacted to the agency's planning with a sense of unity and purpose which caused the agency's planning to be abandoned. The barrio's struggle for survival, however, took 10 years.

This proposed relocation of the barrio was directed at a group of people who shared several common characteristics: (1) the majority of the people were retired and elderly; (2) the people of the community were predominantly Chicano; and (3) the overwhelming majority of the barrio's members were poor.

The proposed relocation program would have forced these people to leave homes they themselves had built and that they owned with pride, and with a sense of belonging to a closely knit neighborhood whose basis was friendship, mutual cooperation, and the sharing of a culture, as well as the struggle of being an oppressed group within the larger society. With the relocation monies offered them, most of the barrio's residents would have been unable to buy new or even adequate homes, and, also, this closely knit social grouping of people in the neighborhood would have been scattered, splintered, and spread to the corners of the city, losing the connection of the social fabric and even of the culture which had united them, causing economic deprivation and distress. Most would have been forced to rent apartment units or houses, and would no longer be able to be owners of small separate houses. With the limited income most of the families had, the added economic burden of having to pay for housing would have created critical economic situations, all the more ironic since they had already jointly built their houses with their own hands and had been able to solve the one problem of housing in their otherwise deprived economic conditions.

The proposed relocation ignored the social and psychologic needs of the community, which had developed strong emotional, social, and environmental ties over a period of many years. There was a basic security which the residents shared despite deprivation. This consisted of the social fabric which had been painstakingly woven over the years by their joint efforts. The barrio's residents were, in effect, a large extended family. In times of crisis within any one family, the other residents of the barrio responded with all kinds of economic, social, and psychologic support. This barrio, unknown to the urban renewal bureaucrats, was more than a collection of houses. It did not have a typical suburban community's psyche with its stress on anonymity, which usually minimizes the development of a collective social consciousness.

Mobilization of Community Resources

It was clear to the barrio's residents that the fabric of mutuality that made life not only bearable, but possible, would be destroyed if the agency's relocation plan was successfully carried out. A nursing student who had grown up in this community lived with her family in the barrio and was involved from the very beginning in the events of this struggle. She, like other residents of the community, was shocked by the impact of the Urban Renewal Agency plan to relocate all the people and thus destroy the fabric of their lives. She was the only Chicano member of her nursing school class in a school that paid lip service to equal rights and equal opportunities, but which had only admitted and trained a bare handful of minority students in previous years. Her family had over a dozen children, and she was working at a nearly full time job while attending school, in order to make professional training possible. She and some other members of the barrio community went door-to-door to talk to everyone in the barrio about the Urban Renewal Agency's plan to relocate the people. A series of meetings were held and were attended by all of the barrio's residents. They represented the community's initial efforts to organize internally. The residents were beginning to understand that this was a struggle against a bureaucratic agency in order to maintain their own world view and to save their community and themselves.

The nursing student established personal contacts in the local anti-poverty agency, which was then in a formative state. Through these contacts, she met volunteer lawyers who had been brought in by the agency to work on poverty law problems, and learned that the legislation authorizing Urban Renewal projects envisioned the goal of neighborhood rehabilitation and did not necessarily authorize removal of the residents and destruction of the neighborhood. Furthermore, there was a provision for consumer representation and citizen participation in the Urban Renewal Agency plans, and this apparently had been totally ignored by the Urban Renewal bureaucrats. She was instrumental in forming the link between these lawyers in the povery field and the residents of the community.

The residents formed a Citizen's Information Committee, which was directed to act on behalf of the residents. Its role was limited to implementation of policy. Any and all policy decisions were made by members of the barrio in their frequent meetings. The nursing student played a continuing part in these meetings, and in maintaining the communications among the barrio residents which facilitated this initial effort at internal organization of the barrio. Meanwhile, she was struggling to meet standards which the nursing faculty demanded. The majority of the nursing faculty was white and of middle class background. They seemed to equate nursing competence with a certain approach to verbal performance in class and on paper. Often, this had little clear relevance at all to the life of this nursing student, who — besides working with her patients and learning the principles that would apply to her future clinical practice of nursing — was also holding down a job, was threatened with the extinction of her community and the family and social life she had known since her childhood, and was working actively with the residents of the barrio to form the organization which would fight the Urban Renewal Agency.

Example of Advocacy

The majority of the persons elected to serve on the Citizen's Information Committee had little or no previous experience in dealing with bureaucracies. Most were middle aged or older, with one outstanding exception. The community elected a young Chicano to be spokesman for the Citizen's Information Committee. He was a member of the community and also had little, if any, previous experience in dealing with bureaucracies. He did not fit the usual stereotype of a docile, inarticulate "macho" that the white community has created. He was an aggressive, highly intelligent, and strategically brilliant individual. It became clear to the Urban Renewal Agency that this barrio was not going to relocate willingly and that, in fact, they were mobilizing to change the administrative fiat that had condemned the barrio. Further, it became evident as the agency and barrio began administrative and legal sparring, that the indigenous barrio population was developing its own leader and its own strategy. While outside help was sought and was instrumental in achieving the barrio's struggle, the initiative and staying power that was necessary to succeed was provided by the barrio residents themselves.

The involvement of the lawyers represents, in itself, an interesting example of advocacy in a professional tradition. The lawyers were called upon for information, the basic technical expertise of their field. They learned through interaction with the barrio residents that they were not called upon to lead the struggle themselves. The barrio had developed its own indigenous leadership, and skills were learned by people in response to necessity. There never existed a gap between the leadership and the other residents, because both were part of the barrio and both, in essence, were one and the same. It is to the credit of the legal consultants that they could recognize this and stand back from the process. They did not attempt to take over the citizen organization, or even to plan its strategy. They were simply available when needed.

Meanwhile, the nursing student was involved in learning some of the realities of her professional relationships. Coming from a poor background and having English as her second language, she had not developed the verbal facility which enabled some of her Anglo fellow students to speak and write in a manner which impressed the faculty. She was viewed as inarticulate and uninvolved, although her personal involvement both with individual patients and with the needs of her community were much greater than those of her fellow students. Her barely passing grades were the subject of attention by certain faculty members who thought that perhaps they augered a lack of ability in nursing and the future of dangerous nursing practice. Personal interviews with nursing school faculty around her "problem" revealed their subtle racist and ethnocentric view of her, as well as their lack of comprehension of the significance of her community work for nursing.

Initially involved in the community struggle as a resident of the community and as a member of her family, who were very concerned about the loss of their home, she used her work in the community as part of a community project presented for her community health nursing class. This first brought the attention of the faculty to her community involvement, as she generally followed the precept of refraining from seeking approval and attention for her accomplishments, a value which had been ingrained in her by early social training. Her view was that a person should do what he can to help others, and should make this contribution without any verbal effort to call attention to it or expect praise. However, partly because of her self-effacing approach, many of the faculty thought that she could not succeed in nursing, and when her community work did become recognized, it was misconstrued by the faculty.

The most positive way in which they viewed this was that, since she was a poor student and also worked at a job to support herself through school, she did not have time for additional involvements and really ought to quit this business in order to assure that she would be able to pass her nursing courses. Additional viewpoints expressed were that involvement in controversial political issues was dangerous and unprofessional and that, through some personal interpretation which they gave to the tradition of nursing, the nurse should overlook the political and social conditions which oppressed the lives and threatened the physical and mental health of the clients. Therefore, some faculty members considered her community work to be negative and dangerous, and she was the center of administrative pressures in the school to force her to limit and/or stop her community involvement.

Here again, another example of professional advocacy occurred. One minority group faculty member was able to recognize the legitimate professional role of this student's community advocacy and see it as positive, necessary, and an important part of her nursing career. She contacted and influenced enough of the more progressive faculty members to support the nursing student's continuing involvement. In some cases, this intervention by the minority faculty member resulted in some restraint by the other faculty members who were otherwise critical or negative, and this restraint

allowed the student to graduate, though she continued to encounter negative attitudes during and beyond her training career. This nurse, who was
now a graduate, took a position with a mental health agency in the same
city and continued to reside in her barrio and work cooperatively with
other barrio residents as they sought and developed collaborative relationships with key agency representatives throughout the city and county.

She was also instrumental in bringing the attention of mental health
agency personnel to bear on this problem. Thus, the community residents
sought and obtained the advice and special kind of help from a variety of
experts and strategically placed political and agency personnel to further
their effort. They involved the local Legal Aid Society and were able to
obtain further legal help on their own terms, again limiting the role of the
lawyers to their specific areas of concern, while the leadership remained
with the community itself.

Development of Collaborative Relationships

The community developed a strong bond with the local Catholic Church,
since the vast majority of the residents were Catholics and the Church, at
least on the grass roots level, was becoming responsive to the political and
social concerns of its communicants. Beyond providing intangible spiritual
help, the Church supported the community with services that made the
struggle possible. A Catholic nun who was interested in the social aspects
of her calling was able to devote her full time to the struggle of the people
of this barrio, and her work was tireless. As the barrio learned the
intricacies of dealing with groups and government, they expanded their
efforts. School board members were contacted and presented with the
barrio's reasons for wanting to remain in the neighborhood. Although the
school board had as part of the Urban Renewal Project, already voted to
locate a new high school on the land where the community now stood, the
efforts of the community caused a majority of board members to change
their minds as they began to understand the nature of the community that
had contacted them and the real meaning of the Urban Renewal Agency's
desire to destroy this community. As a result of a resolution passed by the
school board to change the location of the new high school, the Urban
Renewal Agency lost a major part of its rationale for insisting that the
barrio residents had to be relocated.

The residents then pressured their neighborhood representatives in local
government to speak and act on their behalf. The result of the expanding
effort forced the Urban Renewal Agency to become defensive. The process
of relocation had not yet been defeated, but the residents' efforts had

slowed the process dramatically. More important, the people of the barrio saw their work create change, and this, in turn, spurred them to further action.

While the barrio had organized itself into a formal unit — the Citizen's Information Committee — the underlying strength of the barrio was to be found in the families, especially the older people. It was the older residents — those who had seen their families grow together — who provided the stability and strength that enabled the younger and less patient residents to maintain their determination to continue fighting. Whenever the barrio suffered setbacks in its "war" with the agency, it was the informal leadership provided by the older residents which enabled the community to absorb the blow and bounce back time after time.

After establishing "key" relationships with various agencies and institutions, the barrio began gathering support from the community at large. Through the media, other community organizations, by word of mouth — the residents utilized as many avenues as possible — they took their message to the larger community. Slowly, the weight of public opinion swung in favor of the barrio. More and more individuals and groups lent their support to the barrio. This gathering stream of support began to pressure governmental officials, and the Urban Renewal Agency found itself increasingly isolated in its still-planned relocation project. It was becoming quite clear to the residents that they had turned the corner, and it soon became evident to the Urban Renewal Agency that its planned relocation had failed miserably.

Planning and Coordinating Community Rehabilitation

The community now had won for themselves the right to make a choice; those who elected to do so could still relocate, while those who wanted to remain in the community and rebuild it were able to do so. While some community residents opted for relocation, the majority of the residents quite naturally chose to renew their community.

The revised Urban Renewal Agency plan now called for new homes, a new park, new sewer lines, and roads which would be paved for the first time ever. The new plan, it must be noted, had been developed with major input from the residents and the nurse. The agency was forced to respond to the residents for the first time, and the barrio's residents proceeded to renew their community with an unbridled enthusiasm.

The community did not reject assistance in planning and rehabilitating their barrio. There were problems in leaving homes that had stood for many years. To compound the problem, the barrio changed outward appearances as new homes were built. Many of the residents felt an initial sense of panic to see their old homes demolished, even though they appreciated and enjoyed their new ones.

To allay this stress, the indigenous population again was instrumental in solving their own problems. The fabric of interaction which had created a sense of community helped the residents to overcome their stress. They relied on each other, and in so doing, continued the personal interaction they had always shared and soon overcame their initial disorientation. Residents helped each other plan their new homes. They helped each other settle in their new homes, and housewarmings were commonplace as first one family and then another moved into new quarters.

As the residents worked on their barrio, they utilized the help of individuals and agencies throughout the city to help them create change according to the wishes of the community. All the major decisions on the rehabilitation of the barrio were made by the residents themselves. Slowly, a consensus on major decisions was reached one step at a time. Each family sought aid in determining what home would best fit their living needs. One widow who had supported herself with a small rental unit, for example, was able to plan and build a modern duplex. This enabled her to live in one apartment while renting the other. Every family was treated with the same sensitivity. Again, this was because it was members of the community who dealt with all aspects of the rehabilitation process.

The process of coordinating the different city, county, state, and federal agencies was handled by the Citizen's Information Committee, as well as by the nurse. She continued to play a major role in making every effort to utilize the services of as many agencies and social groups as possible. The services the community sought went beyond just the physical rehabilitation of the community. Health care, recreation, care for the elderly, youth projects, and a myriad of other activities were designed and implemented. The success the community had realized in saving their barrio had spurred activity in all other aspects of their lives. All of these activities were carefully structured to insure their continuity. The Citizen's Committee carefully checked into agencies and their programs before inviting them into the community. The results of the barrio's success in rehabilitating and saving their community, not only physically, but mentally and emotionally as well, changed the community.

The residents are developing a transportation system to the barrio to help those individuals who are too elderly to drive or who have no transportation of their own. They have taken a greater interest in the educational system. They have become actively involved in the local PTA and are influencing the curriculum their children are taught. Recreation has become a major interest, for the elderly as well as the youth. Barrio-wide recreation programs include arts and crafts programs for the elderly and

Table 11.3
Objectives for Patient Advocate Model

COURSE OBJECTIVE	BEHAVIORAL OBJECTIVE	TEACHING STRATEGY	EVALUATION
1) To provide instruction on the "rights of patients."	Student demonstrates knowledge of "patient rights," by informing patients of their rights and providing protection of patient rights.	Provide a copy of the patient bill of rights. Assist the student in understanding the rights.	The nurse can verbalize and write the patient bill of rights and its implications for patients and her as a nurse.
	Identifies infringements of patients' rights and involves appropriate staff in resolution of the infringement.	Provide time for the discussion of the implications and meaning of the patient bill of rights to the nurse.	
	Identifies patients expectations regarding health care and communicates the expectations to appropriate staff.	Provide clinical opportunities for teaching patients the bill of rights.	
	Integrates patients' expectations into the total plan of care from assessment to intervention		

2) To develop within the student the knowledge and skills needed to assess the patient's need for an advocate to facilitate the meeting of his needs.

The student identifies the patients' need for assistance.

Use clinical experience that provides nursing student with the opportunity to function in an advocacy role.

Given a clinical situation the nursing student can determine if the patient needs assistance.

Provide instruction on utilization of the data base in the construction of a plan of action.

3) Given the data collected, the nurse is able to construct a plan of action.

The student collects appropriate data and develops functional plans of action.

Provide the nurse with the necessary information about the collection and an analysis of patient data.

Provide the nurse with the necessary information for the construction of a care plan.

Provide time for discussing the implications of relevant data collection and care plan construction to the patient and nurse.

Provide clinical opportunities for the nurse to practice data collection and care plan writing.

Provide clinical opportunities to implement a plan of action.

Given a clinical example, the student nurse is able to collect appropriate data and construct a plan of action.

255

Table 11.3 (cont.)

COURSE OBJECTIVE	BEHAVIORAL OBJECTIVE	TEACHING STRATEGY	EVALUATION
4) To prepare the student to act as an advocate. To provide the nurse with knowledge on organization theory, conflict resolution/confrontation techniques, teaching/learning, external and internal resources.	The student intervenes in behalf of patients who are unable to act on their own behalf.	Utilize simulation, role playing to involve students in discovering systems organization modes of operation of the actors within the system. Support and guide the nursing student through the intervention process. Use positive reinforcement when advocacy roles are assumed by students. Involve the student in the process of patient education. Involve the student in the analysis of the system/organization. Plan field experiences for the identification of resources utilizing the "discovery approach."	Given a clinical situation, the student's intervention is directed toward furthering patient interest. The student's behavior results in the patient's movement toward self-reliance.

organized sports for the youth. Family activities are also encouraged, such as picnics and educational trips.

The various city agencies no longer do planning for the barrio without first consulting the community. In the important area of human services, the barrio has become a potent force that can no longer be ignored by city agencies. Previously, the city had always ignored the residents and had operated independently of the people's wishes. This no longer occurs. The barrio has, through their long struggle, gained the respect of city government and city officials.

The long struggle for survival has created a community which has developed an enormous amount of political "savvy" and practical knowledge of governmental operations. Local politicians can no longer operate in isolation from the community. Their actions are closely scrutinized by the community, and political subsystems are well known to the residents. The effect has been that the residents now have a larger voice in determining their future. As they continue their efforts to improve their barrio and their lives, the residents are assuming more and more responsibility for themselves. They are determined to control their destiny and, if present activity is any indication, the future will bring even more community participation in shaping their lives.

The objectives in Table 11.3 may serve as preliminary guides toward the development of a nurse who is a patient advocate.

SUMMARY

A patient advocate is a nurse who acts on behalf of the poor or ethnic patient of color in situations where they are unable to act. The action may be as simple as informing the patient that his family may order a tray and eat with him during mealtime or as complex as questioning the judgment of superiors when that judgment seems to be in conflict with the interest of the patient. The skills she needs are the basic technical, communication, interpersonal, conflict-resolution and confrontation skills, knowledge of systems/organization theory, and of resources within and without the institution. The development of the courage necessary to be a patient advocate progresses through supervised clinical practice and adequate role models. Through the patient advocate role, it is hoped ethnic people of color will receive, at least, fair treatment from health care professionals.

References

1. Bullough B, Bullough V: Poverty, Ethnic Identity and Health Care. New York, Appleton, 1972, pp 18–37
2. Gordon M: Assimilation in American Life. New York, Oxford Univ Pr, 1964
3. Idem, p 29
4. Idem
5. Paul BD: Anthropological perspectives on medicine and public health. In Skipper J, Leonard R (eds): Social Interaction and Patient Care. Philadelphia, Lippincott, 1975, pp 199–200
6. Valentine C: Culture and Poverty. Chicago, Univ of Chicago Pr, 1968, p 3
7. Duvall E: Family Development. Chicago, Lippincott, 1957
8. Bell NW (ed): A Modern Introduction to the Family. Glencoe, Free Press, 1960
9. Wagner N, Huang M (eds): Chicanos Social and Psychological Perspectives. St. Louis, Mosby, 1971
10. Staples R (ed): The Black Family: Essays and Studies. Belmont, Wadsworth, 1971
11. Hill R: The Strength of Black Families. New York, Emerson Hall, 1971–1972
12. Billingsley A: Black Families in White America. Engelwood Cliffs, Prentice-Hall, 1968
13. Scanzoni J: The Black Family in Modern Society. Boston, Allyn and Bacon, 1971
14. Bloch B: Health Care and the Black patient. In UCSF News (University of California, San Francisco school newspaper) Vol. II, No. 7, February 1975

Bibliography

Cooper SS: Contemporary Nursing Practice. New York, McGraw-Hill, 1970

Fuerst EV, Wolff L: Fundamentals of Nursing, 3rd ed. Philadelphia, Lippincott, 1959

Johnston DF: Total Patient Care Foundations and Practice, 3rd ed. St. Louis, Mosby, 1972

Kiev A: Transcultural Psychiatry. New York, Macmillan, 1972

Kosik S: Patient advocacy or fighting the system. Am J Nurs 4:694–98, April 1972

Luce G: Body Time. New York, Bantam, 1971

Matheney RV, Nolan BT, Ehrhart AM, Griffin GJ: Fundamentals of Patient-Centered Nursing. St. Louis, Mosby, 1968

Moss, T: The Probability of the Impossible. New York, New American Library, 1974

Ornstein RE: The Psychology of Consciousness. San Francisco, WH Freeman, 1972

Price AR: The Art, Science and Spirit of Nursing, 3rd ed. Philadelphia, Saunders, 1965

Roper, N: Principles of Nursing. Edinburgh, Livingstone, 1967

Ross JS, Wilson KJW: Foundations of Nursing. Edinburgh, Livingstone, 1956

Watson, L: The Romeo Error; A Matter of Life and Death. London, Hodder and Stoughton, 1974

Woolsey AH: A Century of Nursing. New York, Putnam's Sons, 1950

Index

Entries that refer to footnotes are followed by an italic "n."